NATURAL RIGHT
AND THE AMERICAN IMAGINATION

NATURAL RIGHT
AND THE
AMERICAN IMAGINATION

*Political Philosophy In
Novel Form*

CATHERINE H. ZUCKERT

ROWMAN & LITTLEFIELD PUBLISHERS, INC.

ROWMAN & LITTLEFIELD PUBLISHERS, INC.

Published in the United States of America
by Rowman & Littlefield Publishers, Inc.
8705 Bollman Place, Savage, Maryland 20763

British Cataloging in Publication Information Available

Library of Congress Cataloging-in-Publication Data

Zuckert, Catherine H., 1942–
Natural right and the American imagination :
political philosophy in novel form / Catherine H. Zuckert.
p.   cm.
Includes bibliographical references and index.
1. Political fiction, American—History and criticism.
2. Political science—United States—Philosophy.
3. Philosophy of nature in literature.   4. Nature in
literature.   I. Title.
PS374.P6Z97   1989
813.009'358—dc20   89–34917 CIP

ISBN 0–8476–7611–0 (alk. paper)

5   4   3   2   1

Printed in the United States of America

TM The paper used in this publication meets the minimum requirements of
American National Standard for Information Sciences—Permanence of
Paper for Printed Library Materials, ANSI Z39.48–1984.

To Michael
without whom this book
would never have been written

Contents

Preface

In some ways, this is an "untimely" book: It is a frankly thematic study oriented toward the thought and ideas of the authors at a time when thought, authors, and themes are being read out of literary studies by the newest wave of critical practice. Having written previously on Friedrich Nietzsche's *Untimely Considerations,* I have learned that untimeliness may be a virtue, even if—as here—my untimeliness sets me at odds with movements of which Nietzsche himself is in part the originator.

My untimely approach is necessitated by my purpose in studying these literary works. As a political scientist—or, to be more precise, as one of that small and hardy band concerned with political philosophy—I have approached these novels as forms of American political thought. It is the burden of the book to argue that understanding the novels this way both enriches our sense of them as oeuvres and—at the same time—enriches our understanding of the political philosophy on which the American regime rather explicitly rests. Because these novels are works of political *thought*—I shall attempt to show—they are also political *acts* of an important kind. Indeed, the most characteristic theme that arises from the studies here might be the way in which the novelists' often differing theoretical reflections have led them nevertheless to agree on the need for a peculiarly democratic kind of literary political teaching. Suffice it to say that most of my brethren in political science departments slight this sort of political action. This is—then—an interdisciplinary study that may be welcome to practitioners of neither discipline, but that, in its untimely way—I hope—say something of value to both.

The dual audience for this volume creates certain rhetorical problems. I cannot assume the same background information or approach in my readers. Where political theorists may find the introductory account of various arguments about the state of nature philosophy unnecessary, literary critics may think that I have spent too much time recounting plots. Although I have tried to provide my different readers with background information that they might lack, I should emphasize that the restatements of both philosophers' and novelists' positions are interpretative. The originality of the readings may not be so clear as it could, because—to avoid a tedious "review of the literature"—I have often relegated accounts of my specific differences with other critics to the notes.

A prefatory word on the selection of novels analyzed is probably also in order. Because "political" readings like political novels have so often been dismissed as mere propaganda, it seemed desirable to show that the deepest reflections on American political principles have occurred in works of acknowledged literary merit. I did not select the works studied in subsequent chapters merely because they have been accepted into the canon, however. (The whole concept of a "canon" has recently come seriously into question.) I selected the works because they all depict a withdrawal from civil society as well as some kind of return. On grounds of literary merit alone, I might have included Willa Cather's *O Pioneers* or Richard Wright's *Native Son*. Both also deal with political issues: the process of settlement, in the first instance; and race relations, in the second. But neither embodies the characteristically American motif that—I argue—parallels and recasts the movement of thought in the "classic" statement of American political principles in the Declaration of Independence.

A study of this kind generates many debts, both personal and intellectual. Most of these will be documented in the footnotes; but without meaning to be invidious, a few might be mentioned here. While I am moving in other directions from much recent literary theory, I would like to thank several teachers who helped this (mostly) autodidact to understand and to appreciate "the road not taken." The late Paul de Man first encouraged me in literary studies at Cornell University; Jane Tompkins led a faculty seminar on feminist literary theory at Carleton College; Jack Irwin offered another on comparative literature. My debts to Leo Strauss will be obvious to all my readers in political philosophy; also my debts to students of his who have worked on politics and literature, including Allan Bloom and Harry Jaffa. Other political theorists like Michael Rogin and Wilson Cary Mc-

Williams have helped pave the way by showing how literature can be used to broaden our understanding of politics.

Two institutions have also contributed significantly to this study: Carleton College has been a wonderful place to work and has supported my scholarly endeavors in more ways than I can detail here. The National Endowment for the Humanities was kind enough to aid this project with a year's fellowship for a "Younger Humanist." They have also allowed me to try out and—I hope—refine many of the interpretations offered here by leading two summer seminars for secondary school teachers.

I would also like to thank the editors of *Polity* and *Proteus* for permission to reprint sections of the chapters on Hawthorne and Twain that previously appeared in these journals. Earlier versions of some of the general arguments have appeared in articles that I published in the *Journal of Politics* and in *Empire sans Empereur* (volume 2, forthcoming from the University of Paris).

Finally, my family. My children have—in a sense—grown up with this project and have shown themselves to be remarkably patient. My husband started me studying American literature as a form of American political thought. Without him, this study would never have been conceived—much less, completed.

1

The State of Nature in Classic American Fiction

Many commentators have pointed out a recurrent theme or motif in the American literature of the United States: the hero who withdraws from civil society to live in nature. Where previous critics have described this as a reflection of adolescent escapism, the historical experience of settling the frontier, deep-running cultural contradictions, or the Puritanic origins of the republic, I shall argue that American novelists have used this motif in reflecting on the "state of nature" philosophy on which this nation was explicitly founded.[1]

In these novels, the departure of the hero clearly signals his dissatisfaction with established society; but the implicit, if not explicit, criticism is not simply negative.[2] Once "heroes" like Natty Bumppo and Huck Finn find themselves free from the constraints of conventional society, they almost immediately establish new kinds of social relations. In depicting their protagonists' return to the state of nature, the authors of novels like *Huckleberry Finn* and *Moby Dick* not only dramatize a fictional rebellion against established laws and customs. They are also seeking the grounds on which a just community might be founded.

The withdrawal from civil society portrayed by these authors is not merely a celebration of the freedom that human beings enjoy in the absence of conventional restraints. In fact, no canonical American author has presented life in the state of nature as completely satisfying or simply desirable. On the contrary, these authors have seen that, with the veneer of civilization removed, the state of nature can repre-

1

sent a setting in which certain truths about human beings become evident—truths that readers of the books could use to order their own more civilized lives.[3]

By portraying their protagonists' withdrawal to nature and then subsequent return to civil society, classic American novelists have—in effect—been exploring the central issue of political philosophy: the question of the relation between nature and convention.[4] And read in light of that question, these novels provide reflections on the philosophic basis of American political institutions—otherwise lacking in the canon of American political thought.

Books like *The Federalist, Notes on Virginia,* and *Congressional Government* were written by active statesmen who concerned themselves primarily with institutional responses to practical problems, rather than with more fundamental questions about the basis and ends of political life. Classic American novels like *The Blithedale Romance, Moby Dick,* and *Go Down, Moses*—on the other hand—clearly did raise questions about the natural foundations of political order. These novels encouraged their readers to ask not only what was natural, but also whether nature provided an adequate foundation for human community or freedom. By showing how canonical American novels addressed these questions, I hope not only to expand the range of American political thought, but also to enhance our appreciation of the intellectual merit of these literary works.[5]

To inquire into the relation between nature and convention is to ask whether there is a standard of right or good inherent in human life by which all the different laws and customs that the various peoples have established for themselves by agreement (convention) can be judged good or bad—just or unjust.[6] The issue of nature and convention is thus the question of political philosophy as such, but different philosophers have raised that question in different ways.

In order to discover what human beings were like "by nature," early modern political philosophers such as Thomas Hobbes and John Locke suggested that it would be useful to see what human beings were like outside or beyond the effective range of law. Going one step further, Jean Jacques Rousseau tried to deduce—if somewhat hypothetically—what human beings were like before they were affected by society at all. In the works of the "social contract" theorists, the "state of nature" thus had two distinct—although related—meanings. First, it referred to the relations among human beings where there was no effective law enforcement—for example, down a dark alley in the city. Second, it referred to a prehistorical condition that could not be literally documented since there would have been no writing nor history. As we shall see, classic American novels have depicted individuals living in the state of nature in both of these senses.

Like Rousseau, some American novelists concluded that human existence is naturally good, and hence worth preserving. Like Hobbes, other novelists suggested that life in the state of nature is "solitary, poor, nasty, brutish, and short." In either case, nature provided not only the reason for establishing civil society in the first place, but also a standard with which to determine the justice of existing institutions.

State of nature philosophy was particularly influential on the American Founding, for two quite different reasons. First, the experience of settling the frontier made the notion of a "state of nature" eminently plausible to the American public. They themselves had left civil society and established political order anew in a more or less natural setting. Second, the break from Britain forced American political leaders to make the principles of their practice explicit; and in defending the Revolution, these leaders used arguments drawn from the social contract theorists.[7] One reason there has been so little political philosophy in the United States may be that these early leaders came to a consensus about the first principles or ends of their polity at the very beginning, in the Declaration of Independence. Later on, partisan political debate tended to concern alternative institutional means of achieving these ends, rather than the ends themselves.[8]

If we look at the initial statement of the American political creed, the parallel between the characteristically American return-to-nature literary motif and American political principles becomes clear.[9] In the Declaration of Independence, we see the same movement of thought that we find in the novels: An appeal to nature justifies withdrawal from civil society as currently constituted, and is then followed by an attempt to find the principles of a truly just society in nature herself. Stating the reasons for their separation and withdrawal from the British Empire in the first sentence of the Declaration, the colonists appeal to "the law of nature and nature's God." And in the second paragraph, the Americans lay out the "self-evident truths" that they have found in nature. These are the truths on which just government—government conducive not only to the safety, but also to the happiness, of the people—must be founded.

Like ancient myths, therefore, the varied versions of the American story have depicted different understandings of the foundations or origins of the American regime. However, there is an important difference, also: The origins of ancient regimes preceded recorded history, so they were remembered only through stories of the deeds of gods and heroes. The foundations of the American regime are a matter of public record—stated explicitly in the Declaration of Independence. And in the Declaration, the philosophical origins of U.S. political principles in social contract theory are rather clear. Whereas ancient myths were gradually reinterpreted into more prosaic political or philosophical terms, the process was just the reverse in America.[10] What had been explicitly rationalistic or argumentative propositions in the Declaration were then intentionally transformed by James Fenimore Cooper into stories meant to teach his compatriots the true meaning of American political principles. In so transforming the propositions of the Declaration, Cooper also self-consciously reinterpreted them. And novelists like Twain, who subsequently reinterpreted Cooper's story, knowingly reexamined the meaning of American political principles at the same time.

Thomas Jefferson's list of "self-evident" truths in the Declaration actually constitutes an extremely compact history of the institution of civil society, from its origin to its demise.[11] In their prepolitical condition, human beings are "created equal": That is, no one rules anyone else "by nature." Subject to no authority, they are free by nature, as well. In their "natural condition," human beings have certain "inalienable rights." Apparently, these rights are not naturally very effective, however, since human beings must institute government in order to secure them. And once established, government itself becomes a powerful threat to these same rights. So, Jefferson concludes, "whenever any form of government becomes destructive [of these rights] it is the right of the people to alter or to abolish it"—a return, if only temporary, to the anarchic state of nature.

Jefferson did not specify the grounds for his extremely concise argument, however. Had human beings fled the state of nature because it was ruled by force and fraud, as Hobbes maintained?[12] Or were they driven into civil society by the competition and anxiety that arose from the accumulation of property—which the invention of money had facilitated—as Locke argued?[13] Do human beings retain a loyalty to their community and obey its laws primarily on the basis of a calculation regarding mutual self-interest? Or do they continue to live together primarily on the basis of sentimental ties developed over time, as David Hume suggested?[14] Is human nature so malleable that it is corrupted by civilization? Must the contract therefore be ever drawn up anew, as Rousseau urged?[15]

Because Jefferson took some key phrases of the Declaration from the works of John Locke, most interpreters have looked to the latter's *Second Treatise of Government* to find a fuller explanation of the Declaration's "self-evident" truths.[16] Unfortunately, the moral meaning and status of the doctrine of natural rights in Locke's philosophy was by no means unambiguous. But whatever Locke himself intended, his arguments have been taken to justify the unfettered search for economic gain.[17]

Observing the problematic consequences of an attempt to establish a polity wholly and unabashedly on an appeal to economic self-interest, Cooper used the opportunity created by Jefferson's inability to specify the reasons for his claims in a public creed to reinterpret the principles of natural right on which the American regime had been founded. And Cooper reinterpreted them in an evidently Rousseauian—as opposed to Lockean—direction.

Cooper originated the return to nature motif, in his depiction of Natty Bumppo. And in Natty, Cooper presents an image of the simple goodness of a "plain, unl'arned man" living by himself in nature. Like Rousseau's noble savage, Cooper's homely hero is intended to serve not as a literal model, but rather as an embodiment of the natural right on which a just democratic society could be formed in the future. In fact, pressure from the ever-increasing white population makes Natty's way of life difficult for the old woodsman himself to maintain, and impossible for others to sustain in the future. Nevertheless, as the author shows, Natty's self-restraint and compassion can be duplicated inside—as well as outside—civil society. Indeed, Cooper suggests that Americans would never live together in peace or liberty unless they were to adopt Natty's sentiments.

The novelists who subsequently used and reinterpreted Cooper's return to nature motif did not agree with him—or with each other—about the distinctive characteristics of human nature and their relevance for the construction of a just civil society. Indeed, Cooper's work initiated a literary debate of sorts not only about the character of the human psyche and its political implications, but also about the basis and wisdom of the whole notion of returning to nature. Whereas Cooper, Melville, and Hemingway all suggested that the most important function of the literary artist is to provide a fictional illustration of the essential and rational goodness of human life, Hawthorne, Twain, and Faulkner formed a countertradition and objected that such idealized depictions of human life in the state of nature have dangerous political effects.

To a certain extent, these two sets of novelists were exploring two apparently contradictory lines of thought initiated by Rousseau. Those who emphasized the goodness of human life in the state of nature were following the line of thought that Rousseau presented in his "Discourse on the Origins of Inequality" when he declared that he himself would return to the state of nature, if he could.[18] To these authors, nature provided at least a standard or norm of freedom and happiness—one that ought to be emulated or recreated in civil society to the greatest extent possible. On the other hand, those who objected that human beings could not—in fact—return to the state of nature and that the desire to return indicated both failure and an unwillingness to learn from historical experience were duplicating the line of thought that Rousseau emphasized in *On the Social Contract*. To them, civil liberty was superior to natural liberty.[19] Having developed both reason and morality in civil society, human beings could now use these socially developed faculties to construct a new form of government that would avoid the oppressive tendencies of political associations in the past.

In either case, the American novelists who depicted a return to the state of nature were asking whether there were natural foundations on which a just civil society could be constructed and whether such a construction would ever represent an improvement on man's natural condition. That is, they wondered whether progress were possible. Not all concluded that it was.

The imaginative reconceptualizations of the state of nature found in classic American novels were thus by no means uncritical of American political principles or their philosophical foundations. On the contrary, these fictional returns to nature represent repeated attempts to refound the American polity on a truer, more adequate view of nature— including preeminently human nature—as well as of the civilized world of culture in which we find ourselves.

These fictional returns to the state of nature were political, more- over, not only in origin and subject matter, but also in potential effect. As a nation of immigrants, Americans have always been united primar- ily by their adherence to the principles of the Declaration, rather than by a common ethnic origin or historical heritage. In America, one can become an American, and one does so by learning the political princi- ples of the regime. To the extent to which these novelists' depictions of the state of nature reshaped popular understanding of the nation's principles, their works transformed the self-understanding and so the very constitution of the American people. As Rousseau argued in *On the Social Contract*,[20] the fundamental "law" governing the life of any people is not to be found in any document specifying the basic structure of the government. It is rather to be found in the "mores"—the opinions, habits, attitudes, and sentiments—that define a people's distinctive way of life. The canonical novelists were not merely describing American mores; in trying to reshape these mores, they were engaging in an important—if little appreciated—form of political leadership.

Notes

1. D. H. Lawrence, *Studies in Classic American Fiction* (New York: Thomas Seltzer, 1923); Henry Nash Smith, *The Virgin Land* (Cambridge, Mass.: Harvard University Press, 1950); Richard Slotkin, *The Fatal Environment* (New York: Atheneum, 1985); Leo Marx, *The Machine in the Garden* (New York: Oxford University Press, 1964); R. W. B. Lewis, *The American Adam* (Chicago: University of Chicago Press, 1955); Sacvan Bercovitch, *The American Jeremiad* (Madison: University of Wisconsin Press, 1978).

2. See A. N. Kaul, *The American Vision* (New Haven, Conn.: Yale University Press, 1963), and Kenneth Lynn, "Welcome Back from the Raft, Huck Honey!" *American Scholar* 46 (Summer 1977): 338–47, on the nonrevolutionary aspects of the withdrawals. Myra Jehlen, *Class and Character in Faulkner's South* (New York: Columbia University Press, 1976), has pointed out an important difference between European and American pastoralism: "Americans do not as a rule yearn to return to wilds; they are nostalgic for the opportunity to civilize."

3. Philip Fisher, *Hard Facts: Setting and Form in the American Novel* (New York: Oxford University Press, 1985), has also argued that "the wilderness is a privileged setting of beginnings, both national and individual" (p. 11). But Fisher presented this setting primarily in terms of the displacement of the Indians and the guilt that displacement provoked—not in terms of a hypothetical removal of the marks of civilization, intended to reveal the truths of nature.

4. See Leo Strauss, *Natural Right and History* (Chicago: University of Chicago Press, 1953), p. 93: "The discovery of nature or of the fundamental distinction between nature and convention is the necessary condition for the emergence of the idea of natural right. But it is not its sufficient condition: all right might be conventional. This precisely is the theme of the basic controversy in political philosophy: Is there any natural right?"

5. John Conder, *Naturalism in American Fiction* (Lexington: University of Kentucky Press, 1984), has also emphasized the role of philosophic ideas in American fiction. Since Conder was primarily concerned with "naturalistic" or "realistic" novelists like Crane, Norris, and Dreiser, however, Faulkner is the only author whom we both treat.

6. Consent is not adequate to establish the justice of any set of laws or customs, because the consenting majority may merely be forcing the minority to obey the unjust preferences of the larger number. Likewise, an armed or otherwise powerful minority may persuade the majority to consent to the existing regime. On the problem of the conditions under which consent may produce just results, consider John Rawls, *A Theory of Justice* (Cambridge, Mass.: Harvard University Press, 1971).

7. Charles Howard McIlwain, *The American Revolution* (New York: Macmillan, 1923); Alexis de Tocqueville, *Democracy in America* (Garden City, N.Y.: Doubleday, 1964), vol. 1, ch. 4.

8. Both founders of the first two U.S. political parties—Thomas Jefferson and John Adams—had a hand in writing the Declaration of Independence. Therefore, the document expressed the consensus on the basis of which all later argumentation and division took place.

9. See Ralph Barton Perry, "The Philosophy of the Declaration," in Robert Ginsberg, ed., *A Casebook on the Declaration of Independence* (New York: Thomas Y. Crowell, 1967), pp. 166–73, and Martin Diamond, *The Democratic Republic* (Chicago: Rand McNally, 1966), pp. 3–5, on the status of the Declaration of Independence as a statement of the American creed.

10. According to Roland Barthes, *Mythologies* (New York: Hill and Wang, 1972), political myths emerge when the controversial aspects of actual historical events are suppressed in stories that make these events into examples of inexorable natural laws. In the United States the authors of the specific historical event that was the American Revolution did explicitly appeal to "the law of Nature and of Nature's God."

11. See Michael Zuckert, "Self-Evident Truths in the Declaration of Independence," *Review of Politics* (Fall 1987).

12. Concerning the influence of Hobbes on the American Founding, see George Mace, *Locke, Hobbes, and the Federalist Papers: An Essay on the Genesis of the American Political Heritage* (Carbondale: Southern Illinois University Press, 1979), and Frank Coleman, *Hobbes and America: Exploring the Constitutional Foundations* (Toronto, Canada: University of Toronto Press, 1977).

13. On Locke's influence, see Carl Becker, *The Declaration of Independence* (New York: Knopf, 1942), and Ginsberg, *Casebook*. Locke's influence on the American Founding has been questioned by J. G. A. Pocock, *The Machiavellian Moment* (Princeton, N.J.: Princeton University Press, 1975), pp. 506–52; "The Myth of John Locke and the Obsession with Liberalism," in J. G. A. Pocock and Richard Ashcraft, eds., *John Locke* (Los Angeles: Clark Memorial Library, 1980), and his *Virtue, Commerce, and History* (Cambridge, England: Cambridge University Press, 1985), pp. 47–52, 64–71; Garry Wills, *Inventing America* (Garden City, N.Y.: Doubleday, 1978), and Morton White, *The Philosophy of the American Revolution* (New York: Oxford University Press, 1978). Kenneth P. Lynn, "Falsifying Jefferson," *Commen-*

tary (October 1981); Ronald Hamowy, "Jefferson and the Scottish Enlightenment," *William and Mary Quarterly*, 3rd series, 37 (1979); and Harry V. Jaffa, "Inventing the Past," *St. John's Review* 33 (1981), 3–19, have all responded to these critiques. For the purposes of this volume, it is sufficient to see that, in reinterpreting the principles of the Declaration of Independence the novelists could draw on a variety of philosophical doctrines.

14. See David Hume, "Of the Origin of Government," and "Of the Original Contract," in *Moral and Political Philosophy* (New York: Hafner Publishing Company, 1948); also Cary McWilliams, *The Idea of Fraternity in America* (Berkeley: University of California Press, 1973).

15. Rousseau's works were widely read both before and after the American Founding. See Paul M. Spurlin, *Rousseau in America* (University: University of Alabama Press, 1969), pp. 34–35.

16. In *The Second Treatise of Government* (New York: Liberal Arts, 1952), ch. 9, Locke spoke of the rights to life, liberty, and estates—all of which he grouped together as "property." In his *Essay on Human Understanding* (London: Dent, 1961), bk. 2, ch. 21, secs. 51–62, however, Locke used the phrase "pursuit of happiness."

17. John Tully, *A Discourse on Property* (Cambridge, England: Cambridge University Press, 1980), and Nathan Tarcov, *Locke's Education for Liberty* (Chicago: University of Chicago Press, 1984), argue that this is not an accurate reading of Locke; but see Robert A. Goldwin, "Locke," in Leo Strauss and Joseph Cropsey, eds., *The History of Political Philosophy* (Chicago: Rand McNally, 1962), and C. B. Macpherson, *The Political Theory of Possessive Individualism* (Oxford, England: Oxford University Press, 1972).

18. Jean Jacques Rousseau, "Discourse on the Origins of Inequality," note (i), in *The First and Second Discourses* (New York: St. Martin's Press, 1964).

19. Jean Jacques Rousseau, *On the Social Contract* (Indianapolis: Hackett, 1983), bk. 1, ch. 7.

20. Rousseau, *Social Contract*, bk. 2, ch. 12.

2

Natty and Natural Right

The connection between the return to nature motif in American fiction and the principles of the Declaration of Independence has been lost, at least partly because the works of James Fenimore Cooper have fallen into disrepute.[1] Everyone recognizes that Cooper originated the return to nature theme through his brilliant depiction of Natty Bumppo; and Cooper was very explicit about the didactic aims of his literary works. In *A Letter to His Countrymen,* Cooper described himself as "an American who wished to illustrate and enforce the peculiar principles of his own country by the agency of polite literature."[2] When he thought that his readers had misunderstood the political significance of his fiction, Cooper even stopped writing novels for a time and turned to a directly argumentative explication of the Declaration of Independence, in *The American Democrat.*

Properly understood—Cooper argued—the principles of the Declaration are the principles of natural right. Unfortunately, many of his compatriots did not understand those principles properly. It was to teach them the true meaning of the central propositions of the Declaration "by the agency of polite literature" that Cooper dramatized his understanding of the natural principles of justice in stories about the character Nathaniel Bumppo.[3]

Concerned more about the conception of natural right that Natty represented than about the development of his character per se, Cooper did not present the tales of the Leatherstocking in the chronological order of the protagonist's life.[4] In *The Pioneers,* he introduces Natty as a crotchety old woodsman who not only raises questions about the justice of the American Revolution but also expresses doubts about whether there be a natural basis for law. Then, in *The Last of the Mohicans,* Cooper uses his protagonist's adventures as a scout in the French and Indian War to ask by what right the whites had displaced the original possessors of the land. And in *The Prairie,* he suggests that the future peace and prosperity of the American republic would depend on a popular acceptance of the kind of natural religion that Natty preaches at his death.[5]

In *The Prairie,* Cooper has Natty articulate the meaning of the natural standard of justice he embodies more explicitly than in the first two novels in the Leatherstocking series. In the state of nature, force rules. The institution of law is necessary, therefore, to protect the weak and vulnerable. Natty the old trapper maintains his independence from the law only by relinquishing all claims to property and—what is even more fundamental—by severing all family ties. His own solitary way of life will not be possible—nor, indeed, would it be desirable—for people in the future. Human existence under the reign of natural necessity is both arduous and lonely, Cooper emphasizes. What is attractive about Natty is not so much his life as a hunter, but his character. Cooper does not depict the life of a man living essentially by himself in nature to celebrate that man's freedom from all conventional restraints. He seeks, rather, to demonstrate that—free from the distorting manners and ambitions developed along with civil society—human beings are moved by two simple but good natural sentiments: an attachment to their own existence, or *preservation;* and a *compassionate concern* for the suffering of other sentient creatures. By contrasting Natty with both the Indians and the other "more civilized" pioneers, Cooper shows that people who forget their nature in a competition for the external marks of distinction that society spawns do not attain happiness and peace.[6] Laws—which reinstate Natty's natural sentiments as standards of right in civil society—are not only advantageous, but also just.

The Pioneers

If nature is good, then the conquest of nature must always appear problematic. Cooper brought out the problematic aspects of the American conquest of the frontier in *The Pioneers,* by combining magnificent descriptions of the upstate New York landscape with serious questions about the legitimacy of private appropriation of the land.[7] He organized the plot of *The Pioneers* around two different disputes concerning property; and both disputes raise questions about the true meaning of the principles of the American Declaration of Independence.[8]

The first conflict that Cooper described involves young Oliver "Edwards" challenging the right of Judge Marmaduke Temple to appropriate the estate of the young man's prerevolutionary British patron and friend, Maj. Oliver Effingham (Edwards's grandfather). This dispute points directly to a question about the grounds and justice of the rights asserted in the Declaration. Since King George and the British Parliament legally ruled the colonies, there had been no appeal in law—ultimately—against their authority, because they declared what the law was. The colonists had appealed, therefore, to "the law of nature and nature's God" in order to maintain the justice of their cause. By declaring and then fighting for their independence, however, the colonists had in effect seized the land from the British. Did the American War for Independence merely constitute robbery of the British landlord? Did it represent a mere exercise of might, cloaked with doctrines of "natural right"? Natty thinks so. Early in *The Pioneers,* he complains, "Might often makes right, here as well as in the old world" (p. 22); and later, "Might makes right, and the law is stronger than an old man" (p. 135).[9]

According to the Declaration, governments derive "their just powers from the consent of the governed." Natty had never consented to the institution of government at Templeton, however, because he does not believe that settlements and property are either desirable or necessary. If all human beings were to take only what they need from nature, he argues, government would not be necessary to secure anyone's rights. By what right, then, does Judge Temple enforce the law against him?

Thus, the second conflict in the novel—between Judge Temple and Natty—raises the same question posed by the revolutionary struggle, but at a broader or more general level: By what right does any person or people claim a part of the earth for exclusive use? In *The Pioneers,* Cooper concentrated on the question of the legitimacy of the American settlement of land previously held by the British. In *The Last of the Mohicans,* he then took up an even more fundamental question: By what right had the European whites seized the lands of the original inhabitants?

By presenting Judge Temple rather sympathetically, Cooper suggests not only that Americans had declared their independence as a matter of right (not merely self-interest), but also that the institution of law had been necessary to secure the rights for which the Americans fought. Temple bases his law on the very natural foundation or morality of self-restraint ("no waste") that Natty himself embodies. When Natty bemoans the waste and destruction resulting from a massive haul of fish engineered by the judge's cousin Richard Jones, Temple generously responds, "Your reasoning is mine: for once, old hunter, we agree in opinion; and I heartily wish we could make a convert of the sheriff. A net of half the size of this would supply the whole village with fish for a week at one haul." Natty, however, refuses to be drawn into an alliance with the representative of law and organized society. "No, no; we are not much of one mind, Judge, or you'd never turn good hunting grounds into stumpy pastures" (p. 266).

Readers who identify the opinions of the author with those of his most famous character would thus be mistaken. Cooper began *The Pioneers* with a celebratory description of the changes wrought by civilization in the valley where the novel is set. Later, when he stated his political principles under his own name in *The American Democrat,* Cooper declared emphatically in favor of civilization and for property as a necessary means to that end. Without property—he argued—there would be universal poverty, if not famine. Looking down from Mount Vision in *The Pioneers,* Temple reminds Natty that there had been famine in the Susquehanna Valley before he—the judge—came and settled it. Insofar as Temple's laws have secured the preservation of more people, they are compassionate; thus, they embody and make effective both of Natty's natural sentiments. Natty's untutored instincts are right—Cooper indicates—but his explicit opinions are wrong.

The law that Natty specifically objects to in *The Pioneers* is the one setting limits (seasons) on deer hunting. This law does have a basis in nature—Natty admits—because deer are too lean to provide good meat during their mating season and they must be allowed to mate, ensuring a future supply. Nevertheless, Natty insists that, since he kills only when and where it is necessary for his own self-preservation, he does not need to be regulated. He was the first settler in the region, so the judge has no right to impose law on him.

Recognizing Natty's self-restraint, Judge Temple grants to the old woodsman an unlimited right to shoot on his lands. Natty's self-restraint was the exception, however. Cooper shows all too clearly the need to check the wasteful and destructive tendencies of most of the settlers: Billy Kirby's reckless hacking of the maples to obtain their syrup kills the trees within a few years; Temple's own cousin and a servant haul three huge nets of fish out of the lake, only to see three-quarters of them rot on the shore; and the whole town turns out to shoot down flocks of pigeons. Natty walks among the dying birds that litter the ground. He shakes his head at human wickedness, but will not admit the need to restrain people from their wickedness by means of external force.

Perceiving both the goodness and the discipline that nature had enforced through famine so strongly in himself, Natty does not appreciate the extent to which other human beings have to substitute foresight for sentiment. But—Cooper shows—even Natty loses self-control and runs afoul of the law as a result of the excitement of the chase (after a deer on the lake). And although Judge Temple regularly bemoans the waste involved in needless destruction, he too gets caught up in the excitement of the pigeon shoot.

Through the plot, then, Cooper shows that Natty was wrong. Law is necessary to restrain the excessive and excitable passions of human beings. Even the best people occasionally succumb. However, as demonstrated in the subsequent invasion of Natty's cabin by Sheriff Richard Jones's associates, merely instituting and maintaining legal forms will not suffice to protect either person or property. The law has to be executed in the proper spirit, on the basis of an understanding of both its necessity and its purpose.

Cooper brought the dispute between Natty and Judge Temple to a climax when the old hunter is brought to court and convicted not only for shooting a buck out of season, but for resisting an officer of the law. As it happened—when the posse arrived at his cabin—Natty had recognized the justice of the law prohibiting hunting out of season by throwing the deer pelt out the door and promising to pay the fine. Since this law had a natural foundation, he was prepared to honor it. Also by giving Billy Kirby the evidence, Natty was purposely removing any reason for further investigation. Moved by his commonsensical notion of right, Kirby then decided to accept the pelt as a fair response, and moved to depart. Armed with a search warrant and curious to see the interior of the secluded cabin, Hiram Doolittle persisted in his attempt to enter. To protect the anonymity of Oliver's grandfather, who was secretly housed there, Natty was forced to keep the deputy out of his cabin with a gun.

At the trial, Temple refuses to be lenient, although Natty had once saved the life of the judge's daughter. Believing that his reputation as an impartial judge is at stake, he resists all pleas for compassion, as well as his own obligation of gratitude. Ignoring the extenuating circumstances—the known character of the defendant, Natty's lack of education, the sentiments of the community, and the promptings of his own heart—Temple decides the case "on principle": Representatives of the law may not be resisted with force.

When the judge's own daughter and his servants then conspire to help Natty escape from jail, we have Cooper showing that, when laws are in violation of the community's sense of what is right, they will not be effective. And when Sheriff Jones and Deputy Doolittle call out the militia in order to recapture the escaped convict, Cooper is reminding his readers that—separated from its natural foundations and purpose— the rule of law is no better than the rule of superior force.

Laws are not necessary to rule men like Natty who live so close to natural necessity; they are necessary to check the passions of men like Sheriff Jones who do not exercise any form of self-restraint. In nature, the latter see only material to be exploited. They certainly do not listen to the sermons of such as the weak, sickly, and somewhat formal Anglican minister, the Reverend Mr. Grant. To Jones, "Christianity" and "civilization" merely represent excuses to persecute the original inhabitants: the Indians, and their friend Natty. Jones and his associates use the law to further their own commercial ventures and are willing to endanger the lives and property of others in asserting and pursuing their own interests.

Judge Temple sees the need for law, but he does not prove able to use it effectively in controlling his subordinates. Like Locke, he has overestimated the power of rational, long-term calculations of economic interest and has underestimated the divisive, potentially violent character of the competitive desire for distinction. As a result, Temple does not sufficiently question his own motives in rigorously enforcing the law against Natty. Nor does he judge the character of his subordinates accurately. Temple had appointed his cousin as sheriff because he believed (correctly) that Jones wanted the office. Apparently, he had no inkling of how Jones would employ such a license to use force.

As Cooper shows by way of a turkey shoot, the desire for distinction can be checked by mutually agreed upon rules that award honor to those who prove their superior talent. Such rules express a common understanding of what is fair and right—not merely the mutual self-interest of the participants. Cooper indicates that, in a heterogeneous community like Templeton (or the United States)—composed of immigrants and religious dissenters—neither tradition nor sectarian religion can provide a source of agreement. The law must be based on some common sentiment or "natural right" belonging to human beings as human beings, without need for special revelation or experience.

Cooper illustrates the natural principles of right along with the competitive source of dissension in the first confrontation scene between Natty and Judge Temple. Both claim to have shot a deer. The judge pursues his claim because he wishes to show up his cousin Dickon, who had tried and failed seven times to bring home venison. When his claim to have shot the deer is challenged, the judge offers to buy the venison and make up a story about its capture. Because he is more anxious to have the honor than to prove his actual ability, he is willing to deceive others.

Natty, on the other hand, takes pride in his skill as a marksman and his knowledge of weapons. He points out that the judge could not possibly have killed the buck with a scattershot gun. Natty does not insist on getting credit for the shot that killed the deer, however; here— as always—he ultimately subordinates the thrill of the hunt to its purpose: obtaining food. Concerned primarily with the requirements of self-preservation, Natty suggests that it would be more profitable to look elsewhere for food than to stand around arguing over the carcass.

Because Natty is not a man of words or reason, it is not he who finally proves that the judge did not fire the decisive shot. Oliver Edwards shows Temple four scattered bullets that hit a tree; the fifth had come to rest in the youth's own side. Reason is necessary to articulate the principles or consequences of natural right—Cooper here indicates—but it is compassion that makes people respect them. When the judge discovers that he has wounded a fellow human being, he exclaims, "Good God! Have I been trifling here about an empty distinction, and a fellow creature suffering from my hands without a murmur" (p. 24). By reminding people of their shared vulnerability, fellow feeling might actually counteract the divisive effects of the search for preeminence and so provide a natural foundation for more peaceful—even charitable—social relations.

Oliver Edwards has not yet learned to take a charitable view of his fellow human beings, however. Full of suspicion, Edwards believes that the judge is a dishonorable pretender who took the money left in Edwards's keeping by his grandfather to buy the old Effingham estate for himself. Edwards is loath, therefore, to concede that Temple has any principles at all beyond economic self-interest. However, at the end of the novel, Judge Temple proves that he is a just man by showing to the youth the will in which he has left half of his property to the heirs of Effingham, even though—as a matter of strict legality—the judge has title to it all. And—in contrast to his public treatment of Natty in court—in private, Temple recognizes that obligations incurred through friendship and past benefits extend beyond mere obedience to the law.

Oliver Edwards's father, on the other hand, had not been willing to recognize the reciprocal obligations of friendship. Although he helped Temple early on, the second Effingham was not willing to accept aid or friendship in return from his American "inferior." He had, therefore, returned—unopened—all the letters and money that Temple sent after the war. Like his nation, Effingham refused to recognize the equality of the colonists and their consequent right to institute a government in the form that they thought would be most conducive to their own safety and happiness.

Once the British did recognize American equality and independence, there was then no reason that the two nations should not live in amity and peace—as Cooper indicates through the marriage of the Effingham heir to the judge's daughter Elizabeth.[10] Sharing a common civilization, the two peoples belonged—in fact—to the same "family."

Thus, in *The Pioneers,* Cooper shows that it is necessary—as stated in the Declaration of Independence—to institute government in order to secure people's natural rights to life, liberty, and the pursuit of happiness. Government serves its just purposes, however, only if the people living under it share basically the same understanding of right, and consequently treat each other with compassion as equals.

The Last of the Mohicans

In *The Pioneers,* Cooper had only partially solved the questions that he raised concerning the natural foundations of the American republic and the property rights that the regime protected. It was much easier to justify the colonists' claim to equality with the British than to justify the destruction of the original inhabitants of the North American continent. In the second Leatherstocking tale, Cooper thus pursued two further questions: (1) Why were the Indians—universally acknowledged to be fierce warriors—unable to unite and expel the white settlers? (2) Better still, why were the red and the white races not able to amalgamate, settle down, intermarry, and share the land, like members of the various nationalities who came to this country from Europe? Are not all human beings basically—that is, by nature—members of the same species, and hence members of the same family? Is that not the meaning of the Declaration's claims "that all men are created equal" and "that they are endowed by their Creator with certain inalienable rights"?[11]

It was not nature that kept the two races apart, Cooper indicates. The "last of the Mohicans"—Chingachgook's son, Uncas—not only falls in love with a white woman, but dies attempting to save her from an Iroquois brave. We see that members of the two races were indeed sexually attracted to one another and able to mate. Natty Bumppo shakes his head in disapprobation, however, when the Indian girls mourning Cora and Uncas suggest that the couple's close proximity in death means that they will be united in the afterlife. Different social conventions can have so great an effect that uneducated people like Natty tend to mistake them for natural differences. And these cultural differences were what made amalgamation of the two races impossible. Indian mores not only prevented them from uniting to expel the European immigrants by setting tribe against tribe. They also made it impossible for the Indians to retain their distinctive ways and still live peacefully among whites in the new settlements.

Cooper dramatizes the fundamental opposition between Christian civility and Indian mores in the abortive peace that the Marquis de Montcalm negotiates with Colonel Munro in the middle of the novel. Having given Munro written proof (a captured letter) that General Webb would not be relieving the otherwise doomed British battalion, Montcalm convinces Munro to cease all opposition and to withdraw peacefully from the fort. They "signed a treaty, by which the place was to be yielded to the enemy, with the morning; the garrison to retain their arms, their colors, and their baggage, and consequently, according to military opinion, their honor" (p. 166).[12] However— refusing to recognize the force of European conventions of war—the Indian allies of the French attack and massacre the small troop of British men, women, and children as soon as they leave the walls of the fort.

The Indians had joined the French to obtain scalps and honor—and scalps they have, before the end of battle. Indians can be "civilized"— Cooper suggests—only at the expense of their pride as warriors. By using the Indians to defeat the British, Montcalm has sacrificed his own honor—not that of the Indians—because his means are inappropriate for himself and his country. So soon after signing the treaty, Montcalm has discovered how little he is able to control his Indian allies, and Cooper does not think that he is free from blame.

Already his fair fame had been tarnished by one horrid scene, and in circumstances fearfully resembling those under which he now found himself. As he mused he became keenly sensible of the deep responsibility they assume who disregard the means to attain their end, and of all the danger of setting in motion an engine which it exceeds human power to control. (pp. 70–71)

Standing inexplicably inactive while the Indians butcher their helpless victims, the French have managed to acquire military advantage at the expense of their morals.

Despite this massacre scene, Cooper actually presents a very positive view of Indian morality and culture.[13] Throughout *The Last of the Mohicans,* he shows Indians of both major tribes as being physically and even intellectually superior to the whites. The red men are able to see and to hear much more than their white companions, because the Indians listen to nature. They have a religion that teaches them to be just, lest they suffer in the afterlife; and they demonstrate extraordinary self-command. They are true to their promises. They display exact and exacting notions of honor and justice—for example, when the Delawares return Cora to the Iroquois brave as his property until they can recapture her fairly through battle. Despite their overwhelming desire to revenge any wrong, they also exhibit charity and compassion—for example, in their treatment of those whom they regard as mentally incompetent, like the pacifist psalmodist David Gamut. All is fair in war for the Indians—hence, the butchering—but only when they are officially at war.

The conflict between Cooper's reds and whites is not simply between barbaric "savages" and "civilized" human beings or races. The problem—as the massacre at Fort Henry reveals—is that the mores of the Indians are not compatible with the mores of the whites. Indians qua Indians cannot be incorporated into the broader American political community. The tribes have to repulse the white settlers or be destroyed as a community themselves.

Converting the Indians to Christian morals requires that they cease being warriors, Indians, and even men—according to Indian notions of what it is to be a "man." They honor themselves and others according to prowess demonstrated in battle; they prove to themselves and others that they are "men"—capable of ruling, rather than being ruled like "women"—by killing others and taking their scalps as proof. They do not take slaves because they are not interested in luxury or comfort; but they treat those who are unable to go into battle—namely, their women—as slaves. Because Christians refuse to fight to the death for honor and to recognize that "all's fair in war," and because they bow to women rather than forcing them to serve their husbands, the Indians condemn them. "The palefaces are dogs"—and not, therefore, worthy foes. Thus, the Indians seek honor primarily by fighting other Indians.

Although Cooper's Indians have a religion that resembles Scripture in many respects—as Natty often emphasizes—they believe that Manitto will reward them in the afterlife as He does on earth, according to their prowess on the warpath. The Indians' faith in the divine places no restraints on violent competition for distinction, therefore. On the contrary, their faith serves to support their intertribal hostility and to prevent their uniting as one people against the whites.

The Indians were defeated—Cooper suggests—not simply or even primarily by the superior fighting ability of the whites, but rather by the effects of their own—in some respects, extremely praiseworthy—mores. For these mores not only made it impossible for the tribes to unite against their antagonists, but also kept the number of Indians relatively low compared to the ever-expanding white population.

In *The Last of the Mohicans,* an Iroquois chief attempts to unite his tribe with the Delaware tribe against the white invaders of their territories. But Cooper portrays this attempt as bound to be a failure. Not only does the Iroquois' ambition turn him against other chiefs as potential competitors; but—more fundamentally—neither he nor they can maintain a sense of Indian identity without retaining the Indian sense of honor, and that notion of honor inevitably turns red against red. So it is that not a white—but another brave—kills Uncas. And the last and most decisive battle in the book is waged between the bands of Iroquois and Delawares who had previously been allied. It—like the fight between the Pawnees and the Sioux in *The Prairie*—ends in the slaughter of the defeated party.

Cooper concludes *The Last of the Mohicans* with the cementing of a famous friendship between Natty and Chingachgook. Then there is the despairing benediction of the aged Delaware chief Tamenund, who laments that Manitto is continuing to turn His face away from His red children. The whites have conquered. The two events follow logically as well as narratively because—Cooper indicates—friendship, peace, and amity between the Europeans and the natives can exist only on an individual level.

Friendship between whites and reds was not possible on the level of races or peoples because the two peoples were defined by their different customs, mores, or morality.[14] And it was not possible between the sexes and individuals in the form of marriage because marriage produced children, heirs, families—and, hence, eventually tribes or settlements. The child of a white–red combination was neither white nor red. He or she had no home and no people. Such a half-breed would necessarily become a solitary figure who could at most only adopt the ways and children of others, as Natty attaches himself to Uncas and the Delawares without ever truly becoming one of them.[15]

The friendship of Chingachgook and Natty embodies the natural principles on which human society is and ought to be based—mutual respect for the integrity of the other, combined with a unity of feeling or sentiment. The friendship between these individuals could not be generalized in civil society, however, because society requires marriage, children, and—hence—settlements with their necessary distinctions between mine and thine, ours and theirs, friends and enemies. The friendship of Chingachgook and Natty thus points to a fundamental paradox of human existence: We are all of one species; yet we can survive as a species only by dividing up into families, tribes, and peoples. The friendship does not merely reveal a suppressed American preference for unconventional homosexual relations—a desire to escape from conventional sexual morality—as Leslie Fiedler would have it;[16] nor simply a romantic dream of union superseding even sex, as D. H. Lawrence suggested.[17] Rather, it signifies that society is necessary for human survival—on a moral and psychological level, if not a purely physical one. This friendship represents the absolute—if saving—minimum kind of social union between human beings. "I am alone," concludes Chingachgook. "No, No," Hawkeye cries. "No, Sagamore, not alone. The gifts of our colors may be different, but God has so placed us as to journey in the same path. I have no kin, and I may also say, like you, no people" (p. 349).

Families are necessary to produce future generations, however, and families require settlements and property—as Cooper displays even more clearly in *The Prairie* and *The Pathfinder*. Among the Indians, women with children cannot roam freely through the woods; hence, we see that the different tribes have various territorial claims. Cooper's Indians set up houses—whether in the form of tents or huts—where the women stay while the men hunt and fight. Before the white settlers arrived, the tribes avoided decimation through war by living in widely dispersed areas; but as the whites push them westward, the Indians come into conflict with each other over the land. They cannot live in such high density as the whites, because the Indian men of both the woods and the plains refuse to till the soil like squaws. Like Natty, they define their freedom and their manhood in terms of the ability to hunt. Their pride prevents them from being producers. Then, too, because the whites live in a far less transient manner, these newcomers are able to raise many more children than the natives.[18] Thus, the white population grows and presses increasingly on the Indians.[19]

According to Cooper, the white Christians are able to live concentrated in greater numbers because their mores tend to make them more pacific than the Indians. Whereas conflict among tribes or nations is the inevitable result of Indian morality, it is not a necessary product of Christianity, although Christian precepts alone will not prevent men (and women) from fighting. As Cooper shows in *The Pioneers* through the reconciliation of British and American heirs in marriage, peace is possible if and when people(s) are willing to recognize the inherent equality, desire for dignity, and independence—the "rights," so to speak, or claims—of others. In this respect, Christian civilization seems to be superior to the apparently more purely natural morality of the Indians—both ethically and effectively. In teaching the limits of one's claims on personal honor (or pride) and of justice as revenge, Christianity seems both more conducive to the preservation of human life and more compassionate.

In order to be the source of an effective personal and political morality, however, Christian precepts must be built on a natural foundation. As the novelist indicates in the contrast between Natty Bumppo and David Gamut, Christianity can sometimes make men (and women) pacific at the expense of their ability to defend themselves. Gamut gives the Bible precept "Thou shalt not kill" a very literal reading. Therefore, he is a pacifist. Like the lilies of the field, he depends on Providence to take care of him. In fact—as Cooper tells it—Gamut is preserved as a result of the nonpacific endeavors of his associates and the compassion of the Indians.

By contrasting Natty with Gamut, Cooper portrays natural morality as working where bookish learning does not. Unlike the psalmodist, the scout bases his faith on experience and reflection—not on the merely human authority of the printed word. When Gamut demands that Natty cite chapter and verse to support his religious convictions, the scout responds that he has read the only book and worshipped in the only temple made directly by God's hand: the book and the temple of nature. He himself is a creation of God and worthy of being preserved. He kills only to preserve life, but he does kill. It is necessary to use force against those who would use violence to achieve their own selfish ends. This necessity—Cooper repeatedly demonstrates—constitutes the natural foundation and justification for government. Like Gamut, those who depend solely on Providence without acting or taking responsibility for their own actions are not only ineffective; ironically—by refusing to take responsibility themselves— pacifists like Gamut allow force rather than right to determine what happens.

Just as Cooper uses the contrast between Gamut and Natty to show that Christianity can constitute an effective foundation for personal and political morality only when its precepts are combined with a recognition of natural necessity, so he uses the contrast between the scout and the Indians to show that compassion can be the sole truly natural source of morality only when it results from the same merger of natural sentiment with Scriptural teaching (Natty's Christian "gifts").

Perhaps sensing his own imperfections and limitations, Cooper suggests that such a "naturalized Christian" would be tolerant of both the different ways and the defects of others. Like Natty, he or she would see that there were red gifts as well as white; like Natty, he or she would be compassionate, and even merciful. Rather than test the mettle of an enemy's self-discipline like the Indians by prolonging his death through torture, he would—like Natty—"waste" the precious ammunition that he needs for his own defense in order to put an enemy out of his misery. Unlike the Indians, Natty never attempts to prove his superiority. They respect him for his prowess as a warrior—that is, insofar as he meets their norms. He respects them for serving their own notions of justice—even when he does not share those notions. As a popular image of natural virtue, Natty thus represents the superiority of toleration to sectarianism—a vice much more prevalent among Cooper's Christian countryfolk than among the Indians, and a vice that Cooper thought particularly inimical to the preservation of both personal liberty and democracy.[20]

Thus—as in *The Pioneers,* so also in *The Last of the Mohicans*— Natty embodies the prudent standard of natural right. As Cooper recognizes in his depiction of Indian mores, one's natural attachment to self-preservation—as well as one's compassion for others—can be virtually eradicated by social convention, especially through an attachment to honor. If civil society would be based on natural standards of right and justice, people must rediscover the goodness of their own natural inclinations. They do not act on such sentiments automatically, however. They have to be taught. Cooper leaves the moral teaching that Natty represents more or less implicit within his character and deeds in the first two Leatherstocking tales. Then, in the third, he moves the old hunter to articulate an explicit doctrine. Cooper may be hoping to counteract the concern for reputation and status that caused so much conflict among the Indians as well as the European settlers, when—in *The Prairie*—he has Natty preach a natural and tolerant religion that emphasizes the limits of all human achievement.

The Prairie

Cooper accented the unconventional character of Natty's existence within the state of nature in the first two Leatherstocking tales, by showing him living with his Indian friend Chingachgook. In *The Prairie,* the author stresses the fundamentally solitary character of life outside civil society, by showing Natty facing death entirely alone.

Cooper emphasizes Natty's solitude in order to bring out the true significance of his protagonist's withdrawal from civil society. In *The Prairie,* it becomes evident that—contrary to the impression some readers might have gotten from *The Pioneers*—the old trapper has not fled from the settlements merely out of a misanthropic dislike for the society of other human beings, or a resistance to legal regulation. He is able to live without the protection of law only because he has no family, and hence needs little—if any—property. The conditions of his life in the state of nature are not desirable for most human beings, nor does Cooper wish his readers to follow Natty's example literally by leaving town to live in the woods. Although Natty is able to preserve himself, the conditions of his existence are obviously not conducive to the propagation and preservation of the human species. It is not his solitary existence in itself—but the opinions and sentiments fostered by his solitary existence in nature—that are the repository of natural right and are so exemplary.

In one part of the third tale, Cooper contrasts Natty's opinions and deeds with those of a doctor that he meets on the prairie. The contrast proves that Natty's virtues (his courage as well as his compassion) have been produced and preserved not simply by his solitude, but by his meditations on the grandeur of Creation—meditations encouraged by his solitude. Although people in civil society could not duplicate Natty's physical independence, they could share his opinions and attitude. Indeed—Cooper suggests—the future freedom and justice of the American republic would depend on the popular inculcation of such views.

Having fled his beloved woods to avoid the settlements that seem to spring up in his wake, Natty is dismayed to see the wagons of the Bush clan on the prairie. "Is the land filled on the other side of the big river? . . . Or why do I see a sight I never thought to behold again?" (pp. 16–17).[21] When Natty actually meets the old pioneer patriarch, however, the latter appears to be a kindred spirit. Like Natty, Ishmael Bush left the settlements to avoid unnecessary legal restraints on his liberty. "I have come old man, into these districts," Ishmael explains, "because I found the law sitting too tight upon me and am not overfond of neighbors who can't settle a dispute without troubling a justice and twelve men." And like Natty in *The Pioneers,* Ishmael justifies his resistance to law—especially the law of property—through an appeal to nature. When Natty suggests that in the absence of law the Sioux have a right to claim anything they might find on the prairie, Ishmael expostulates:

> Owners! . . . I am as rightful an owner of the land I stand on as any governor of the States! Can you tell me, stranger, where the law or the reason is to be found which says that one man shall have a section, or a town, or perhaps a country to use and another have to beg for earth to make his grave in? This is not nature, and I deny that it is law. That is, your legal law. (p. 61)

Nevertheless—Cooper shows—the two old pioneers have withdrawn from civil society to live on the frontier for fundamentally different reasons. And they embody very different conceptions of natural right. Ishmael Bush represents the more typical pioneer experience—in terms of which Cooper's readers tend to misconstrue the significance of his hero, Natty. In this last of what was initially intended to be a Leatherstocking trilogy, Cooper thus dramatizes the difference.

Where Natty has withdrawn from civil society because he does not require its protection, Ishmael came to the frontier in search of unowned land on which to support his family. Despite their similarities, the situations of the two pioneers are fundamentally different. Without dependants and able to support himself, Natty has little need for property and—consequently—for legal protection. When Ishmael remarks on Natty's lack of baggage, the latter responds thus: "At my time of life, food and clothing be all that is needed; and I have little occasion for what you call plunder, unless it be now and then to barter for a horn of powder or a bar of lead" (p. 22).

And Natty points out the contradiction in the old settler's position in their very first conversation. Laws are established to protect property, the old hunter observes. Having left the protection of the law,

Ishmael has no right to complain about the Sioux taking his animals. Unlike Natty, Ishmael needs possessions in order to feed and protect his dependants. Without recognizing it, he actually needs the law, which serves not merely to secure property rights, but—more importantly—to protect the weak from the strong.

Encountering Bush's adopted ward Ellen Wade walking alone on the prairie, Natty demands of her:

> Why do you venture in a place where none but the strong should come? Did you not know that when you crossed the big river you left a friend behind you that is always bound to look to the young and feeble like yourself?

"Of whom do you speak?" she responds. And Natty explains,

> The law—'tis bad to have it, but I sometimes think it is worse to be entirely without it. Age and weakness has brought me to feel such weakness at times. Yes—yes, the law is needed when such as have not the gifts of strength and wisdom are to be taken care of. I hope, young woman, if you have no father you have at least a brother. (p. 27)

Although he does not need the protection of law himself, Natty has come to see that it is necessary for families.

If women and children must have the protection of a man in order to survive in the state of nature, then the family appears to be necessary for survival of the species and—hence—to be a natural form of association. Ishmael therefore concludes that—by nature—as head of the family, the father has a right to rule. The contrasting notions of natural right that are represented by the two old pioneers reflect their different situations. Able to support himself, Natty does not seek to rule others any more than he concedes the right of anyone else to rule him. On the other hand, perceiving the need to keep a large family— almost a tribe—together if they are to survive, Ishmael insists on the primacy of paternal authority.

By tracing the development of internal dissension within the Bush clan, Cooper shows Ishmael to be wrong. As Locke had argued against Sir Robert Filmer, parental authority does not extend—effectively, or as a matter of right—to grown sons.[22] Ishmael himself is aware of the problem.

> United to their parents by ties no stronger than those which use had created, there had been great danger, as Ishmael had foreseen, that the

overloaded hive would swarm and leave him saddled with the difficulties of a young and helpless brood, unsupported by the exertions of those whom he had already brought to a state of maturity. The spirit of insubordination which emanated from the unfortunate Asa had spread among his juniors, and the squatter had been made painfully to remember the time when, in the wantonness of his youth and vigor, he had, reversing the order of the brutes, cast off his own aged and failing parents to enter into the world unshackled and free. (p. 143)

To help him raise his youngest children and to support him in his old age, Ishmael requires the assistance of other adults. But why should they help? Why should his older children stay to be ruled by an arbitrary old man when they can set out on their own? Where neither property nor inheritance rights are respected—Cooper indicates— intergenerational family ties are also loose.

Not only is the purportedly "natural" foundation of the paternal authority claimed by Ishmael found to be defective; so is the associated conception of justice as "an eye for an eye; a tooth for a tooth." Like the Indian understanding of right in terms of revenge, the Old Testament notion of a justice that would inflict equal damage in response to injury is essentially divisive.

Ishmael's son Asa—who resentfully remains under the thumb of his elders—not only questions his father's wisdom in bringing the clan into such dangerous territory, but also slaps his maternal uncle when the latter makes a nasty comment about the family. The uncle, Abiram—afraid as he is to face the severity of the head of the household, as well as the physical strength of the patriarch's son—waits to take his revenge in secret and shoots Asa in the back. When Ishmael discovers that it is not Natty—as first suspected—but his own wife Esther's brother who has killed his son in cowardly cold blood, Ishmael dismisses Esther's pleas for clemency and insists that a life must be paid for a life. By clinging to his notion of right without favoritism, Ishmael displays a stern—if rough—nobility; but his action also serves to decimate the clan further.

The only truly natural foundation for political community—Cooper suggests—is to be found in the respect for the rights of others that Natty represents. Because his compassionate attempts to save lives leads him to help the very settlers who have displaced him and made his way of life impossible, Natty's sentiments might appear to be self-defeating and irrational. His solitary way of life contributes nothing to the propagation of the species, as Cooper has already indicated; it would not be tenable in the future, nor is it particularly desirable in itself. Cooper's point in writing these novels was not to urge readers to follow the woodsman's example literally. It was, rather, that Natty embodies the natural moral standards on which a peaceful, prosperous civil society could be constructed.

Thus—as in *The Pioneers,* so also in *The Prairie*—the men and women who have benefitted from Natty's services and who recognize his excellence of character later return to civil society. They have learned the lesson that Cooper designed Natty to teach. Having observed the value of both self-control and service to others, they are fit to govern a democratic people. Both young men whose brides Natty helped rescue from the Bushes would eventually be elected to public office, the narrator informs us at the end of the novel. Duncan Uncas Middleton becomes a U.S. senator, while the beekeeper Paul Hover is elected to the lower house of a state legislature.

Cooper never really placed his hope for the future of the American republic in the character of its governors, nor in the laws and institutions that they design and administered, however. As shown in *The Pioneers,* people will not obey laws that they do not think are just or necessary. Public opinion is the strongest force in a modern democracy, Cooper later argued explicitly in *The American Democrat.* Thus, through his depiction of Natty, Cooper tried to shape popular opinion. In *The Pioneers,* he used the crusty old woodsman to convince readers not to regard nature simply as a source of materials to be greedily exploited, but rather as a source of right standards. In *The Last of the Mohicans,* he then dramatized Natty's friendship with the Indians in order to describe grounds for toleration of cultural differences based on a fundamental recognition of the unity of the natural species. And in *The Prairie,* he highlights Bush's inability to preserve and support his family without legal protection in order to show that there are natural grounds for instituting the rule of law.

Cooper recognized that it is not merely shortsighted economic interest or the resentful desire not to be ruled by another that prevents people from perceiving the natural foundations and necessity of political rule. In the modern world, there are two different teachings about nature: Regarded as the source of human freedom and equality, nature is respected as a source of moral standards or norms. Regarded merely as an object of scientific inquiry, however, nature becomes a source of material to be exploited as human beings wish. Although these two doctrines were often articulated by the same philosophers, the two teachings about nature nevertheless exist in tension—if they do not simply undermine one another.

Cooper dramatizes this tension in *The Prairie* through the interaction between Natty and one Dr. Obed "Bat" Battius. If public opinion is the most powerful force in a modern democracy, then popular notions about "nature" constitute *the* most decisive political fact. Cooper's satirization of Bat would suggest that popular adulation of science's power to transform the cosmos can easily undermine any possibility of establishing and maintaining a regime based on standards of natural right. By promising human beings the possibility of complete knowledge, science prompts them to dream of complete mastery. Rather than restraining human greed, ambition, and consequently conflict— Cooper seems to be saying—science feeds it. At the same time, the promise of material knowledge and power that science holds out can undermine the more naive (but hence perhaps more natural) reflections on one's own experience that—Cooper demonstrates in Natty—are the source not only of all self-knowledge, but also of the self-restraint essential for maintaining a self-governing democracy. Bat is the parody of a scientist. A true scientist or philosopher would be the first to admit the limits of his knowledge, Cooper recognizes.[23] In fact, it is the parody or the popular misconception that concerns the author, because it is this popular misconception that threatens to have such pernicious moral and political effects.

Dr. Obed Battius has come to the prairie in the company of the Bush clan in order to make his fame by identifying and describing its previously unclassified flora and fauna. And just as Cooper comically played Natty's naturally armed religion against David Gamut's bookish ineffectiveness in *The Last of the Mohicans,* so in *The Prairie* the novelist sets the old trapper to debating with the ridiculous Bat on the nature of man to show the moral wisdom of natural religion.

"Am I man enough!" the doctor expostulates when Natty asks whether he has the courage to face Asa's corpse in the thicket. "I claim to be of the class Mammalia, order primates, genus Homo! Such are my physical attributes; of my moral properties let posterity speak!" (p. 180). For the doctor, knowledge consists in the categorization of externally observable characteristics. He knows nothing of courage or of compassion; and as he himself ironically indicates, he knows nothing of his own moral properties.

Cooper shows Bat to be a craven coward who uses others as well as his precious knowledge merely as a means of securing his own life, comfort, and fame. He is by no means the selfless seeker of wisdom that he pretends to be. When he is pleading with Natty not to slit the throat of the ass who bore him thither lest the animal's bray reveal their hiding place to the Indians, Battius appears to be a man of compassion—concerned with preserving life and rewarding service. Science—particularly, medicine—has been justified as a means of relieving the human condition; it could be regarded as an expression of human compassion for the sufferings of the species, which then extends to other living creatures. But, as Cooper indicates through his bitter ridicule of Bat, science pursued for the sake of science is not so simply motivated. Bat saves the life of the ass, that the animal may carry him another day. And when he flees from the Indians in terror, the good doctor literally runs his loyal servant to death. Although more concerned with collecting information and acquiring fame than with healing human beings, the doctor is nonetheless acquainted with the soothing effects of opiates. Thus, when Ishmael's wife cannot sleep from worry over her missing son, Bat administers a heavy dose to the grieving woman—not so much to relieve her, however, as to secure himself a good night's rest.

Although Bat recognizes that human beings have a common animal—and hence, sensitive—nature, he is more concerned with what distinguishes humans from animals and from each other than with their shared properties or concerns.

> A Homo is certainly a Homo . . . so far as the animal functions extend . . . but there the resemblance ends. Man may be degraded to the very margin of the line which separates him from the brute, by ignorance; or he may be elevated to a communion with the great master spirit of all, by knowledge; nay I know not, if time and opportunity were given him, but he might become the master of all learning, and consequently equal to the great moving principles. (pp. 180–81)

By extending man's lifetime, Bat dreams, science might one day make human beings like unto God. Shaking his head, Natty responds,

> This is neither more nor less than mortal wickedness. . . . Your larning, though it is man's boast, is folly in the eyes of Him who sits in the clouds and looks down in sorrow at the pride and vanity of his creatures. . . . Say, you who think it so easy to climb into the judgment seat above, can you tell me anything of the beginning and the end? Nay, you're a dealer in ailings and cures; what is life, and what is death? (p. 181)

True enlightenment would lead human beings to recognize the limits of their knowledge, not to glory in it.

Looking outside himself, Natty perceives the existence of an order that he himself did not create. In the arches formed by the tree branches in the forest, he has observed the temple of God. And his faith has strengthened both his natural inclination to take only what he needs from nature to survive and his compassionate concern to preserve all forms of life. Natty appreciates Creation too greatly to see any part of It destroyed unnecessarily. Unlike the other pioneers, he has never mistaken the human transformation of things—whether physical or intellectual—for Creation. He has recognized the limits not only of his own but of all human achievements by contemplating the beauty and grandeur of God's work. Aware of his own limitations, Natty is much less willing to judge harshly the faults of others than either Dr. Obed Battius or Ishmael Bush. Natty's self-knowledge is thus also the source of his toleration.

In his first two Leatherstocking tales, Cooper suggested that amour propre—or the desire for personal distinction—is the primary source of human conflict; and in *The Prairie,* he indicates rather directly that science constitutes the worse form of this divisive desire. Natty's natural religion, on the other hand, makes him relatively immune from this invidious force.

Natty is not altogether indifferent to considerations of reputation, however. When the old trapper (improbably) meets Lt. Duncan Uncas Middleton in the midst of the prairie, Natty is surprised and happy to learn that the sons and grandsons of Maj. Duncan Heyward (a young friend of Cora—and Natty—in *The Last of the Mohicans*) now bear the name of the young Mohican: "He was not too proud, then, to call the Indian his friend? . . . It was well done! Like a man, Aye! And like a Christian too!" (p. 113). Natty is perhaps even more pleased and astonished to discover that his own name has also been preserved and handed down by the Heyward family. "What, the name of a solitry unlarned hunter? Do the great, and the rich and the honored and, what is better still, the just—do they bear his very, actual name?" (p. 115). Middleton offers to place a gravestone over Natty's remains—which also pleases the old man. Nevertheless—Cooper emphasizes—Natty would not have asked that his name be so preserved, and he admonishes his assembled friends and beneficiaries: "Put no boastful words on the same, but just the name, the age, and the time of the death, with something from the holy book; no more, no more" (p. 384).

The precious science of Dr. Obed Battius had not only made him ridiculously boastful and slavishly subservient to the opinions of others, but it also failed to provide him with courage in the face of death. Natty's faith in the beneficence of the Creator enables him to face his end resolutely and with dignity. If his compatriots were to adopt Natty's attitude—Cooper seems to be saying—then they too would serve others with courage and compassion. Esteeming God's creations above human works, they would respect the natural equality and liberty of all human beings. They would recognize the need for instituting government to secure their inalienable rights, but they would not expect government—nor human beings themselves—to do more than try to protect and preserve what Providence has dispensed.[24] Thus, Natty's religion illuminates both the grounds and the content of natural mores—the opinions and attitudes that Cooper believes to be necessary for maintaining a democracy.

Notes

1. Now that—in the wake of the New Criticism—political readings have come back into fashion, Cooper's work has received more attention. But debate continues over the merit of that work. Wayne Franklin, *The New World of James Fenimore Cooper* (Chicago: University of Chicago Press, 1982), argues that Cooper is an artist of the first rank, and therefore has been unjustly neglected. On the other hand, Robert Erwin, "The First of the Mohicans," *Antioch Review* 44 (Spring 1986): 149–60, gives a brief history of the critical treatment of Cooper in the twentieth century to show that the novelist has received altogether too much praise as a source or origin.

2. James Fenimore Cooper, *A Letter to His Countrymen* (New York: John Wiley, 1834), p. 98.

3. Cooper himself thought that "all fine writing must have its roots in ideas." James Beard, ed., *The Letters and Journals of James Fenimore Cooper* (Cambridge, Mass.: Harvard University Press, 1960–68), Vol. 4, p. 350. George Dekker, *James Fenimore Cooper, The Novelist* (London: Routledge and Kegan Paul, 1967), also emphasizes the importance of Cooper's ideas—although not the idea incorporated in Natty himself.

4. Critics like Allen M. Axelrod—"The Order of the Leatherstocking Tales," *American Literature* 54 (May 1982): 189–211—who argue that the tales should be read in the chronological order of Natty's life rather than the order in which the novels were written, miss the conceptual development. Annette Kolodny makes a similar point when she observes, "The problem with this kind of approach is that it reads the novels in the order of Natty's development, from youth to old age, and ignores the *real* development of the character's meaning, which occurs in the author's mind as he proceeds from one novel to the other in the course of composition." *The Lay of the Land* (Chapel Hill: University of North Carolina Press, 1975), p. 170; emphasis in original.

5. William P. Kelly, *Plotting America's Past* (Carbondale: Southern Illinois University Press, 1983), also notes the change of characterization that accompanies Natty's increasingly explicit didactic role, although Kelly associates this change primarily with the last two novels in the Leatherstocking series.

6. Much of the critical controversy about whether Natty represents a literal model (see Kelly, *Plotting*, pp. 56, 72), an ideal used to criticize the society that Cooper found around him: see Marius Bewley, *The Eccentric Design: Form in the Classic American Novel* (New York: Columbia University Press, 1957), p. 107; A. N. Kaul, *The American Vision* (New Haven, Conn.: Yale University Press, 1963), p. 118; R. W. B. Lewis, *The American Adam* (Chicago: University of Chicago Press, 1955), p. 103, or an adolescent dream of escape from the complexities of conventional society altogether—but especially from women: see D. H. Lawrence, *Studies in Classic American Fiction* (New York: Thomas Seltzer, 1923), pp. 50–66—arises from a failure to see the way in which Cooper used Natty's solitary condition to reveal his natural virtues—virtues that could be recaptured in civil society, if in different form, because they are natural and thus at least potentially belong to all human beings qua human beings. As an exemplar of natural virtue, Cooper could use Natty both to criticize the deleterious tendencies of most human beings living in society and to illuminate the foundations of a better form of human life, both for individuals and for communities.

7. Although critics since Ralph Waldo Emerson have complained that Cooper did not write good dialogue, Douglas Anderson has argued that the magnificent visual pictures that Cooper presented justify his place in the canon. "Cooper's Improbable Pictures in *The Pioneers,*" *Studies in American Fiction* 14 (Spring 1986): 35.

8. Because Cooper so clearly raised the question of the relation between nature and convention in terms of rights of property in *The Pioneers,* John McWilliams has argued that the novelist's teachings must be understood in terms of the philosophy of John Locke. *Political Justice in a Republic* (Berkeley: University of California Press, 1972). I, too, believe that Cooper's Leatherstocking tales ought to be read in light of state-of-nature theory. But I shall argue that, in this novel as well as in the Leatherstocking tales as a whole, Cooper moves from a Lockean concern with economic development toward a more Rousseauian emphasis on the divisive effects of the desire for distinction and on the need for a community to share a common understanding of right.

9. Citations are from James Fenimore Cooper, *The Pioneers* (Albany: State University of New York Press, 1980).

10. Most critics have missed the thematic significance of the Effingham plot, and therefore dismiss it as a stock element of a conventional romance. See Donald Ringe, *James Fenimore Cooper* (New York: Twayne, 1962), pp. 32–33; Henry Nash Smith, *The Virgin Land* (Cambridge, Mass.: Harvard University Press, 1950), p. 61; D. E. S. Maxwell, *American Fiction: The Intellectual Background* (New York: Columbia University Press, 1963), p. 127.

11. Philip Fisher, *Hard Facts: Setting and Form in the American Novel* (New York: Oxford University Press, 1985), p. 22, has also pointed out that the "hard fact" of the need to rid the land of the Indians contradicted the promise or "theory" of the Declaration. But Fisher does not recognize Cooper's self-conscious attempt to address that contradiction.

12. Citations are from James Fenimore Cooper, *The Last of the Mohicans* (Albany: State University of New York Press, 1983).

13. Whereas Cooper's account of the battle at Fort Henry is scrupulously accurate, Robert Clark has shown in *History and Myth in American Fiction, 1823–52* (New York: St. Martin's Press, 1984), that his depiction of the Indians—with each other as well as with the Europeans (especially the relations between the Iroquois and the Delawares)—departs significantly from historical fact. Clark does not correctly perceive the reason that Cooper gives such an ahistorical picture, however. Clark thinks that it is the result of a not altogether conscious attempt on Cooper's part to justify white expansion. Since Cooper causes Chingachgook to raise explicit questions about the justice of white conquest in his first exchange with Natty, I find it hard to believe that Cooper was unconscious of the issue. And in order to settle it without prejudice to either party, he apparently thought that he should give the best picture of Indian life possible. As repeatedly indicated in Cooper's depiction of John Mohegan in *The Pioneers,* Maqua in *The Last of the Mohicans,* and Mahortee in *The Prairie,* the mores of Indians who came into regular contact with whites tended to weaken and become corrupt—to a large part, as a result of their introduction to alcohol. To give an historically accurate rendition of the Indians as people on the frontier actually encountered them would not have painted the most flattering picture. Cooper therefore tried to imagine them and their mores as they were or could have been before they were corrupted by whites. As Clark himself points out, "The fact that [Cooper] represented the Last of the Mohicans as a man of noble sentiments enraged some of his critics, Lewis Cass in particular." Cooper defended himself by insisting on the right of the romancer "to represent the *beau ideal* of his character to the reader" (p. 49).

14. Because one individual, Natty, overcomes the divisions between groups—Kay Seymour House, *Cooper's Americans* (Columbus: Ohio State University Press, 1966), pp. 235–36, saw—these divisions do not represent contradictions in Cooper's thought, as "cultural" critics like Henry Nash Smith and Leo Marx had claimed. But House does not explain the social and political reasons why only the individual—not groups—can overcome cultural dividing lines.

15. In *The Wept of Wish-ton-Wish* (St. Clair Shores, Mich.: Scholarly Press, 1970), Cooper depicted the marriage of a white woman (Ruth Heathcote) to the Indian chief (Conachet) who saved her after his tribe had massacred the other whites in the settlement. When Conachet discovers that Ruth's family has survived, he orders her to forget him and go back. Her family is repelled by the child; and the psychological disjunction between her recent life, includ-

ing her love of Conachet, and Ruth's childhood fear of the dark inhabitants of the woods—which come flowing back in the presence of her family—prove too much for the mother. Father, mother, and child all die in the end. For two excellent analyses of this novel, see Ringe, *Cooper*, pp. 50–53, and Franklin, *New World*, pp. 123–49.

16. Leslie Fiedler, *Love and Death in the American Novel* (New York: Dell, 1969), p. 209. Both Daniel G. Hoffman, *Form and Fable in American Fiction* (New York: Oxford University Press, 1961), pp. 348–49, and George Dekker, *James Fenimore Cooper, The Novelist* (London: Routledge and Kegan Paul, 1967), pp. 81–84, have pointed out the problems with Fiedler's claim that Cooper was merely a racist.

17. Lawrence, *Studies*, pp. 50–66.

18. Fisher, *Hard Facts*, pp. 56–60, has also pointed out the importance of marriage and reproduction in keeping the land.

19. Thomas Jefferson, *Notes on Virginia* (New York: Norton, 1954), query 6, gave a similar if somewhat fuller explanation of the lower rate of reproduction among the Indians and criticized them for their "barbarous" treatment of women:

> The women are submitted to unjust drudgery. This I believe is the case with every barbarous people. With such, force is law. The stronger sex imposes on the weak. It is civilization alone which replaces women in the enjoyment of their natural equality. That first teaches us to subdue the selfish passions, and to respect those rights in others which we value in ourselves. . . . They raise fewer children than we do. The causes of this are to be found, not in a difference of nature, but of circumstance. The women very frequently attending the men in their parties of war and of hunting, child-bearing becomes extremely inconvenient to them. It is said, therefore, that they have learned the practice of procuring abortion by the use of some vegetable; and that it extends to prevent conception for a considerable time after. During these parties, they are exposed to numerous hazards, to excessive exertions, to the greatest extremities of hunger. . . . With all animals, if the female be badly fed, or not fed at all, her young perish; and if both male and female be reduced to like want, generation becomes less active, less productive.

Unlike Cooper, Jefferson thought that the Indians could be amalgamated—in part, because of their lesser numbers—although blacks could not. As Cooper points out, however, Indians would have become "white" as a result; that is, they would have lost both their distinctive appearance and ways or culture.

20. Bewley, *Eccentric Design*, p. 97, has also emphasized the extent to which Natty serves as the embodiment of the virtue of toleration.

21. Citations are from James Fenimore Cooper, *The Prairie* (Albany: State University of New York Press, 1985).

22. John Locke, *The Second Treatise of Government* (New York: Liberal Arts, 1952), ch. 6.

23. Ringe, *Cooper,* p. 47, points out that Bat's name signifies his intellectual blindness.

24. Arthur Mizener has also observed that Natty is "the kind of being democracy ought to produce and indeed must, if it is to justify its existence." Quoted from *Twelve Great American Novels* (New York, 1967), p. 8, in Norman R. Hane, *Nature's Moralist,* unpublished dissertation, University of Chicago, 1968.

3

Cooper's Political Rhetoric

In his initial Leatherstocking trilogy, Cooper had depicted a man living in the state of nature in order to show his readers that there are natural standards of justice. These Natty Bumppo stories had proved to be even more popular than his early tales of the American Revolution. When Cooper left the United States to deal with his publisher in Europe, he thus had every reason to believe that his didactic project was succeeding. By transforming popular American views of the principles of the regime, he could give the republic a new and better moral foundation.

Seven years later, Cooper returned—a disillusioned man. His novels had been popular, he discovered, only so long as they were regarded primarily as celebrations of the settlement of the frontier. When the critical thrust of his works became apparent, his integrity, his democratic sympathies, and even his status as a distinctively American author had been called into question.

Convinced that his literary works had failed their primary didactic function, Cooper quit writing novels for a time and turned to expository prose. Rather than seek to attach his readers' better sentiments to the principles of natural right through the presentation of a sympathetic character, he attempted to instruct them in political truth directly in a brief treatise entitled *The American Democrat*.

Cooper's Temporary Turn to Discourse

What Cooper had suggested in the Leatherstocking tales, in *The American Democrat* he stated baldly: Properly understood, the principles of the American Declaration of Independence are the principles of natural justice. Unfortunately—Cooper believed—those principles are often misunderstood. Responding to the most typical misunderstandings of the Declaration's principles, Cooper made both the problem that he had been addressing and the solution that he had been suggesting in his literary works more explicit.

Americans tended to misconstrue the meaning of the equality and liberty enjoyed by all human beings in the state of nature, according to the Declaration. In the first place, Americans had erroneously taken Jefferson's statement that "all men are created equal" to mean that human beings are and ought to be equal in every respect. Cooper objected:

> The celebrated proposition in the declaration of independence is not to be understood literally. . . . Men are not born equals, physically, since one has a good constitution, and one a bad. . . . Neither are men born equals morally, one possessing genius, or a natural aptitude, while his brother is an idiot. As regards all human institutions men are born equal, no sophistry being able to prove that nature intended one should inherit power and wealth, another slavery and want. (pp. 108–9)[1]

Believing that by nature "one man was as good as another," Americans did not see—as Cooper had attempted to show them in *The Pioneers*—that it is in the public interest to have educated men of good character in office. Instead, they suspected such "gentlemen" of having aristocratic pretensions. Educated men do not rule as a matter of right, Cooper admitted. Because no person is born a master or a slave, popular consent constitutes the only just basis of government. Once the people consent to the institution of government, however, their duty is to obey its decrees, as the gentleman's duty is to serve as their minister.

Popular government or democracy has no effective meaning except through the rule of law, because it is only by making their own laws and electing their own officials that the people exercise their authority.

> As [a citizen] is a "law-maker," he should not be a "law-breaker," for he ought to be conscious that every departure from the established ordinances of society is an infraction of his rights. His power can only be maintained by the supremacy of the laws, as in monarchies, the authority of the king is asserted by obedience to his orders. The citizen in lending a cheerful assistance to the ministers of the law, on all occasions, is

merely helping to maintain his own power. This feature in particular, distinguishes the citizen from the subject. (p. 142)

Rather than regard the rule of law as the enforcement of popular will, Americans tend to view laws merely as restraints on their natural liberty.

Believing themselves to be not only equal but also free by nature, Americans are tempted to deny the legitimacy of government altogether. Like the Declaration itself, Cooper too insisted that it is necessary to establish government in order to secure every individual's inalienable rights.

> Man is known to exist in no part of the world without certain rules for the regulation of his intercourse with those around him. It is a first necessity of his weakness that laws founded on the immutable principles of justice should be framed, in order to protect the feeble against the violence of the strong; the honest from the schemes of the dishonest; the temperate and industrious from waste and indolence of the dissolute and idle. (p. 75)

As Natty argued in *The Prairie,* government does not deprive human beings of their liberty so much as it frees them from the oppression of others. Knowing that they have the power to rule, however, the people tend to become impatient of legal restraints. The besetting vice of democracy is the temptation to substitute the direct pressure of public opinion for the rule of law.

> Men know that the publick, or the community, rules, and becoming impatient of any evil that presses on them, or which they fancy presses on them, they overstep all the forms of law, overlook deliberation and consultation, and set up their own local interests, and not infrequently their passions, in the place of positive enactments and the institutions. (p. 200)

If Americans are to maintain a free, truly democratic government under law—Cooper thought—these two widespread misunderstandings regarding the political significance of humanity's natural liberty and equality would have to be corrected.

Cooper had tried to counteract the potentially vicious effects of these misunderstandings by showing in his Leatherstocking tales that government is necessary to secure the weak from oppression by the strong. Human beings would neither propagate nor prosper if they lived like Natty in natural solitude. Families require property, however; and property requires protection by law. These laws would be justly administered, moreover, only by gentlemen like Judge Temple and Lieutenant Middleton who appreciate the principles of natural justice that Natty represented. In *The American Democrat,* Cooper advocated the "rule of gentlemen" even more explicitly.

Many critics have concluded that, in advocating the rule of educated men, the novelist contradicted his perhaps unconscious glorification of the man of the woods.[2] I am arguing, on the contrary, that Cooper's fictional and prosaic accounts of the meaning of American political principles are internally consistent. Indeed, Cooper's defense of the rule of gentlemen makes his own vocation as a popular teacher of the principles of justice even more evident.

If government were actually to secure the rights of all citizens—Cooper reminded his readers—great differences would necessarily result.

> By possessing the same rights to exercise their respective faculties, the active and frugal become more wealthy than the idle and dissolute; the wise and gifted more trusted than the silly and ignorant; the polished and refined more respected and sought, than the rude and vulgar. (p. 137)

These differences are not necessarily invidious, however. In fact, by protecting the rights of all people to the fruits of their labor, government contributes not only to the prosperity, but also to the "civilization" or education of the public as a whole.

Were human beings satisfied merely with the requirements of self-preservation, they would continue to live as "savages"—like Natty. But most are not content to live at the level of subsistence. To produce more than they need, however, they have to be assured that they will profit from their labor. "Were it possible to have a community of property, it would soon be found that no one would toil, but that men would be disposed to be satisfied with barely enough for the supply of their physical wants, since none would exert themselves to obtain advantages solely for the use of others."[3] Because labor is painful, "the principle of individuality or . . . selfishness lies at the root of all voluntary human exertion" (pp. 186–87). Human beings work only when they are reasonably sure that the fruits will belong to them or those dearest to them. If any community is to rise above the level of economic subsistence, increase its population, and improve its standard of living, it has to guarantee private claims.

Property rights should be guaranteed not only to promote public prosperity, but also to encourage the growth of civilization—especially education. "Property is desirable as the ground of moral independence, a means of improving the faculties, and of doing good to others and as the agent in all that distinguishes the civilized man from the savage" (p. 191). Property should thus be protected as the ground for social and individual improvement—not recognized or given political privileges in and for itself. "Property always carries with it a portion of indirect political influence, and it is unwise, and even dangerous to strengthen this political influence by adding to it constitutional privileges; the result always being to make the strong stronger, and the weak weaker" (p. 189). Large property holders should be treated like any other citizens; they should make their influence felt politically as individuals—according to their merit, and not their wealth.[4]

The people needed leaders and would elect them from the wealthier, more educated classes.

> There can be no question that the educated and affluent classes of a country, are more capable of coming to wise and intelligent decisions in affairs of state, than the mass of a population. Their wealth and leisure afford them opportunities for observation and comparison, while their general information and greater knowledge of character enable them to judge more accurately of men and measures. (p. 113)

The rule of gentlemen is thus definitely in the public interest. "If one head is necessary to direct the body, so is the head of society (the head in a social, if not a political sense) necessary to direct the body of society" (p. 148).

To serve the public in his most important capacity—Cooper suggested—a gentleman need not hold office. Educated men can have a decisive effect on the community merely through their own private endeavors.

> Anyone may learn the usefulness of a body of enlightened men in a neighborhood, by tracing their influence on its civilization. Where many such are found, the arts are more advanced, and men learn to see that there are tastes more desirable than those of the mere animal . . . ; they acquire habits which contribute to their happiness by advancing their intellect . . . and obtain juster notions of the nature and real extent of their rights. (p. 148)

By developing their intellect and providing them with "juster notions of the nature and real extent of their rights," private gentlemen enable the people as a whole to govern themselves.

Since teaching the true principles of government is not apt to be so popular, elected politicians are not so apt to do it. A gentleman's wealth makes him somewhat independent of public opinion, however; therefore, his influence can be largely private—exercised more in the social realm of the arts, manners, and opinion than through partisan politics.[5] In explicating the grounds and meaning of the rule of gentlemen in *The American Democrat,* Cooper thus articulated his own sense of duty more clearly than he had in either his novels or his travelogues.

Literary men or intellectuals could have more influence on politics than they had in the past—Cooper thought—because their influence is exercised largely on opinion, and public opinion has much more power in modern democracies than it had in ancient regimes.

> The influence of opinion on governments has been greatly aided by the wars and revolutions of the last [two centuries] in which privileges have been diminished, and the rights, as well as, what is perhaps of more importance, the knowledge of their rights among the people, have been greatly augmented. (p. 77)

Because the majority retain the power to alter and even abolish the government in a democracy, institutional or legal restraints do not suffice to protect individual rights. The majority must be convinced of the need to restrain its own power and to obey its own laws. That is exactly what Cooper was trying to do.

Cooper stressed the educated man's public duty rather than his right to be recognized as an embodiment of human excellence, finally, because knowledge of the "true principles of government" necessarily involves an appreciation of human limitations—including, preeminently, one's own. Because the government of the United States is based on natural principles of justice, reflection on specifically American conditions should teach the observer the limits of all human institutions and endeavors.

> As the tendency of the institutions of America is to the right, we learn [from the presence of slavery within its borders], the power of facts, every question of politics being strictly a question of practice. They who fancy it possible to frame the institutions of a country on the pure

principles of abstract justice, as these principles exist in theories, know little of human nature, or of the restraints that are necessary to society. . . . It is hopeless to aspire to any condition of humanity approaching perfection. The very necessity of government at all arises from the impossibility of controlling the passions by any other means than that of force. (p. 108)

As in the Leatherstocking tales, Cooper concluded *The American Democrat* by emphasizing the limits both of human beings and of governments, in an appeal to the sort of natural religion that Natty preached. "There is but one true mode of viewing life, either in a religious, or in a philosophical sense, and that is to remember it is a state of probation in which the trials exceed the enjoyments" (p. 232). Cooper did not urge the importance of recognizing the limits imposed by human mortality so much for the sake of securing eternal salvation, however, as for the sake of preserving a liberal polity. He had a very specifically democratic problem in mind.

If there is no pure and abstract liberty, no equality of condition, no equal participation in the things of the world that we are accustomed to fancy good, on remembering the speck of time passed in the present state, the possibility that what to us may seem a curse, may in truth be a blessing, the certainty that prosperity is more corrupting than adversity, we shall find the solution of all our difficulties. (p. 232)

In both his prose and his fiction, then, Cooper addresses his final appeal to our sense of the smallness of all things human in the face of the Eternal—the recognition of which should counter the democratic tendency to undermine the rule of law in the name of abstract or absolute (and hence impossible) equality and liberty.

Cooper's Return to Fictional Teaching

Cooper's turn to discursive prose may thus be understood as an attempt on his part to come to terms with the limits of his influence as a writer, as well as with the problems of American democracy. Acutely aware of the fallibility of human reason, he did not try for very long to instruct his readers through argument. His attempt to use "polite literature" to teach his compatriots the principles of their polity had not been so successful as he had once hoped. Contradicting wide-spread errors is not apt to make an author popular, he now saw. He still considered such popular instruction to be the primary duty of a gentleman, however. Therefore, in the 1840s Cooper returned to the writing of novels. He even revived his most successful character. And in the last two tales of the Leatherstocking series, Cooper tried to show his readers that Natty's solitary existence outside the bounds of civil society was not in itself desirable or exemplary, by dramatizing two possible marriages.[6]

The Pathfinder

Natty's solitude is not—it turns out—entirely by choice; he has simply not encountered a suitable woman. Like other creatures, he feels a natural desire to mate. The women that he has guided through the forest—Natty explains—"were always too much above [him] to make [him] think of them as more than so many feeble ones [he] was bound to protect and defend" (p. 130).[7] Not so Mabel Dunham. She is of his own class, and her father Sergeant Dunham assures Natty the Pathfinder that his daughter will perceive and appreciate the scout's merits.

The prospect of marriage works remarkable effects on Natty—a man of nearly 40 years in this novel. Where once he had been as proud of his skill as a marksman as he was cognizant of his limitations, Natty now comes to doubt his own value entirely. "I'm afeared I'm too rude and too old and too wild like to suit the fancy of such a young girl. . . . I never knew my own worthlessness, perhaps, until I saw Mabel" (p. 130). To remain in her company, he withdraws from going out on forward patrols. As a result, a French spy escapes, and Natty reflects,

> I'm sometimes afeared that it isn't wholesome for one who is much occupied in a very manly calling, like that of a guide or scout, or a soldier even, to form friendships for women—young women in particular—as they seem to me to lessen the love of enterprise, and to turn the feelings away from their gifts and natural occupations. (p. 189)

Even more remarkable, the man who never cared for distinctions except those clearly based on personal merit (for example, bravery, ability, and honesty) now wishes above all to find favor in the eyes of a young woman:

> I have often thought myself happy, Mabel, when ranging the woods on a successful hunt . . . filled with vigor and health; but I now know that it

has all been idleness and vanity compared with the delight it would give
me to know that you thought better of me than you think of most others.
(p. 270)

Natty never cared for gold or property. "I can easily believe, by what
I've seen of mankind," he reflects, "that if a man has a chest filled
with either, he may be said to lock his heart up in the same box."
Nevertheless, he admits that, during the last peace when he collected
so many pelts, he found his "right feelings giving way to a craving
after property; and if I have consarn in marrying Mabel, it is that I
may get to love such things too well, in order to make her comfortable"
(pp. 432–33). Natty definitely plans to build a home and furnish it; he
would join the settlers on the edge of the wilderness when he married.

In *The Pathfinder,* Cooper thus demonstrates that he regards the
desire to mate to be natural, and that this natural desire is at the
foundation of society (or "the settlements") as well as of its problematic effects. When Mabel responds to Natty's first advance by observing, "I believe that you are happier alone, Pathfinder, than when
mingling with your fellow creatures," Natty counters

> I have seen the time when I have thought that God was sufficient for me
> in the forest, and that I have craved no more than His bounty and His
> care. But other feelings have got uppermost, and I suppose natur' will
> have its way. All other creatures mate, Mabel, and it was intended man
> should do so too. (p. 266)

Natty loses Mabel with great pain, therefore, to the younger, hand-
somer, and more articulate Jasper Western—a friend of Natty and
otherwise very much like the older scout. He respects both Mabel's
right to choose and the power of nature too greatly to hold her to the
promise of marriage that her father extracted before his death. When
he discovers that Jasper loves Mabel just as well as he does, Natty
forces Mabel to choose. He would be her guardian—not her tyrant. He
has always suspected that Jasper would make a more appropriate mate
for the lovely young girl. "Like loves like," he thinks; this is the
reason—he tells Mabel—that he never sought an Indian squaw. His
reason and his judgment tell him that "I wasn't fit for her; that I was
too old, too ignorant, and too wild-like." But "the Sergeant *would*
have it otherwise" (p. 457; emphasis in original); and Natty reflects
that our desires allow us—like him—to be persuaded of what we want
to believe, against our better judgment.

Although Natty's lonely life is not desirable in itself—Cooper shows us—his solitude has enabled the scout to preserve certain pristine virtues that most human beings lose when they enter civil society.

> In short, it was said of the Pathfinder, by one accustomed to study his fellows, that he was a fair example of what a just-minded and pure man might be, while untempted by unruly or ambitious desires, and left to follow his feelings, amid the solitary grandeur and ennobling influences of a sublime nature; neither led aside by the inducements which influence all to do evil amid the incentives of civilization, nor forgetful of the Almighty Being whose spirit pervades the wilderness as well as the towns. (p. 135)

The first of these virtues "was the entire indifference with which he regarded all distinctions which did not depend on personal merit." Living all by himself in the woods, Natty has no reason to concern himself about what others think—of him or anything else. He is therefore free to judge the people that he meets for himself; and when he does, he does so on the basis not of class, but of character.

> A disbeliever in the ability of man to distinguish between good and evil without the aid of instruction would have been staggered by the character of this extraordinary inhabitant of the frontier. His feelings appeared to possess the freshness and nature of the forest in which he passed so much of his time; and no casuist could have made clearer decisions in matters relating to right and wrong. (p. 134)

Because he listens so immediately and directly to his own natural impulses and sentiments, Natty is not deceived by appearances or impressed by conventional distinctions. He neither resents authority, therefore, nor slavishly obeys.

> He was respectful to his superiors from habit; but had often been known to correct their mistakes and to reprove their vices with a fearlessness that proved how essentially he regarded the more material points, and with a natural discrimination that appeared to set education at defiance. (pp. 135–36)

Natty thus represents the ideal citizen of a democracy. He is able to recognize differences of ability and obey orders without sacrificing his own self-respect, independence of thought, or sense of right. Natty's virtues could not be maintained in their pristine, relatively unselfconscious form in civil society, however. Even Natty begins to lose his indifference to the opinions of others when his natural desire to mate has been strongly aroused. If his natural virtues are to be recaptured by the citizens of a "civilized" nation—Cooper indicates—they would have to be recaptured on the basis of intelligent understanding.

Although Natty himself is as emphatically "unl'arned" and common as he is natural, Cooper shows that Natty's virtues are recognized more by military officers and by gentlemen like Judge Temple than they are by rough settlers or more ordinary citizens like Ishmael Bush and Hiram Doolittle. Because his virtues are matters of internal motivation and judgment rather than externally visible skills or achievements, they are not apparent to most of the people that Natty encounters on the frontier. In the Leatherstocking tales, all the whites who come to honor and love the old woodsman are the likes of Sergeant Dunham, Benjamin Pump, and Elizabeth Edwards—whose lives he had saved. The Indians honor "La Longue Carabine" for his prowess as a hunter and warrior—that is, insofar as he matches their standards of human excellence. They do not respect his distinctive character nearly so much. It requires the very civilized art of the novelist to bring out Natty's inner beauty—and educated readers, to appreciate it.

The Deerslayer

In his last and perhaps best tale of Leatherstocking—*The Deerslayer*—Cooper again indicates that Natty has not remained outside society simply because his plain appearance and rough natural manners make him unattractive to members of the opposite sex. On the contrary, the beautiful Judith Hutter prefers the Deerslayer to another much more handsome frontiersman, "Hurry" Harry March. She even goes so far as to offer the Deerslayer her hand! Indeed, Cooper uses the contrasting reactions of Thomas Hutter's two daughters to the two young white frontiersmen to show that it requires both intelligence and experience with the dishonesty produced by civilization to appreciate Natty's charms.[8]

Simple-minded Hetty cannot see beyond Harry's good looks into his more problematic soul. Because she sees only what is on the surface, she does not perceive the evil in Harry or in her own father, who would scalp unarmed Indian women and children in order to get bounty from the Colony of New York. Nor does she comprehend the crafty ferocity of the Indians, who did not touch her only because they see her as a "non-compositer" (Natty's expression for mentally retarded). Judith—on the other hand—had been seduced by the officers' flattery, because she loves being admired. She has discovered—sadly, only through experience—the deceit and condescension that often lie behind pleasing words. Having been stung by her own pride and attraction to beautiful appearance, she therefore values Deerslayer's truthfulness much more than Hurry's looks or the officers' social status and wealth.

Deerslayer will not accept the marriage offer of a woman who has lost her innocence, however. And commentators have subsequently berated both youth and novelist for prudish cruelty. Since Judith had clearly learned her lesson, should she not have been forgiven?[9]

To object to the resolution of the story in this fashion is, however, to miss the thrust of the entire Leatherstocking series. Throughout these tales, Cooper tried to show that undue regard for external marks of social distinction was *the* ultimate source of social dissension, among the American pioneers as well as the Indians. The lesson that he was attempting to teach through his depiction of the life of the solitary man of the woods was that the liberty and equality enjoyed by human beings in the state of nature could be recognized and preserved in civil society only by overcoming this particular vice. Therefore, Judith is severely punished, to make the lesson clear. At the same time—Cooper indicated—Natty is a creature solely of the past; his is a life literally without a future. If he does not marry, there will be no more of his kin and kind. He is an image of pristine human goodness—not complete human satisfaction or virtue. He is a figure from a prehistoric past that can be recalled only through art.

Rousseau in America

By suggesting that concern for reputation and honor is *the* cause of social and political dissension, Cooper was dramatizing the distinctive thesis of Jean Jacques Rousseau's political philosophy. And comparing Cooper's Leatherstocking tales with the major outlines of Rousseau's thought brings out not only the comprehensive, cohesive character of Cooper's political vision, but also the rhetorical advantages of its novelistic presentation.

Like Cooper, in the "Discourse on the Origins of Inequality" Rousseau had presented an explicitly hypothetical (and hence somewhat "fictional") depiction of the solitary life of a human being in the state of nature, in order to show certain natural standards of right on which a just civil society could be founded.[10] Living alone—Rousseau reasoned—human beings would have neither speech nor reason; they would therefore have neither the foresight nor the powers of calculation required to think of their future exigencies (and hence the desire to stockpile the means or material property to serve them) or to conceive of other human beings as potential threats. Both the anxiety and the competitive hostility that Hobbes and Locke had attributed to human beings in their natural condition were really products of society. By nature—Rousseau concluded—human beings are moved by two and only two native sentiments: attachment to their own existence, and compassion for the suffering of other sentient animals. So long as they lived alone, human beings would thus have abided in peace and without property. Having no use for anything beyond the requirements of their subsistence—like Natty in *The Pioneers*—they would find it more trouble than it was worth to maintain a claim to possession. They would simply look for food and shelter elsewhere.

Because nature was bountiful, however, the numbers of human beings multiplied. And once human beings lived in regular association with others, their character began to change markedly. Comparing others as possible mates—like Natty in *The Pathfinder*—they began to be concerned about their own image in the eyes of others. The natural self-love rooted in the pleasure that a human being takes simply in feeling alive became transformed into vanity or amour propre.

Like the Indians that Cooper depicted, people in primitive societies were characterized by stringent notions of honor and violent conflict, because their members tended to take offense at any slight. Nevertheless—Rousseau speculated—because people at this stage of their development first came to experience "the sweetest sentiments known to men: conjugal love and paternal love," this must have been the happiest period of human existence.[11] Like Natty, primitive human beings found that they preferred living in families to solitary freedom.

Because tribal life represented the happiest period of human existence—Rousseau concluded—people would have abandoned this stage only as a result of some external accident; and that accident—he thought—was the discovery of iron. With the discovery of iron, agriculture became dependent on metallurgy; and when individuals became economically dependent on others, the desire for distinction became a source of falsification and hypocrisy. Having to please others in order to survive, human beings began to conceive of their own worth solely in terms of the way in which they appeared to others.

They forgot their own authentic feelings and concerned themselves solely with the impression that they were making. It did not matter whether that impression were based on fact or not, so long as it was advantageous. Like Judge Temple, they were willing to lie in order to receive honor for the accomplishments of others. Like Sheriff Jones, they were willing not only to corrupt office and profession, but also to invade the rights of others in order to foster their own economic interests and consequent social status.

Once the race had multiplied and people were accustomed to living in settled societies—Rousseau acknowledged—human beings could not return to living solitary lives in the woods. They could not again become economically independent. Economic interdependence is only the proximate—not the ultimate—cause of the moral and physical degeneration of human beings in society, however. As Rousseau had observed in his analysis of their natural condition, human beings are inherently lazy. They work to amass property only when they find the property to be useful—that is, only when they have to. In civil society, human beings tend to use their property not to guarantee their survival so much as in a competitive attempt to "best" and glory over others. It is not "property" per se, but the desire for honor or distinction, that is the ultimate cause of social conflict.

By contrasting the hypocrisy, dependency, exploitation, and oppression of commercial society with the contented, pacific life of a solitary human being in nature, Rousseau tried to convince his contemporaries of the desirability of overcoming this invidious desire for distinction, by projecting an image as well as an argument. In Natty Bumppo, Cooper presented as effective an image of the advantages of freeing oneself from the desire for social preeminence as an author has ever created. Natty maintains his freedom of action and of conscience—we have seen—precisely because he does not measure his own worth by the opinion of others.

Natty's modesty rests on his religion as well as his natural solitude, however. The two are connected in Cooper's novels, because Natty acquires his belief in God and His goodness from reflection on the natural expanse around him. The immensity of Creation impresses the woodsman with the relative insignificance of his own—and all mortal— existence. The power of nature looks greatest perhaps to one who confronts it all alone.

Rousseau did not mention religion at all in his *Discours sur l'origine de l'inégalité* because he was attempting to give an entirely natural account of the development of society, and so of the distinctively human faculties. When he sought to show how people could regain their natural freedom in society—in both *Emile* and *On the Social Contract*—instruction in "natural religion" very much like that articulated by Natty then became a necessary means.

In the *Emile*, Rousseau attempted to show how human beings could retain their natural freedom if they were educated according to natural principles. Simulating the state of nature, Rousseau brings the boy Emile up on the edge—if not altogether outside—of society until he has reached puberty. By raising the boy all by himself, Rousseau prevents Emile from hearing the superstitious ghost stories of nurses; he also tries to counter the child's imagined fears, through experience. Those who know the area through which they are traveling in the dark have no tendency to be afraid. (Natty was also raised outside white society among the Delawares, who led him—as Rousseau did Emile— to develop his physical strength and to listen closely to the real sounds and appearances of things in order not only to find his way through the woods, but also to become a courageous and able warrior.) When Emile is tempted to boast so as to gain the praise of others (he being not altogether removed from other people), Rousseau sees to it that the boy is brought to shame. But with puberty—Rousseau argued—the imagination can no longer be checked. Emile is drawn into society by his at first inchoate desire for a mate. Comparing others with regard to their attractions for him, he becomes concerned about his own appearance in the eyes of his beholders. Rousseau first attempts to transform Emile's growing eros and imagination into sympathy, rather than envy, by allowing him to view the great suffering in human society at all levels. Finally, when Emile's imagination is irrepressibly aroused, Rousseau introduces his pupil to religion.

Rousseau does not offer this religious instruction in his own name, however, but through the voice of a Savoyard vicar. Emile first learns of God—we note—overlooking a magnificent mountain vista, and the religion taught by the priest begins with a recognition of the limits of his own knowledge: He knows insofar as he feels his own existence and senses things outside and around him. The religion of reason has its origin in feelings—in the sentiments of the heart become self-reflective. This is explicitly a religion of nature, because the order that the priest perceives around him has led him to infer the existence of a Deity—a good God—whom he cannot know any more directly. Unlike the testimony of his own heart and his perception of the natural order, all purportedly "supernatural" revelations have only the authority of human beings behind them.

I shall never be able to conceive that what every man is obliged to know is confined to books, and that someone who does not have access to these books . . . will be punished for an ignorance which is involuntary. . . . Were not all books written by men? Why, then, would man need them to know his duty, and what means had he of knowing them before these books were written? (p. 303) [12]

All claims to privileged truths are, in fact, merely testaments to human pride. "I therefore closed all the books," the priest reports. "There is one open to all eyes—it is the book of nature" (p. 306). The priest's religion is altogether nonsectarian, because the truth of any and all religions—as he understands them—lies in their general core. There is no reason to seek the conversion of others. One should, rather, pursue the kernel of truth in the religion of one's fathers, and attempt to imbue the external forms with the inner truth of sincere faith. The priest could have been speaking of Natty when he concludes, "Good young man, be sincere and true without pride. Know how to be ignorant. You will deceive neither yourself nor others" (p. 313). The religion and morality of the Savoyard priest is, in sum, the religion and morality of Natty Bumppo.

Like Natty, the priest lives on the edge of society. He was originally disgraced and so exiled from the Church because he could not maintain the vow of chastity and was too honest to deny or disguise his faults. Reflections on his experience and the truth of the heart or nature revealed therein have led him to perceive the limits of human reason and the goodness of the Divine. The boy Emile is not able to maintain his sexual solitude any better than Natty or the priest. Rather than vainly try to suppress this strongest of all the natural passions, Rousseau attempts to attach Emile's budding eros to an image of innocent beauty. And in his description of Sophie, Rousseau stresses the importance of making the image of innocence that attracts both men and women to marriage (and therein their social duties) an image of a common—not extraordinary—individual. If the image would serve as an embodiment and guide to popular morality, it must be attainable by common people. Otherwise they might despair, or ultimately despise the illusion. (As a moral creation, Natty was also emphatically common, rough, and uneducated—though never crude or vulgar.) If Emile had no desire to marry—Rousseau the author indicated—he could continue to live as a free individual. He has learned a trade (as a carpenter) whose tools he can carry with him, to work and to exchange for what he needs. Only the acquisition of dependants—a wife and children—forces Emile to acquire land, and so necessarily to come under the authority of some government and its laws. The steps into social and political bondage are exactly those that Cooper later depicted in *The Pathfinder*. Natty remains free of law and property because—against his own inclinations—he remains unmarried.

But if Cooper's fiction was so Rousseauian, should not his politics have been more revolutionary and radical? By comparing Rousseau and Cooper, we discover not only what a deep-running understanding of the relation between nature and civil society the American novelist had, but also how conservative principles that seem revolutionary in the context of an absolute monarchy look in a postrevolutionary and essentially democratic regime.

Because human beings are free and equal by nature—Rousseau argued—no one is obliged to obey any government or law to which he or she has not consented. To be free, one must rule oneself. To rule oneself means, however, substituting reason for mere natural inclination. In order to establish government, it is necessary for all future citizens to cede all their natural rights to the body politic in order to be ruled by a "general will" equally applicable to all. If anyone (like Natty) were to reserve some of his or her natural rights and so refuse to agree to the "social contract," that person would continue to be ruled by his or her particular desires, interests, or inclinations—not by the generalized rule of reason. By refusing to be governed by the same rules that he or she would apply to others, such an individual would not have acquired the "moral liberty, which alone makes him truly master of himself. For to be driven by appetite alone is slavery, and obedience to the law one has prescribed for oneself is liberty" (bk. 1, ch. 8, p. 27).[13] "Instead of destroying natural equality," by making all citizens subject to the same law, "the fundamental compact substitutes a moral and legitimate equality [for] whatever physical inequality nature may have . . . imposed upon men" (bk. 1, ch. 9, p. 29). Like Cooper, Rousseau thus argued that natural liberty and equality can only be secured—finally—in civil society on the basis of a rather explicit, intelligent understanding of these natural rights.

Like Hobbes and Locke before (and Cooper after) him, Rousseau distinguished the social contract on the basis of which government is instituted from the form of government itself. The only proposition to which the people must agree unanimously is the fundamental compact; each person has to decide for himself or herself whether to become a member of the body politic. After that, the majority rules, and the individual is obliged to obey. Moreover, the way the majority ought to exercise its power is through elections. Indeed—Rousseau suggested—an "elective aristocracy" is the best form of government. It resembles the "natural aristocracy" among savages and yet represents an improvement, insofar as elections prevent the degeneration of the rule of the best into the hereditary rule of the wealthy—if and so long as the elections are regulated by law. "It is the best and most natural arrangement that the wisest should govern the many, when it is assured that they will govern for its profit, and not for their own" (bk. 3, ch. 5, p. 60). Rousseau thus advocated something very much like Cooper's "rule of gentlemen."

Rousseau's famous critique of representation—as well as his insistence that the larger a government, the more oppressive it will be—has led many commentators to infer that the French philosopher advocated direct democracy. In fact, in *On the Social Contract,* he stated,

> Taking the term in the strict sense, a true democracy has never existed and never will. It is contrary to the natural order that the majority govern and the minority is governed. It is unimaginable that the people would remain continually assembled to handle public affairs; and it is readily apparent that it could not establish commissions for this purpose without changing the form of administration. (bk. 3, ch. 4, p. 58)

Rousseau drew a very sharp line between the social contract, or the constitution of the body of the people (to use Cooper's phrase)—which remains sovereign—and the administration of its affairs, or government.

> Since the law is merely the declaration of the general will, it is clear that the people cannot be represented in the exercise of the legislative power. But it can and should be represented in the executive power, which is merely force applied to the law. This demonstrates that, on close examination, very few nations would be found to have laws. (bk. 3, ch. 15, p. 75)

Rousseau considered most of what we call "laws" to be administrative decrees; one of his examples of a law that is *not* part of the social contract itself—nor of the same status—is the constitution of any particular form of government.

If the fundamental governing compact is not to be found in what we consider the "fundamental law of the land," or the Constitution—we might well ask—what and where is it? It is to be found in the mores—

Rousseau responded—in the characteristic opinions and attitudes that make a people a people, and on which the enforcement and administration of all particular legislation ultimately depend. Sharing such a Rousseauian understanding of politics, in his Leatherstocking tales Cooper had, therefore, concentrated on popular American notions of natural right. And in many respects, his novels were better suited to conveying fundamentally Rousseauian lessons than the philosopher's own treatises.

Cooper mentioned Rousseau specifically only in his travel writings and journal. However, by connecting Jean Jacques not only with the city of Geneva (where Rousseau was born, and whose civic virtues he praised in the dedication to his "Discourse on the Origins of Inequality"), but also with the island to which Rousseau withdrew late in life to live in solitude and revery, Cooper indicated that he was actually familiar with a wide range of the philosopher's works.[14] One of the major lessons that Cooper had been trying to convey through his depiction of Natty Bumppo was the value of thinking for oneself—on the basis of one's own experience—rather than attending primarily to the opinions of others. To have appealed to the authority of the French philosopher would, therefore, have undermined Cooper's didactic purpose.

By reinterpreting the Lockean language of the Declaration in a Rousseauian direction, Cooper nevertheless changed the meaning of its principles in two important respects. Beginning with *The Pioneers,* he suggested that the natural right of self-preservation need not entail economic exploitation of the environment or cutthroat competition for the means of survival. On the contrary, to recognize the right of self-preservation is to recognize the value not merely of human, but of all life—and thus, of nature as a whole. To be sure—Cooper emphasized—human beings must establish governments to secure their natural liberty and equality. And once established, these governments represent the greatest threat to the maintenance of that same liberty and equality. Whereas Locke (and the American framers of the Constitution) had argued that political power could be limited by institutional checks and balances, however, Cooper concluded that public opinion constitutes the only really effective restraint on popular government. If all political power belongs—ultimately—to the majority, the only way the use of that power can be limited is through internalized norms of the majority itself. Cooper thus concentrated on popular opinion or attitudes about what is right, because he saw that these mores would determine not merely the actual operation of American government, but the character of American society as a whole.

The Advantages and Limitations of Cooper's Art

If it be true that human beings are moved more by their passions than their reason—as Hobbes, Locke, and Rousseau all argued—appeals to their emotions are apt to be more persuasive than logical argumentation. As Cooper perceived, novels might therefore represent a more effective way of communicating the truths on which this nation was founded than the philosophical treatises from which the "self-evident" truths of the Declaration had been originally drawn.

Believing that human beings are fundamentally equal—Alexis de Tocqueville observed of Cooper's America—democratic people resist anyone who tries to tell them what to think. They do not, therefore, take well to "teaching" in any form.[15] Not wanting to accept opinions on authority, democrats tend to judge things on the basis of their own experience. But—Cooper saw—this trait could make novels at least potentially a more effective means of public teaching in a democracy than argumentative tracts or treatises.[16] By vicariously extending the readers' own experience through their empathy with the characters of fiction, a novelist could speak to a democratic audience more effectively than a lecturer. Leaving readers free to judge for themselves, the novelist could still indirectly guide their thought by showing what happens to specific sorts of characters with specified opinions under certain circumstances. By actively involving the reading audience in figuring out the complexities of their stories and personae, these novelists might affect readers' understandings of themselves, their nation, and its principles more profoundly—if more subtly and indirectly—than any expository analysis could. Surely, the novel represented a more accessible and thus more democratic way of presenting fundamental political truths than philosophic argumentation.

Philosophic writings—properly speaking—have never been truly popular. For example, although Rousseau himself wrote novels and his ideas appear to have been especially well suited to a literary mode of presentation insofar as he emphasized the priority of feeling over reason, Rousseau presented his understanding primarily through arguments directed to intellectuals—arguments that seem unintelligibly abstract to many readers. Cooper's novels had a much wider audience. By enlisting his readers' empathy, the novelist engages their sentiments more than their critical reason. The major voice in Cooper's novels is not that of a philosopher—or even that of the educated author—but rather an explicitly "unl'arned" man whose goodness obviously exceeds that of his social and intellectual "superiors." If the point was to show that human beings are by nature good and that social or conventional marks of distinction are not truly important, Cooper's presentation was certainly more successful than that of his philosophic predecessor.

Not only was Cooper's presentation more popular, but his view of politics was also more consistently democratic. Whereas in his autobiographical writings Rousseau undercut his own attachment to civil society and the morality or self-restraint necessary to maintain it—by making himself an exception to the rules that he proposed for others—the American novelist did not. Although Cooper was much criticized for personal egoism—especially in connection with his libel suits against critics—he was ultimately much more modest than the French philosopher, because Cooper truly believed that human beings could not know the answers to the most fundamental questions about the meaning of life and death. In his "First Discourse," Rousseau vehemently criticized "civilization" in the form of the popular "Enlightenment" of the eighteenth century; but he excepted Descartes, Bacon, and Newton from his attack, on the grounds that they had pursued and obtained true knowledge. Cooper excepted no one in his attacks on the pretensions of human knowledge; he saw learning as valuable only insofar as it contributed to the quality of life of the individual or benefitted the general public by promoting economic prosperity and popular understanding of the principles of just politics.

Cooper captured the imagination not only of his contemporaries, but also of his most notable literary successors with his image of the solitary man withdrawing from civil society to live in the woods. He did not succeed so well as a political teacher. By showing that human life is good by nature, Cooper hoped to ground the right of self-preservation and to convince his readers to respect it in others. Further, he hoped to convince readers that the rule of law is the best means of securing their fundamental rights. By protecting the rights of property, the rule of law creates conditions under which natural resources can be made to support many more people than under anarchism. People will live together in peace, however, only if they learn to tolerate religious, cultural, and individual differences. Through Natty, Cooper thus tried to show his readers that human excellence does not lie in any kind of social or conventional distinction. He tried to make them more modest and less resentful by having his protagonist remind them that all human achievements look paltry compared to Creation. However, these less sentimental lessons appear to have been lost on most readers.

And if we ask why Cooper failed in his broader intention, the answer seems to be that he did not manage to give his more specifically political lessons a sufficiently literary form to shape the minds and hearts of his readers without their knowing what was happening. Although Natty is a sympathetic figure, most of Cooper's characters are stereotypes, whose interactions with one another were designed to illustrate or refute certain social and political theories. In his novels, Cooper thus appealed more to his readers' intellect—than to their empathy, compassion, or emotions generally. Because Cooper nevertheless left many of his arguments implicit in the action rather than making them explicit in dialogue or narrative, the lessons that he wished to teach are much less clear in his novels than in his far less popular political treatise.

Cooper's failure may thus have been one of the major reasons for Hawthorne's conclusion that, if romances do have any discernible effect, it is through more subtle means than direct moralizing. By imbedding the political lessons completely in the basic elements of the literary structure—in the interplay of plot, setting, characterization, and imagery—Hawthorne hoped not only to write better fiction, but also to teach "the truth of the human heart" more successfully.

Notes

1. Citations are from James Fenimore Cooper, *The American Democrat* (Baltimore: Penguin, 1969).

2. The "classic" commentator on Cooper's contradictory mind is Vernon Louis Parrington, *Main Currents in American Thought* (New York: Harcourt, Brace, and World, 1927), vol. 2, pp. 214–16, 229. His description—along with Mark Twain's satirical piece on Cooper's "literary offenses"—has shaped the critical literature ever since. Psychological studies like D. H. Lawrence, *Studies in Classic American Fiction* (New York: Thomas Seltzer, 1923), and Stephen Railton, *Fenimore Cooper: A Study of His Life and Imagination* (Princeton, N.J.: Princeton University Press, 1976), insist even more strongly on the contradictory character of Cooper's thought, which they then attempt to explain.

3. See Aristotle, *Politics,* (Chicago: University of Chicago Press, 1984),

passages 1261b–63b, for a similar argument on the need to attach the individual's self-love to his or her familial responsibilities and economic endeavors.

4. Wealth gives human beings the opportunity to educate and improve themselves, but there is no necessary correlation or connection: "Men may be, and often are, very rich without having the smallest title to be deemed gentlemen. A man may be a distinguished gentleman [on the other hand], and not possess as much money as a footman" (p. 174).

5. Marius Bewley has suggested that we ought to see Hawthorne, Melville, and James as what Cooper had in mind—more so than Daniel Webster or Henry Clay. *The Eccentric Design: Form in the Classic American Novel* (New York: Columbia University Press, 1957), p. 68.

6. Annette Kolodny, *The Lay of the Land* (Chapel Hill: University of North Carolina Press, 1975), pp. 105–12, also stresses Cooper's concern with Natty's sexuality in these last two tales, but she argues that Natty remains infantilely attached to his "mother": nature.

7. Citations are from James Fenimore Cooper, *The Pathfinder* (Albany: State University of New York Press, 1981).

8. In the initial conversation between the two frontiersmen, Natty's companion shows that he certainly does not value Deerslayer's famed "innocence." When Harry asks whether Natty has ever used his rifle on a truly dangerous and honorable target, young Natty soon gets "the better of false pride and frontier boastfulness" and states that he has not yet had occasion. "I hold it to be unlawful to take the life of men, except in open and generous warfare" (James Fenimore Cooper, *The Deerslayer* Albany: State University Press of New York, 1987, p. 19). Harry responds, "Shooting an Indian from an end-bush is acting up to his own principles, and now we have what you call a lawful war on our hands, the sooner you wipe that disgrace off your character" (p. 21), the better. Like the Indians that he contemns, Harry himself believes that a man proves his manliness primarily by besting another. Taking their cue from Harry's initial comment, both Yvor Winters and David Noble have argued that the novel ought to be read primarily as the story of a youth's coming of age. They thus concentrate on an analysis of the scene in which Natty kills his first man and earns a new epithet—ignoring the romantic plot altogether. Yvor Winters, "Fenimore Cooper or The Ruins of Time," from *In Defense of Reason* (Denver: Allan Swallow, 1960), and David Noble, "Cooper, Leatherstocking, and the Death of the American Adam," *American Quarterly* 16 (1964): 419–31. But did Cooper agree with Harry's definition of what it means to become a "man"? These otherwise fine essays unfortunately represent a preeminent example of the tendency of the critics—rather than the novelists themselves—to read women out of the classic American story. See Nina Baym, "Melodramas of Beset Manhood," *American Quarterly* 33 (Summer 1981): 123–39.

9. See Donald Davie, *The Heyday of Sir Walter Scott* (New York: Barnes and Noble, 1961), p. 127, and Joyce M. Warren, *The American Narcissus* (New Brunswick, N.J.: Rutgers University Press, 1984), p. 99.

10. Jean Jacques Rousseau, "Discourse on the Origins of Inequality," in *The First and Second Discourses* (New York: St. Martin's Press, 1964).

11. Rousseau, "Discourse on Inequality," pp. 146–47.

12. Citations are from Jean Jacques Rousseau, *Emile* (New York: Basic Books, 1979).

13. Citations are from Jean Jacques Rousseau, *On the Social Contract* (Indianapolis: Hackett, 1983).

14. See journal entry of 14 July–August 1828, James Fenimore Cooper, *Letters and Journals,* James Franklin Beard, ed. (Cambridge, Mass.: Harvard University Press, 1960), vol. 1, p. 272; and his *Gleanings in Europe: Switzerland* (Albany: State University Press of New York, 1980), pp. 25, 249.

15. Alexis de Tocqueville, *Democracy in America* (Garden City, N.Y.: Doubleday, 1964) vol. 2, pt. 1, ch. 2.

16. Michel Foucault has pointed out the general tendency in modern writing for the author to fade into the background—that is, to efface his or her individual characteristics. The advent of this tendency can be dated, moreover; it occurred along with the emergence of science and liberal democratic politics in the seventeenth century. By submerging his or her individuality, a writer at once minimizes a potentially offensive claim to personal superiority (or argument by authority) and implicitly asserts the broader validity or authority of the presentation on the grounds of its impersonality—if not literal objectivity. As such, the author's view may be shared by the reader. "What Is an Author?" in *Power/Knowledge* (New York: Pantheon, 1980), pp. 141–45, 149. Foucault's own attempt to expose the "author-function" as well as the growing body of "reader-response" criticism may be seen as an extension of this democratic— that is, egalitarian—impulse. See, for example, Geoffrey H. Hartman, *Criticism in the Wilderness* (New Haven, Conn.: Yale University Press, 1980); Jane P. Tompkins, ed., *Reader-Response Criticism: From Formalism to Post-Structuralism* (Baltimore: Johns Hopkins University Press, 1981). Kenneth Daubner, "The American Culture as Genre," *Criticism* 21 (Spring 1980): 104–6, points out the consonance between the appeal for consent in American politics and in American literature.

4

Hawthorne's Politics of Passion

Nathaniel Hawthorne stated his skepticism about the efficacy of literary moralizing just as explicitly as Cooper had declared his intention to teach. In an oft-quoted section of his Preface to *The House of Seven Gables,* Hawthorne observed,

> Many writers lay very great stress upon some definite moral purpose at which they profess to aim their works. Not to be deficient in this particular, the author has provided himself with a moral . . . and he would feel it a singular gratification, if this Romance might effectually convince mankind (or, indeed, any one man) of the folly of tumbling down an avalanche of ill-gotten gold . . . on the heads of an unfortunate posterity. . . . In good faith, however, he is not sufficiently imaginative to flatter himself with the slightest hope of this kind. When romances do really teach anything, or produce any effective operation, it is usually through a far more subtle process than the ostensible one.[1]

Hawthorne did not object to teaching in itself; he thought that it had to be done more indirectly. And the substance of his teaching seemed to differ as much from Cooper's as the style of presentation.[2]

Cooper had depicted a plain woodsman living by himself on the frontier to show that human beings are good by nature—they are corrupted by society. Hawthorne presented a secularized version of the Puritanic doctrine of original sin to reveal the black "truth of the human heart."[3] If we look at prime examples of evil in Hawthorne's tales, however, we find that he frequently associated it—as in Ethan Brand, Rappacini, and Aylmer—with pride of intellect and sexuality.

Like Cooper, Hawthorne thus located the source of human unhappiness and social conflict in the form of selfishness that Rousseau called "amour propre."[4] But unlike Cooper, Hawthorne suggested that this vice is not merely a product of society. If the human race cannot survive without sexual relations, it is totally unrealistic to suggest that, by nature, human beings are meant to live in asexual solitude.[5] To found civil society on a conception of human nature derived from the picture of a solitary man living in isolation is to base it on a dangerous illusion that ignores the most powerful human passion.[6]

Hawthorne thus implicitly criticized both Cooper's presentation of the state of nature and his conception of the political role of literary art. Cooper had suggested that it took the quite civilized art of the novelist to reveal the goodness of humanity's original sentiments, because these sentiments are neither externally visible nor easily articulated by uneducated men and women. If the "nature" that we are most concerned with lies in the human "interior"—Hawthorne responded—a writer ought to delve into the complexities of the human psyche, rather than describe the interaction of social stereotypes in a magnificent physical environment.

Hawthorne's own romances have a clearly psychological focus. But there is a generally neglected political thrust, as well. If human beings are selfish and contentious by nature, the question arises: How can they best organize civil society to overcome their natural faults?

The Puritans' attempt to reform human beings with strict moral legislation had not worked, Hawthorne reminded his readers in *The Scarlet Letter*. Sexual passions are sometimes too strong to be repressed by religious dogma or public regulation. And when such adulterous desires burst through conventional restraints, they threaten to destroy not only the mores of the theocratic republic, but also the psychic integrity of the individuals involved.

In *The Blithedale Romance,* however, Hawthorne demonstrated that letting human passions run wild in a virtual state of nature has even more disastrous results than stringent moral legislation. Because individual human beings are not equally attracted to all others, their sexual passions lead them into competition; and if these conflicting desires are not regulated by law or custom, the competition can have deadly effects.

Because human beings are passionate by nature—Hawthorne concluded—they must institute government to restrain themselves. But in *The House of Seven Gables,* he suggested that basing government on popular consent will not suffice to protect everyone's right to life, liberty, and the pursuit of happiness. People in power can use their position and influence to promote their own self-interest at the expense of the rights of others, in a democratic republic as well as under a Puritan theocracy.[7] If Americans would live together in peace and freedom, they must learn to restrain themselves not only as a body politic, but also as individuals.

Like Cooper, Hawthorne thus tried to inculcate a popular sense of self-restraint through his romances. Whereas Cooper sought to remind his readers of the limits of all things human by having Natty preach a natural religion, however, Hawthorne attempted to moderate the extravagant political expectations of his nineteenth-century readers by leading them to reflect on their nation's history.[8]

As Hawthorne saw it, the characteristic American political vice lies in a tendency to try to forget the past and begin entirely "from scratch"—like the Puritans establishing a new commonwealth in the wilderness. Wherever they go, human beings take the source of their problems with them. It is no particular set of institutions, but they themselves who are the cause of injustice and oppression. In order to institute a government that will really secure justice, Americans first have to learn "the truth of the human heart." Only by confronting the domineering force of the passions within do people learn the need for self-restraint.

But, Hawthorne saw, dwelling on the faults of human nature itself has given rise to a second, even more dangerous American political temptation: the desire to re-form human beings entirely—which can again be observed in the Puritanic origins of the republic. No matter how well intended, that reformist urge is inherently tyrannical precisely because it recognizes no natural limitations on human power. Fortunately, such idealistic moral reforms are doomed to failure, because they deny the basic facts of human nature. However, the repeated failure of efforts to reform human beings is itself apt to produce cynicism and despair.

Hawthorne attempted to counteract not only the reformist urge, but also the despair that tends to follow its frustration, by revising the terms in which people understood the fundamental social contract. Human beings form communities to supply what they lack or want as individuals; but their needs extend far beyond protection, to sympathy and support. The social contract should not, therefore, be conceived merely in terms of an economic exchange of some of the liberty that individuals would enjoy in the state of nature in return for a certain amount of security or public service. The foundation of political union should, rather, be understood more like the compact underlying a middle-class marriage: as an expression of a joint desire to live together, based on the free choice of the parties, in light not only of their individual failings but also of their complementary strengths and talents.

Doubting the efficacy of literary moralizing, Hawthorne did not state his teaching explicitly. On the contrary, in each romance he left the lesson implicit by letting the plot serve as his commentary on the political setting. In order to capture his overall understanding of the state of nature and its relation to civil society, therefore, we must first make these lessons explicit and then—so to speak—add them up.

The Scarlet Letter

Believing that human beings are indelibly flawed by "original sin," America's Puritanic forefathers tried to create a "community of saints" by carefully controlling all aspects of the lives of all their members. But—Hawthorne showed—such stringent moral legislation does not work. Public regulations can neither entirely root out nor repress human passions—especially sexual desire. Nor is it desirable to do so. Bodily desire and intellectual activity are mysteriously connected. Although Puritanic punishment never makes Hester Prynne repent her adultery, it does have an unintended effect: It makes her a freethinker. Obversely, Hawthorne reports in his ironic introduction that associating with people who were devoted primarily to sating their most animal desires was killing his own imagination. While working in the Customs House he could not write.[9] The extent to which the public or political environment can shape or control an individual's inner life is not merely a matter of historical interest. Although Hawthorne addressed the question primarily in an historical context in *The Scarlet Letter,* he made its contemporary relevance clearer in his two subsequent major romances.

Unlike some modern readers, Hawthorne does not condemn the Puritans for punishing a crime of passion. Rather, he begins his story with the observation: "The founders of a new colony, whatever Utopia of human virtue and happiness they might originally project, have invariably recognized it among their earliest practical necessities to allot a portion of the virgin soil as a cemetery, and another portion as the site of a prison" (p. 47).[10] What he does criticize is the undifferentiated severity of Puritanical punishment and the publicity given it.

In describing the crowd gathered at the foot of the scaffold where the convicted adulteress stands holding her baby, Hawthorne observes,

> Amongst any other population, or at a later period in the history of New England, the grim rigidity that petrified the bearded physiognomies of these good people would have augured some awful business in hand. It could have betokened nothing short of the anticipated execution of some noted culprit, on whom the sentence of a legal tribunal had been confirmed by the verdict of public sentiment. But, in that early severity of the Puritan character, an inference of this kind could not so indubitably be drawn. It might be that a sluggish bond-servant, or an undutiful child, whom his parents had given over to the civil authority, was to be corrected at the whipping-post. (p. 49)

Puritan laws aimed at purifying the entire character. All sins were equally in need of correction to the mind of "a people amongst whom religion and law were almost identical, and in whose character both were so thoroughly interfused, that the mildest and the severest acts of public discipline were alike made venerable and awful" (p. 49). This conjunction of religion and law in the Puritan regime precluded a distinction in the law between private and public; the concern for the salvation of the soul could not be limited to public actions. Breaches of family rule constituted as serious crimes as heresy or murder, for all were transgressions of God's will as well as of human regulations. All had to be publicly confessed and publicly punished lest sin kept secret not only prevent the erring individual from truly repenting and thus finding salvation, but also pollute the community. Hence the importance of the scaffold in Puritan America and in Hawthorne's story.[11] Although he praises the dignity with which the Puritan people observed public displays that might—in less severe times—have produced an even crueler ridicule, he condemns the destruction of the private entailed in Puritan instruction and institutions.[12] "There can be no outrage, methinks, against our common nature . . . more flagrant than to forbid the culprit to hide his face for shame" (p. 55).

The Puritan regime depicted in *The Scarlet Letter* does indeed succeed in forming the character of the people: It makes them serious—but grim, solemn, and unsympathetic. By seeking to destroy the private, it tends—in Hawthorne's terms—to destroy the heart as well. The publicity and severity of its punishments are supposed to counteract the human tendency to take pride in public appearances. There is to be no secret sin. Yet—Hawthorne shows—these institutions produce just the pride that they are designed to discourage. If people are as easily tempted as the Puritans believe, it might seem that they would have more compassion for those who succumb. But, precisely because they feel themselves tempted and yet resist the temptations, the Puritans tend to be cold, self-righteous, and superior.

When they are even tempted, the Puritans believe that they have sinned as much as the confessed malefactor. They can hold themselves superior only through a certain hypocrisy. That is the reason the Reverend Arthur Dimmesdale so perfectly embodies the Puritan regime: He is—until the very end—the complete hypocrite. Although he repeatedly and publicly bemoans his own sinfulness in general, he cannot bring himself to confess his very specific adulterous activities.

> The minister well knew—subtle, but remorseful hypocrite that he was!—the light in which his vague confession would be viewed. He had striven to put a cheat upon himself by making the avowal of a guilty conscience, but had gained only one other sin, and a self-acknowledged shame, without the momentary relief of being self-deceived. He had spoken the very truth, and transformed it into the veriest falsehood. (p. 144)

Hypocrisy finally destroys all self-knowledge, because—as the Puritans recognize—human beings cannot maintain a permanent division between their public professions and their private beliefs.

> "At least, they shall say of me," thought this exemplary man, "That I have no public duty unperformed, nor ill performed!" Sad, indeed, that an introspection so profound and acute as this poor minister's should be so miserably deceived! . . . No man, for any considerable period, can wear one face to himself and another to the multitude, without finally getting bewildered as to which may be the true. (p. 212)[13]

Although the Puritans perceive the indissoluble link between public and private, they do not see the way in which the attempt to police the "private" directly leads not to the purification of private life—as intended—but to the pollution of the public with the attempt to deceive. Public pretense finally destroys even the knowledge of private prevarication on which it is based. Puritan practices are supposed to be founded on the doctrine of original sin; but their claim to purify humans through a humanly instituted regime denies that very doctrine, by suggesting that human beings can be living saints.[14]

Hawthorne, in contrast, reaffirms that original truth—if in secular form—in his opening statement: There will always be crimes and death in the human community. Human beings are finite and hence fallible by nature. This is the fundamental self-knowledge that the Puritans both enunciated and lost. If they truly believed and lived their own doctrines, they would—like Dimmesdale at the end—have put their trust in God's mercy and not in the power of their own institutions. Hawthorne, then, is not a Puritan; although—as he often stated—he is their descendant and has learned from their example.[15] Among other things, his story shows that Puritan institutions do not work.

When the community brands and ostracizes her, Hester is forced outside the bonds of faith as well as those of association and affection. She not only comes to see the hypocrisy of those who accuse and lecture her—consider Dimmesdale's public appeal that she reveal her partner if she think best—but she also starts to question the very standards and presuppositions of the Puritan community that both she and her accusers have failed to meet. "Standing alone in the world . . . , she assumed a freedom of speculation, then common enough on the other side of the Atlantic, but which our forefathers, had they known it, would have held to be a deadlier crime than that stigmatized by the scarlet letter" (p. 164). Hester is a human being almost without human society; and as Aristotle observed, such a person must become either a beast or a god.[16] In the course of the novel we see the scarlet letter become transformed in the community's mind from a feared mask of bestial, damned passion to the revered sign of an angel of mercy (p. 161).[17] Knowing what it is to suffer, Hester gently nurses the sick and dying. Although the community's reception of Hester gradually alters—if not explicitly or completely—her attitude does not. She never repents or denies the passion through which she initially set herself outside and against the norms of the Puritan community. Hawthorne concludes that "the scarlet letter had not done its office" (p. 166).

Had the elders taken her child away as they once threatened—the novelist speculates—Hester might have become an open revolutionary. She would not have been able to achieve happiness through political action, however, any more than the elders had succeeded in reforming her with laws. Such a great revolution in inherited attitudes would be necessary to produce free and equal relations between the sexes, that a would-be reformer was apt to despair.

> She discerns . . . such a hopeless task before her. As a first step, the whole system of society is to be torn down, and built up anew. Then, the

> very nature of the opposite sex, or its long hereditary habit, which has become like nature, is to be essentially modified, before woman can be allowed to assume what seems a fair and suitable position. (p. 165)

Changing male attitudes do not constitute the most fundamental difficulty that feminists face, moreover. The most serious problem lies in the nature of the woman herself. She cannot take advantage of public or political reforms, Hawthorne thinks,

> until she herself shall have undergone a still mightier change; in which, perhaps, the ethereal essence, wherein she has her truest life, will be found to have evaporated. A woman never overcomes these problems by any exercise of thought. They are not to be solved, or only in one way. If her heart chance to come uppermost, they vanish. (pp. 165–66)[18]

Hester herself obviously does not care so much about her public position or reputation as she does about the particular people she loves. Keeping the identity of both her bookish lover and her husband secret to protect them from public humiliation while she herself suffers castigation in isolation, she shows herself to have a stronger character than either man. If women act more on the basis of the "heart," and men on the basis of the "head"—Hawthorne thus indicates—eradicating the differences between the sexes will not constitute a real improvement. If—as Hester hopes at the end of her life—"at some brighter period, when the world should have grown ripe for it . . . , a new truth would be revealed, in order to establish the whole relation between man and woman [and, therewith, society as a whole] on a surer ground of mutual happiness" (p. 263), that truth would not consist so much in the fundamental sameness of the sexes as in their complementarity. Nor would that truth be made effective so much through public action as in private life.

Rather than flee the community that has condemned her, Hester remains in an ignominious position to serve the man whom she would have married, and to raise their child. The love that initially separated her from the community ironically ends up tying her to it. Perceiving the spiteful and destructive effects of Dr. Roger Chillingworth's medical treatment of Dimmesdale, however, she persuades her lover to meet her in the forest. There, beyond the bounds of civil society—in nature—she urges him to leave with her and begin a new life in a new community, as man and wife. Their potential happiness does not depend so much on reforming public attitudes—she intuits—as in securing a private family life of their own.

Dimmesdale is not able to leave with her, however. Unlike Hester, the minister has not freed himself from Puritanic dogma. Living under false pretenses with her as his "wife" would have tormented him (that is, his conscience) just as unremittingly as Dr. Chillingworth's "medicine." Rather than flee with Hester, the minister publicly confesses his sin, and expires. As a Puritan, he literally cannot live with his fallible, sexual nature.

A change of attitudes would be necessary "to establish the whole relation between man and woman on a surer ground of mutual happiness"; but those attitudes do not concern the political equality of the sexes per se so much as the relation of body to soul, or the fundamental constitution of human nature itself. The problem with the Puritan regime as Hawthorne portrayed it is not that it treated the sexes differently.[19] Had Hester exposed Dimmesdale, he too would have suffered public ignominy. The problem with the Puritan regime stems, ultimately, from a failure to appreciate the indissoluble natural tie between physical passion and the origin of life or the soul. Although the Puritans' specific set of social regulations has long been abolished—the novelist recognizes—the fundamental misunderstanding of human nature underlying those regulations has not.[20] Hawthorne brings out the destructive consequences of this misunderstanding even more emphatically in his depiction of a contemporary effort at social reform.

The Blithedale Romance

Offended by the economic inequality and exploitation characteristic of the nineteenth-century American commercial republic—as Hawthorne tells it—a group of reformers has withdrawn from the "rusty framework" of civil society, to a farm. There they hope to recapture the liberty and equality that all human beings enjoy in the state of nature, by establishing a community free from all conventional restraints. In place of self-interested competition and a division of labor, the citizens of Blithedale want to institute egalitarian economic cooperation. Rather than regulate affection by legal contract in the form of marriage, moreover, they would permit everyone to love whomever he or she pleased.

As Sigmund Freud suggested almost 100 years later, such an experiment is particularly well designed to reveal the "ineffaceable feature of human nature."

Suppose that personal rights to material goods are done away with, there still remain prerogatives in sexual relationships, which must arouse the strongest rancour and most violent enmity among men and women who are otherwise equal. Let us suppose this were also to be removed by instituting complete liberty in sexual life, so that the family, the germ-cell of culture, ceased to exist; one could not, it is true, foresee the new paths on which cultural development might then proceed, but one thing one would be found to expect, and that is that the ineffaceable feature of human nature would follow wherever it is led.[21]

The Blithedale experiment demonstrates that human beings are ineradicably selfish.

Associating the evils of life in a commercial republic especially with economic competition, the Blithedale reformers are determined to equalize labor.

We meant to lessen the laboring man's great burden of toil, by performing our due share of it at the cost of our own thews and sinews. We sought our profit by mutual aid, instead of wresting it by the strong hand from an enemy, or filching it craftily from those less shrewd then ourselves . . . , or winning it by selfish competition with a neighbor. (pp. 19–20)[22]

Contrary to the expectations of most critics—Hawthorne points out—the farm does not fail economically.[23] "Dreamy" intellectuals can become pragmatic farmers; the problem is rather that, when they become farm laborers, they cease being intellectuals. As the narrator—Miles Coverdale (a poet)—reports,

While our enterprise lay all in Theory, we had pleased ourselves with delectable visions of the spiritualization of labor. . . . [But] the clods of earth which we so constantly belabored and turned over and over, were never etherealized into thought. Our thoughts, on the contrary, were fast becoming cloddish. (p. 66)

By equalizing physical labor among the members of the community, Blithedale threatens to destroy all intellectual or "spiritual" life.

Intellectual activity is incompatible with any large amount of bodily exercise. The yeoman and the scholar—the yeoman and the man of finest moral culture, though not the man of sturdiest sense and integrity—are two distinct individuals, and can never be melted or welded into one substance. (p. 66)

Economic equality is neither the primary goal of the Blithedale experiment nor the essential means of achieving it, however.[24] Blithedale takes its institutional designs from Charles Fourier; and the French reformer would have rewarded unequal contributions of capital and talent as well as labor. He merely insisted that every member of his community be provided with the minimal necessities of a private room and bath! He also counted on competition to increase production and on the desire for distinction to encourage self-restraint in the governing classes, in his system of "harmonizing the passions."[25] Blithedale thus goes far beyond Fourier. The French reformer tried to use human self-interest to achieve the common good, but the Blithedalers want to root out all forms of selfishness. The reform that they contemplate is thus much more radical than Fourier's Harmony, because it involves a fundamental transformation of human nature. As Hawthorne shows in his characterization of the "philanthropist" Hollingsworth, the desire to change human nature is *the* distinguishing character of social and political reform. When one member of the Blithedale community explains the Frenchman's system to another, the latter exclaims, "He has committed the unpardonable sin; for what more monstrous iniquity could the Devil himself contrive than to choose the selfish principle— the principle of all human wrong . . . which it is the whole aim of spiritual discipline to eradicate—to choose it as the master-workman of his system?" (p. 53). "There was far less resemblance," the narrator thus observes, "than the world chose to imagine, inasmuch as the two theories differed, as widely as the Zenith from the Nadir, in their main principles" (p. 53).

Nonetheless—Hawthorne suggests—there is a deeper affinity. Despite their different views of economic self-interest, the community at Blithedale is founded on the same basic misconception as Fourier's Harmony: the notion that, if people would but free their natural passions from artificially imposed social restraints, they would live in perfect harmony. In *The Blithedale Romance,* Hawthorne shows that—on the contrary—liberating the passions entirely has destructive results. When people are allowed to act solely on the basis of their own strongest desires, they immorally use others as expedients to achieving their own ends—in affairs of the heart, as well as in business.

By destroying all social and economic differences, the Blithedale reformers think that they will enable people to love each other free of all artificial barriers.

> The footing on which we all associated at Blithedale was widely different from that of conventional society. While inclining us to the soft affections of the golden age, it seemed to authorize any individual of either sex to fall in love with any other, regardless of what would elsewhere be judged suitable or prudent. Accordingly, the tender passion was very rife among us. (p. 72)

Expecting to live as "brothers and sisters," they fail to perceive the exclusive character of human sexuality. As demonstrated by Hawthorne in the actual relations of the four major characters, however, the love that brings certain people together—by virtue of that very fact—sets them apart from others.[26] On a more general level, Coverdale the narrator observes,

> It struck me as rather odd, that one of the first questions raised, after our separation from the greedy, struggling, self-seeking world, should relate to the possibility of getting the advantage over the outside barbarians in their own field of labor. But, to own the truth, I very soon became sensible that, as regarded society at large, we stood in a position of new hostility, rather than new brotherhood. . . . We were inevitably estranged from the rest of mankind in pretty fair proportion with the strictness of our mutual bond among ourselves. (pp. 20–21)

The bonds tying the members of the Blithedale community together turn out to be not very strong, either. The "emigrants" have come to the farm less from any positive attraction to one another or agreed political principles than from a shared rejection of existing society (p. 63). Once removed from the common enemy (society), the community at Blithedale gradually dissolves. Hawthorne does not describe the process of dissolution, however. Rather—quite characteristically—he indicates the grounds for the sundering of the community at Blithedale through the plot of the novel.

Instead of making his four major characters one big affectionate family, Hawthorne shows in their relations with each other that "free love" produces even deeper, more destructive divisions than society's conventional kind. Hollingsworth—for instance—will have nothing more to do with Coverdale after the poet refuses to help the philanthropist undermine Blithedale in order to construct his own criminal reformatory. To keep Hollingsworth's affections, the feminist reformer Zenobia proposes not only to destroy Blithedale by shifting her financial backing to his reformatory, but also to sell her half-sister Priscilla into a kind of spiritual slavery worse than the economic oppression that she had suffered in the commercial republic. Repelled by the sight of Priscilla's servitude, Hollingsworth banishes Zenobia from his company, and she commits suicide shortly thereafter. Like James Fenimore Cooper, Hawthorne too suggests that competition among human beings is less economic in its origins than it is sexual. And sexual passion cannot be eradicated.[27]

Zenobia clearly embodies such sexual passion. And Hawthorne uses the contrast between the power of her person and the relatively more pallid pretensions of the other reformers to reveal the illusory character of their respective misunderstandings of human nature.[28]

The narrator Coverdale, for example, represents the idealized—and hence, fundamentally false—view of nature characteristic of pastoral poetry. He has come to Blithedale in the hope of producing "something that shall really deserve to be called poetry—true, strong, natural, and sweet" (p. 14). Zenobia greets him—and she strikes him as being woman incarnate: robust, sensual, proud, and almost indecent. She embodies the natural passion that he is seeking for his poetry, but she does not attract him.[29] She is too strong, too independent—he thinks—to need his aid or protection (p. 79). Early in the romance, Hawthorne thus indicates that Coverdale's quest to strengthen his poetry will fail. He is more attached to the puny figments of his imagination than he is to the truth.

Coverdale's artistic failure reveals a moral deficiency, as well. Because he has no animating principle himself, he cannot act; he lives, rather, by observing the lives of others. Although he expects Priscilla to be the tragic victim of Hollingsworth and Zenobia's passionate love, he does nothing to prevent this from happening. Rather, at one point he muses, "If any mortal really cares for her, it is myself; and not even I, for her realities—poor little seamstress, as Zenobia rightly called her!—but for the fancy-work with which I have idly decked her out!" (p. 100). When the poet "confesses his love" for Priscilla in the last sentence, he is merely revealing his bias as a narrator. This love of his has never affected his action; he confesses it only after the object is safely married to another.[30] Like "Zenobia," the narrator's name—also—indicates something about his character and function.[31] Trying constantly to disguise his own lack of feeling, the poet is not honest with himself any more than he is with the reader.

Zenobia may make both the Blithedale experiment and Coverdale's pastoral poetry "show like an illusion" merely by her presence, but she explicitly accuses the philanthropist Hollingsworth of deluding himself. Pretending only to care for others—Zenobia charges—Hollingsworth has in fact cared only for his own pet project.

> It is all self . . . nothing else but self, self, self. . . . You have embodied yourself in a project. . . . You are a better masquerader than the witches and gypsies yonder; for your disguise is a self-deception. (p. 218)

Hollingsworth has been ready to sacrifice everything and anyone to see his reformatory built.

> First, you aimed a death blow . . . at this scheme of a purer and higher life. . . . Then, because Coverdale could not be quite your slave, you threw him ruthlessly away. And you took me, too, into your plans, as long as there was any hope of my being available, and now fling me aside, a broken tool! But foremost and blackest of your sins, you stifled down your inmost consciousness!—you did a deadly wrong to your own heart! You were ready to sacrifice this girl, whom, if God ever visibly showed a purpose, he put into your charge. (p. 218)

As undifferentiated and apparently selfless love of all human beings, philanthropy stands in morally pretentious contrast to the passionate attachment to one man represented by Zenobia. But in Hollingsworth, generalized love proves to be as egotistical as sexual passion; it merely lacks the knowledge of its own foundation and character that Zenobia possesses.

What pretends to be "love of human beings" in Hollingsworth is really a deep hatred of their most basic drives. If it be true that human beings are selfish by nature, then a reformer like Hollingsworth must remake them entirely if they were to become selfless. It should not be surprising if—like Zenobia—they are destroyed in the process. Like Coverdale, the philanthropist—too—prefers his own illusion to the reality of human existence.

In fact—Hawthorne suggests—the reality is not so bad as Hollingsworth fears. Were he to succeed in building his reformatory, the philanthropist would be establishing an essentially tyrannical—even totalitarian—institution.[32] But he himself is not driven by a perverted will to power. A tenderhearted man, he cares deeply for the suffering of other human beings—especially the sick, injured, weak, and lonely. It is for this reason that Hollingsworth is unable to countenance the exploitation and degradation of Priscilla when he is actually confronted with it.

His tender sentiments had given rise to a tyrannical project because Hollingsworth lacks the knowledge of human nature that Hawthorne's romances were intended to supply. No person would hurt another willingly, Hollingsworth believes; people rob and kill others only because they themselves have been degraded and cast out of civil society. Like his fellows at Blithedale, Hollingsworth attributes the failure of human beings to live with each other in complete harmony to external causes, especially to inadequate institutional arrangements. He thus thinks that he can reform criminals "by methods moral, intellectual, and industrial, by the sympathy of pure, humble and yet exalted minds, and by opening to his pupils the possibility of a worthier life than that which has become their fate" (p. 131). He angrily condemns Zenobia for taking advantage of her sister's weakness—without realizing that in condemning her and banishing her from his presence, he is treating her exactly the way society treats the criminal, and for the same reasons: to protect the weak, and to maintain the purity of his society's moral standards. Only after Zenobia's death does Hollingsworth recognize that he, too, is a criminal:[33] He sought to have his own way without regard to the interests, opinions, or needs of others. He was a party to the enslavement of Priscilla as much as Zenobia, but he could not banish himself from his own presence. He marries Priscilla; but her noncomprehending adoration adds to his suffering and self-deprecation rather than alleviating it, because he abhors the selfishness that he has been forced to confront—not merely in others, but primarily in himself.[34]

There is no such thing as selfless love among human beings, Hawthorne seems to indicate. But there is a strong connection between love—of self as well as of the other—and the reformist urge. To desire something is—after all—not only to feel oneself lacking, but also to want to remedy the defect. People tend to delude themselves about the nature of their strongest passions, however. They become confused about the true foundations or source of human community, because their pride makes it hard for them to admit that their noblest desires are rooted in their own most basic faults. As Hawthorne indicates in Hollingsworth's psychological collapse at the end of the romance, it will not suffice merely to lead people to confront their own faults; it is just as essential to show them how to live with their flawed nature. To do that—the novelist suggests—they need a better understanding of the human spirit.

Just as Hawthorne uses the embodiment of sexual passion in Zenobia to unmask the pretenses of pastoral poetry and philanthropic reform, so he uses the contrast between the feminist and her weak half-sister to correct a common American misunderstanding regarding the nature not merely of "woman," but of the human spirit more generally. The adulation of selflessness as the epitome of morality is often associated with praise of passivity in women and a perception of the spiritual as being in opposition to the physical. These views are not only contrary to the facts of human nature, Hawthorne suggests; they also threaten to destroy individual liberty.

On first meeting Hollingsworth's mysterious charge, Zenobia quickly concludes that her pale complexion and slight stature are not signs of superior spirituality so much as physical frailty resulting from economic exploitation.

> She is neither more nor less . . . than a seamstress from the city, and she has probably no more transcendental purpose than to do my miscellaneous sewing. . . . There is no proof, which you would be likely to appreciate, except the needle marks on the tip of her forefinger. Then, my supposition perfectly accounts for her paleness, her nervousness, and her wretched fragility. Poor thing! She has been stifled with the heat of a salamander-stove, in a small close room, and has drunk coffee, and fed upon dough-nuts, raisins, candy and all such trash, till she is scarcely half-alive; and so, as she has hardly any physique, a poet, like Mr. Miles Coverdale, may be allowed to think her spiritual! (pp. 33–34)[35]

But whatever its material causes—the defender of women's rights can see—Priscilla's bodily weakness and consequent psychological dependency have broader social and political significance, as well. Priscilla represents "the type of womanhood, such as man has spent centuries in making," Zenobia complains in a later conversation with Hollingsworth. Rather than elevating themselves by making women poor and subservient so they can rule them, however, men have degraded themselves by claiming to love women who are obviously inferior to them.

Men do not want to lord it over women, Hollingsworth responds; on the contrary, they desperately need feminine sympathy and support.

> [Woman] is the most admirable handiwork of God, in her true place and character. Her place is at man's side. Her office, that of sympathizer; the unreserved, unquestioning believer; the recognition, withheld in every other manner, but given, in pity, through woman's heart, lest man should utterly lose faith in himself; the Echo of God's own voice, pronouncing— "It is well done!" (p. 122)

Should women fail to accept their appointed role voluntarily, however, Hollingsworth is willing to force them back into their proper place:

> Man is a wretch without women, but woman is a monster . . . without man, as her acknowledged principal! As true as I had once a mother, whom I loved, were there any possible prospect of woman's taking the social stand which some of them—poor, miserable, abortive creatures, who only dream of such things because they have missed woman's peculiar happiness, or because Nature made them really neither man nor woman!—if there were a chance of their attaining the end which these petticoated monstrosities have in view, I would call upon my own sex to use its physical force, that unmistakeable evidence of sovereignty, to scourge them back within their proper bounds! (p. 123)

Although he argues that the conventional distinction between the roles of the sexes is a product of both nature and divine will, Hollingsworth nevertheless admits that the distinction is not based on the freely given consent of both parties. Nor—Hawthorne shows at the end of the romance—does it have its desired effect. Hollingsworth is totally unable to find faith in himself from Priscilla's absolutely unquestioning adoration. He knows his own faults too well to believe he is worthy of worship.

What human beings both male and female most want—as Hawthorne demonstrates most clearly in the fate of Zenobia—is the sympathetic support of others. To offer such sympathy, people must have experienced the same passions, and so understand the frustration and failure that necessarily accompany them. People like Priscilla cannot, therefore, provide the desired support. The foundation of a true community based on love does not require the abolition of all passions and self-interest. On the contrary—as the Puritans' earlier experiment in "spiritual" reform ought to have taught later Americans (and as Hawthorne himself had shown in *The Scarlet Letter,* in the fate of Dimmesdale)—the attempt to purify human beings of all bodily desire succeeds only in depriving them of life.

Based on the same mistaken belief in the opposition between soul and body—Hawthorne indicates in *The Blithedale Romance*—contemporary "spiritualism" even more clearly entails the loss of life. The mesmerist Westervelt understands full well the physical basis of Priscilla's susceptibility to hypnosis:

> She is one of those delicate, nervous young creatures, not uncommon in New England, and whom I suppose to have become what we find them

by the gradual refining away of the physical system among your women. Some philosophers choose to glorify this habit of body by terming it spiritual, but, in my opinion, it is rather the effect of unwholesome food, bad air, lack of out-door exercise, and neglect of bathing. . . . Zenobia, even with her uncomfortable surplus of vitality, is far the better model of womanhood. (pp. 95–96)

Westervelt is, nevertheless, cynically willing to take advantage of the popular belief in the opposition of spirit and body, to promote his staged production of Priscilla as the "Veiled Lady" who enables others to communicate with the spirits of the dead. Although he presents such spiritualism as the means of establishing a universal brotherhood of all souls at all times and places—Coverdale observes—Westervelt's lecture is infused with a deadly materialism.

The Professor began his discourse, explanatory of the psychological phenomena, as he termed them, which it was his purpose to exhibit to the spectators. . . . It was eloquent, ingenious, plausible, with a delusive show of spirituality, yet really imbued throughout with a cold and dead materialism. . . . He spoke of a new era that was dawning upon the world; an era that would link soul to soul, and the present life to what we call futurity, with a closeness that should finally convert both worlds into one great, mutually conscious brotherhood. He described (in a strange, philosophical guise, with terms of art, as if it were a matter of chemical discovery) the agency by which this mighty result was to be effected. (p. 200)

And Coverdale leaves no doubt as to the danger represented by such scientific-historical schemes for enforcing the future brotherhood of mankind: "If these things were to be believed, the individual soul was virtually annihilated" (p. 198). All differences would be reduced to one common element.

Both in the form of Westervelt's brand of spiritual union and the Blithedale egalitarian economic experiment, the aspiration toward universal "brotherhood" results in the utter—if unintended—subordination of spiritual individuation to materialistic commonality. Only in death will human beings actually be reduced to one common denominator, and so be completely united. But there is no sympathetic support to be derived from such commonality. On the contrary, as Coverdale observes over Zenobia's grave:

While Zenobia lived, Nature was proud of her, and directed all eyes upon that radiant presence, as her fairest handiwork. Zenobia perished. Will not Nature shed a tear? Ah, no!—She adopts the calamity at once into her system and is just as well pleased, for aught we can see, with the tuft of ranker vegetation that grew out of Zenobia's heart, as with all the beauty which has bequeathed us no earthly representative except in this crop of weeds. It is because the spirit is inestimable that the lifeless body is so little valued. (p. 244)

Nature herself is indifferent to the suffering as well as the survival of the individual. Human beings will never find the compassion and comfort that they want merely by returning to nature or by trying to abolish all individual distinctions in total and complete community.

Although Zenobia revealed the pretensions of her companions, she herself thus finally represents the greatest illusion of all. She embodies the mistaken belief underlying the Blithedale experiment that, if human beings but follow their natural inclinations, they will find happiness.

Zenobia herself attributes her tragic end to her unconventional behavior as a woman in public.

A Moral: Why, this: That, in the battlefield of life, the downright stroke, that would fall on a man's steel head piece, is sure to light on a woman's heart, over which she bears no breastplate, and whose wisdom it is therefore to keep out of the conflict. Or, this: That the whole universe, her own sex and yours, and Providence, or Destiny, to boot, make common cause against the woman who swerves one hair's breadth, out of the beaten track. Yes; and add (for I may as well own it, now), that, with that one hair's breadth, she goes all astray and never sees the world in its true aspect afterwards. (p. 224)

But the narrator observes, "So great was her relative power and influence and such seemed the careless purity of her nature, that whatever Zenobia did was generally acknowledged as right for her to do. The world never criticized her so harshly as it does most women who transcend its rules. . . . The sphere of ordinary womanhood was felt to be narrower than her development required" (pp. 189–90).

Zenobia's unhappy ending results, rather, from her own inability to restrain her impulses. Free to choose her associates for herself, she at first chooses badly. Apparently recoiling from her association with a superficially handsome but "unprincipled" young man (Westervelt) with "no passion, save of the senses," Zenobia joins the agrarian utopians in hope of finding a true response to "her real womanhood" in Hollingsworth.

> What a voice he has! And what a man he is! Yet not so much an intellectual man, I should say, as a great heart; at least he moved me more deeply than I think myself capable of being moved, except by the stroke of a true, strong heart against my own. It is a sad pity that he should have devoted his glorious powers to such a grimy, unbeautiful, and positively hopeless object as this reformation of criminals. . . . To tell you a secret, I never could tolerate a philanthropist before. (p. 21)

Resenting the nineteenth-century conventions that confine women to private life, she supports the Blithedale experiment allowing everyone to love whomever he or she pleases with no artificial restraints. Acting according to those principles, she cannot extract any promise of future affection or any other sort of enduring commitment from Hollingsworth in return for the use of all her wealth in his project—to say nothing of the sacrifice of the Blithedale experiment, her own feminist beliefs, and her half-sister Priscilla.

In Zenobia, Hawthorne thus dramatizes the ill-starred fate of the female reformer—which he had only sketched out in *The Scarlet Letter*. Although able at least partially to combat the inherited prejudices of the opposite sex, Zenobia abandons her principles when her heart chances to come uppermost.[36] And in the end, she confesses,

> I am a woman with every fault, it may be, that a woman ever had—weak, vain, unprincipled (like most of my sex; for our virtues, when we have any are merely impulsive and intuitive), passionate, too, . . . false, moreover, to the whole circle of good, in my reckless truth to the little good I saw before me—but still a woman! A creature whom only a little change of earthly fortune . . . and one true heart to encourage and direct me might have made all that a man can be! (pp. 217–18)

Through her desire to find a man able to move her "by the stroke of a true, strong heart against [her] own," Zenobia nevertheless brings to the fore the true foundations of human community. They are not merely economic, sexual, or intellectual. She wants the company, sympathy, and support of someone who has developed compassion because he himself feels the failures and frustrations that necessarily accompany high aspirations.

She is unable to satisfy her most fundamental desire, because she has not been properly trained or educated:

> In her triumphant progress towards womanhood, she was adorned with every variety of feminine accomplishment. But she lacked a mother's

care. With no adequate control . . . (for a man, however stern, however wise, can never sway and guide a female child), her character was left to shape itself. There was good in it, and evil. Passionate, self-willed, and imperious, she had a warm and generous nature; showing the richness of the soil, however, chiefly by the weeds that flourished in it, and choked up the herbs of grace. (p. 189)

Zenobia does not understand how she can satisfy her deepest desire because she has never experienced life in a family where relations are based on mutual respect and love. Her mother died in shame when her father's excessive attachment to worldly appearances led him into bankruptcy, and thence into crime as well. Zenobia herself thus sees only the way in which conventions are false to nature; she does not understand the way in which conventional relations or agreements in the form of marriage are necessary to satisfy the strongest human passions.

In Zenobia, Hawthorne shows that—contrary to the initial belief of the Blithedalers—nature alone is not sufficient. Zenobia needs to be shaped, guided, even restrained by institutions. The proper institution for checking the wilder impulses of human nature is not, however, a reformatory of the kind that Hollingsworth envisions. Education is and should be a function of the family—an institution founded on particularized, rather than generalized, love.

Zenobia's inability to find happiness at Blithedale thus reveals the illusory character of that social experiment, in two different respects. Not only does she embody the particularistic physical passion that sets human beings in competition with one another, but her faults also point to the necessity of the very institution—the family—that the reformers wish to abolish. Only through a marriage based on the free consent and commitment of both partners can human beings realize their deepest desire for a passionate but enduring union at more than a purely physical level. In *The House of Seven Gables,* Hawthorne makes the significance of that institution even clearer.

The House of Seven Gables

In contrast to the tragic affairs of Hester and Dimmesdale and of Zenobia and Hollingsworth, Hawthorne concludes *The House of Seven Gables* with the happy marriage of Phoebe and Holgrave. The peaceful union of the last descendants of two previously warring families represents the way not only to satisfy sexual passion but also to overcome the class conflict generated by economic inequality that the Blithedalers had sought to abolish. To grasp the broader political significance of the tale, however, we must once again examine the interaction between plot and setting.

American life had changed so much since the Puritan founding that Hawthorne was led to ask what—if any—relevance the past had for life in the contemporary commercial republic. Was there an American heritage? If so, what was it? To answer that question—like Faulkner after him—Hawthorne used a story of the fortunes of a particular family to bring out the several meanings of "inheritance": biological, economic, social, and historical.[37]

The house of seven gables in which Hawthorne sets his tale had been built by a Puritan—Colonel Pyncheon—as an enduring monument to his fame and wealth. When the story opens, however, we see that the last heir living under the now rotting timbers of the family mansion has been forced to open a penny shop to eke out a living. The first question, then, becomes how to explain the decline in the Pyncheon fortunes. And the second, how best to respond to that decline.

Determined to build a family mansion on the site of a well that was owned by the commoner Matthew Maule, Colonel Pyncheon had sought to obtain title to the land in court. When Maule won the lawsuit, Pyncheon contrived to have Maule hanged as a witch. Unable to act against the aristocratic Pyncheons in public, Maule's plebian descendants nevertheless took their revenge—slow but sure. Pyncheon hired Maule's son to erect his mansion. And the carpenter hid the Pyncheon deed to a truly baronial territory in Maine inside a secret panel that he built into the wall behind a portrait of the old colonel. Anxious to be remembered by posterity, the colonel forbade his heirs to move his image, so their claims lay in abeyance until they were finally lost. As a result, the Pyncheon family became poorer and poorer.

The decline in the Pyncheon family fortunes is not, then, simply a reflection of the decay of all things physical. It is a result of the interaction of the colonel's domineering pride with the resentful reaction of those whom he oppressed. And—Hawthorne shows—later generations inherit and act on the basis of both.

Colonel Pyncheon's heritage is not just economic; it is also political and psychological. In changing the American regime, commoners like the Maules denied the aristocratic pretensions of people like the Pyncheons to be better than others by birth. But—Hawthorne suggests—declaring that all "men" are created equal and that governments are instituted to secure their rights is not sufficient to prevent oppression. On the contrary—just as the colonel used the witch trials to serve his own particular interests—so his democratic descendant, Judge Jeffrey Pyncheon, is able to use his position and knowledge of the law in the contemporary commercial republic to obtain what he wants at the expense of the rights of others. Unwilling to share the estate that he has inherited, the judge uses his influence. First, he has his cousin and competitor Clifford incarcerated until the latter is too feeble to fight. Then the judge has Clifford freed so he can pressure him into revealing the secret of the lost Pyncheon estates, which the judge is convinced (erroneously) that Clifford knows.

Contrary to the opinions of most of his contemporaries, Hawthorne seems to feel that making government officials responsible to the people through elections will not suffice to secure individual liberty. There are democratic as well as aristocratic means to dominance. The judge has no "aristocratic" qualms about currying favor with the populace or buying his party's nomination—and thus virtually assuring his election as governor (pp. 230, 268–83).

> As is customary with the rich, when they aim at the honors of a republic, he apologized, as it were, to the people, for his wealth, prosperity, and elevated station, by a free and hearty manner towards those who knew him; putting off the more of his dignity in due proportion with the humbleness of the man whom he saluted, and thereby proving a haughty consciousness of his advantages as irrefragably as if he had marched forth preceded by a troop of lackeys to clear the way. (p. 130)

Americans who believe that they have escaped the oppression of the past by establishing democratic institutions ironically commit the same intellectual error that their Puritan forefathers had. They overestimate the power of institutions to affect human behavior—especially the more self-regarding passions—just as they underestimate the resistance of human nature to external control.

If Americans are truly to absorb the lessons of the past concerning the evil effects of attempts to dominate others, they have to internalize and personalize those lessons. And Hawthorne shows how this might occur through the major plot of the novel. The marriage of the last heir of Matthew Maule—named Holgrave—to the last Pyncheon descendant—Phoebe—clearly represents the final and effective overcoming of past class antagonisms and the true foundation of a liberal, egalitarian regime. To discover how Hawthorne thinks that Americans can truly absorb the lessons of the past (or their heritage), we thus need to investigate the circumstances that made such a union possible.

Phoebe and Holgrave would not ordinarily have been attracted to one another.

> Had they met under different circumstances, neither of these young persons would have been likely to bestow much thought upon the other, unless indeed their extreme dissimilarity should have proved a principle of mutual attraction. Both, it is true, were characters proper to New England life, and possessing a common ground, therefore, in their more external developments; but as unlike in their respective interiors as if their native climes had been at world-wide distance. (p. 175)

External similarities of habit, manners, or appearance will not suffice to create or maintain a community, Hawthorne suggests. It is necessary to deal somehow with the internal or psychological differences of the people composing it.

The first condition necessary for the romantic union here is the relinquishing of the Pyncheons' aristocratic claims to be better than others by birth. Like the shop-keeping Miss Hepzibah Pyncheon—Phoebe's elderly cousin—they must be forced to support themselves by their own labor. Phoebe herself turns out to be the product of a marriage between one of the Pyncheon family's sons and a commoner. As a result, she does not consider herself too good to marry a plebian because of her heritage or inheritance.

Nevertheless—Hawthorne indicates—the levelling of social and economic differences is only a necessary condition for the establishment of a democratic union; it does not suffice. Like Holgrave, common people must overcome their angry resentment of past wrongs and learn not merely to tolerate individual differences—but to appreciate them positively, as well.

Like the average American that he is, Holgrave represents unformed potential. As such, his future is "delightfully uncertain."

> There appeared to be qualities in Holgrave, such as, in a country where everything is free to the hand that can grasp it, could hardly fail to put some of the world's prizes within his reach. But these matters are delightfully uncertain. At almost every step in life, we meet with young men of just about Holgrave's age, for whom we anticipate wonderful things, but of whom even after much and careful inquiry, we never happen to hear another word. (p. 181)

Precisely because Holgrave is so typical, Hawthorne makes his change of attitudes—or "education"—the central action of the romance.

Before his arrival at the house of seven gables, Holgrave has already had a broad range of experiences. He tried his hand at several occupations: teaching school; selling in a country store; writing political editorials; and even dentistry. He toured the New England and Middle Atlantic states as a peddler, and travelled to Europe aboard a packet-ship. Perhaps as a result of this enterprising spirit, he also experimented with living in a Fourierist community (of the kind that Hawthorne depicted in *Blithedale*), and even tried his hand at mesmerism. Holgrave thus embodies both the egalitarianism and materialism of the American spirit of enterprise.

These experiences have convinced him primarily of the mutability of human existence and the need for reform.

> "Shall we never, never get rid of this Past?" cried he. . . . "If each generation were allowed and expected to build its own houses, that single change, comparatively unimportant in itself, would imply almost every reform which society is now suffering for. I doubt whether even our public edifices—our capitals, state-houses, court-houses, city-halls, and churches—ought to be built of such permanent materials as stone or brick. It were better that they should crumble to ruin once in twenty years, or thereabouts, as a hint to the people to examine into and reform the institutions which they symbolize." (pp. 182–84)

Although he has read few books, Holgrave here follows Jefferson, who would have had each generation construct its own system anew every 19 years.[38] Holgrave Maule represents the dominant American tendency—as Hawthorne sees it—to respond to past oppression and present dissatisfaction by attempting to wipe the slate clean and start again from scratch.

Acting on the basis of such a thought or ideology, Americans clearly will not learn anything from the past. In attempting to destroy a heritage of class hatred, they unwittingly condemn themselves to perpetuating a more deeply rooted "natural" cycle of domineering political ambition (if in democratic guise) and sporadic (often disguised) popular reaction against it. Hawthorne thus tries—if very subtly—to suggest a different tack.

As a result of his experience at the house of seven gables, Holgrave's attitudes undergo a profound change. The turning point occurs when he reads Phoebe a short piece that he has written for a magazine—a tale drawn from the history of their two warring families. Disdainfully ordered in his time to help regain the Pyncheon family fortune, Maule's grandson took revenge by hypnotizing Gervayse Pyncheon's beautiful daughter Alice. Intending only to shame her (and her family's aristocratic pretensions), the later Matthew Maule ordered Alice to her death when he commanded her to come out through the damp and cold night to wait on his bride the evening of their wedding. Alice subsequently died of pneumonia, and Maule regretted the incident.

Watching Phoebe nod under the hypnotic effect of his own words, Holgrave refrains from exercising his hereditary power; his story has reminded him of the destructive effects of both possession and revenge. And the narrator praises such self-restraint:

> There is no temptation so great as the opportunity of acquiring empire over the human spirit; nor any idea more seductive to a young man than to become the arbiter of a young girl's destiny. Let us, therefore— whatever his defects of nature and education, and in spite of his scorn for creeds and institutions—concede to the daguerreotypist [Holgrave] the rare and high quality of reverence for another's individuality. (p. 212)

Rather than seeking to dominate or punish, Holgrave falls in love with Phoebe and asks her to marry him.[39] And in so doing, he quite consciously exchanges his former ambition to found a new social system for the ease of prosperity and domestic happiness: "The world owes all its onward impulses to men ill at ease," Holgrave observes. "The happy man inevitably confines himself within ancient limits. I have a presentiment that, hereafter, it will be my lot to set our trees, to make fences,—perhaps, even, in due time, to build a house for another generation,—in a word, to conform myself to laws and the peaceful practice of society" (pp. 306–7).

Where he would once have torn down all to build afresh, at the end of the novel Holgrave thus seeks permanence and stability. He wonders, for example,

> that the late Judge, being so opulent and with a reasonable prospect of transmitting his wealth to descendants of his own—should not have felt the propriety of embodying so excellent a piece of domestic architecture in stone, rather than in wood. Then, every generation of the family might have altered the interior, to suit its own taste and convenience; while the exterior, through the lapse of years, might have been adding venerableness to its original beauty, and thus giving that impression of permanence

which I consider essential to the happiness of any one moment. (pp. 314–
15)

Holgrave has come to see not only the cost of political ambition and
class-based resentment, but also—in terms of the book's dominant
imagery—the true locus of new growth and individual distinction: the
"interior." His marriage to Phoebe is founded on an explicit recognition of their differing perceptions and talents and the advantages of
pooling their resources, rather than demanding the subordination or
conformity of one to the tastes of the other. Holgrave has thus
internalized and personalized what he learned about the evils of
oppression from reflecting on a fictionalized account of the past.

Although initially attracted to reform, Holgrave sees the advantages
of regularity and order by observing Phoebe's effect on all the inhabitants of the dark old mansion. He has come to understand that the
only hope of escaping the crimes and errors of the past is to build with
the materials accumulated—not to repeat those crimes and errors in
destructive revenge and an unchecked desire to rebuild everything
anew in one's own name. He and Phoebe do leave the rotting timber
of the dark old mansion and move to the fresh air of the country; but
they move into Judge Pyncheon's estate. They accept the need for
continuity in external, conventional forms and institutional structures.

On the other hand, it takes exposure to the dark mysteries of the
past to make Phoebe sensible of Holgrave's superior knowledge and
her need in extraordinary circumstances to depend on someone with
such knowledge. By nature, Phoebe is attracted to the regular and
commonplace; repelled somewhat by Holgrave's dissident opinions
and his unusual life-style, she initially keeps her distance from the
daguerreotypist. Confronted with the extraordinary in the form of the
judge's mysterious death, however, she feels her own inability to deal
with the situation and her need to depend on the strength of one with
more understanding of the strange and mysterious. When Holgrave
proposes marriage, Phoebe responds with admirable self-understanding:

"How can you love a simple girl like me? . . . You have many, many
thoughts with which I should try in vain to sympathize. And I,—I, too,—
I have tendencies with which you would sympathize as little. . . . I have
not scope enough to make you happy. . . . And then—I am afraid!"
continued Phoebe, shrinking towards Holgrave, even while she told him
so frankly the doubts with which he affected her. "You will lead me out

of my own quiet path. You will make me strive to follow you where it is
pathless. I cannot do so. It is not my nature." (p. 306)

Yet Holgrave persuades her. She senses that he possesses some
understanding of the dark past and passions that altogether escape and
yet threaten her and her peaceful, prosaic existence.

Because Holgrave is an artist, his marriage to Phoebe indicates
something of what Hawthorne thought not only about the foundations
of a free community, but also about the relation of the artist to
bourgeois society.[40] Such a community will not be possible until its
members rather explicitly give up all desire to dominate others, on a
personal as well as a political level. And it is the peculiar function of
the literary artist to help them internalize this essential lesson from the
past. The artist will reveal the significance of the darker aspects of
human nature for readers who may not feel such passions in themselves but feel threatened by them in others. The artist will also show
those readers who have the desire to correct past wrongs why they
should exercise self-restraint. Just as Holgrave comes to see the evil
effects of revenge by reading a fictionalized account of his own family's
past, so Hawthorne hopes that he can convince his readers of the
limited effects of political reform, by presenting to them fictionalized
accounts of American history.[41]

The Heritage of the Puritans

Hawthorne repeatedly reminded Americans about the Puritanic origins of the republic, because—like Tocqueville—he believed that the
nation's formative experience had a decisive effect on its political
mores.[42] But where Tocqueville stressed the beneficial effects of combining democratic principles with stringent morals (especially with
regard to sexual relations), Hawthorne emphasized the destructive
potential of the example that the Puritans set—first, by withdrawing
from civil society to establish an entirely new polity in the wilderness;
and, second, by attempting to reform human beings they thought were
ineradicably stained by original sin. In nineteenth-century America,
there were—to be sure—relatively few strict Calvinists. Acting on
secularized versions of Puritanic doctrines like the morality of selflessness and the opposition of spirit and body, contemporary American
reformers—like the emigrants to Blithedale—were repeating both of
these earlier errors, with potentially more disastrous results.[43]

Americans will never escape the heritage of past oppression by withdrawing from civil society to begin anew in nature, Hawthorne showed in *The Blithedale Romance*. Because human beings are selfish by nature, they bring the source of competition and conflict with them. To found a just and lasting community, they must come to terms with the passions that make them want to unite with others in the first place.

The problem is that the very same passions that draw certain people together separate them from others. Perceiving the divisive effects of physical passion, Puritanic American reformers tried to purge people of all concern with the body in order to create a community of "souls" or "spirits." But in repressing the passions that initially make human beings want to unite with others, such reforms threatened to destroy the true grounds of community, along with the roots of life itself.

Sensing their limitations as individuals—Hawthorne observed—human beings like Zenobia desperately want the sympathy and support of others. The desire for community is thus rooted in feelings of individual inadequacy that cannot be admitted publicly without the loss of all shame.[44] Because people tend to hide the reasons that they seek company, they become confused about the true grounds of human association.

To force "sinners" into confessing their faults in public—Hawthorne showed in *The Scarlet Letter*—is to lose sight of both the origin and rationale for human association in the first place. Such confessions suggest that human beings can avoid all error. The Puritan's moral regulations thus contradicted their own fundamental doctrine of original sin. To make human beings shameless by allowing them to satisfy their desires any way they can—as at Blithedale—is, however, to destroy all sense of the need for self-restraint.

If people can safely confess their most deeply felt fears and hopes only in private, then the public sphere must be strictly limited. The political analogue of individual respect for the integrity of others is, therefore, the protection of privacy. And it is in the protection of privacy that Hawthorne found both past theocratic and present economic or spiritualistic communitarian alternatives to the commercial republic most lacking. By insisting that the most private desires be made public, all these attempts to further human brotherhood violated the most fundamental truth of the human heart.

Criticism of the commercial republic is often founded on an erroneous notion of human morality as selflessly giving up everything for some other person or goal. As Hawthorne variously illustrated in his depictions of Hester and Dimmesdale and of Hollingsworth and Zenobia, such "selflessness" is fundamentally selfish and unprincipled. It tends, therefore, to be highly hypocritical, as well. True morality is founded—as Hawthorne suggested in his praise of Holgrave—in respect for the integrity of others. Acting on the basis of such respect, no individual would try to manipulate, possess, or dominate another. All true or moral communities are based on mutual consent, freely given, in light of the members' differing, but complementary strengths and weaknesses. That consent must, however, take the form of a lasting commitment to a shared conception of the good life, if the partners are to enjoy the sympathy and support that they desire. So long as an association is based merely on momentary physical attraction or mutual utility, members cannot be confident that it will last when they reveal their worst flaws. Thus, trying to disguise their deepest desires, they continue to lack the compassion that they—like Zenobia—most want.

As Hawthorne demonstrated most clearly in *The Blithedale Romance,* nature alone does not provide human beings with the compassion and concern that they so desperately desire. Therefore, people can neither achieve happiness nor secure their liberty merely by returning to nature. What they need is—rather—to confront the truth about their own nature, so that they will see both the reasons for and the limits of conventional restraints. Human happiness can be achieved only in private, through a union based ultimately on a legal contract. The commercial republic is superior to its apparently more moralistic Puritanic and egalitarian alternatives, because it makes such private unions possible. The social contract underlying a liberal, democratic political order is not based fundamentally on economic exchange and interests so much as on the individual's need for sympathy and support.

Notes

1. Citations are from Nathaniel Hawthorne, *The House of Seven Gables* (Columbus: Ohio State University Press, 1956), p. 2. The irony is compounded, because—as F. O. Matthiessen, *American Renaissance* (New York: Oxford University Press, 1941), p. 332, has pointed out—Hawthorne's romance does not in fact have any such moral since the characters Holgrave and Phoebe eventually benefit from the estate that Phoebe finally inherits as a Pyncheon. Nina Baym, *The Shape of Hawthorne's Career* (Ithaca, N.Y.: Cornell Univer-

sity Press, 1976), p. 170, noted the same discrepancy between the prefatory statement and the evident outcome of the plot. She argued, therefore, that Holgrave's "conversion" is not real. It seems strange to take an obviously ironic introductory statement as a more conclusive indication of Hawthorne's understanding or position than the resolution of the story and the protagonist's explicit comments on it.

2. Sections of this chapter were previously published in Catherine H. Zuckert, "The Political Wisdom of Nathaniel Hawthorne," *Polity* 13 (Winter 1980): 163–83. Reprinted here with permission.

3. The emphasis on Hawthorne's "blackness" originated in Melville's review, "Hawthorne and his *Mosses,*" *Literary World,* August 17 and 24, 1850.

4. According to Lawrence Hall, Hawthorne read Rousseau during the summer of 1848. *Hawthorne: Critic of Society* (New Haven, Conn.: Yale University Press, 1944), p. 162. Hawthorne had studied the works of Rousseau in the 1830s, as well. Marion L. Kesselring, *Hawthorne's Reading* (Folcroft, Pa.: Folcroft Library, 1975).

5. Frederick C. Crews, *The Sins of the Fathers* (New York: Oxford University Press, 1966), has documented Hawthorne's frequent use of sexual imagery. At the time, Crews argued that this imagery reflected Hawthorne's own repressed obsession. Crews has since repudiated his earlier interpretation. "Criticism without Constraint," *Commentary* 73 (January 1982): 65–71. We can nevertheless take his earlier observations to show how pervasive a force in human life Hawthorne thought sexuality was, and how many different forms or reflections it had.

6. Hawthorne may have been thinking not only of his literary predecessor, but also of the prosaic form in which this vision had been put forth by Henry David Thoreau in *Walden and Civil Disobedience* (New York: W. W. Norton, 1966). The only time Hawthorne mentioned Thoreau in his notebooks was in 1842—years before the publication of either *Walden* or "Civil Disobedience"— when he predicted that "the only way [Thoreau] could ever approach the popular mind would be by writing a book of simple observation of nature." (quoted in Matthiessen, *American Renaissance,* p. 196). In *Walden,* Thoreau warned readers away from literally following his example. He put himself forward as a model, however, in his essay on "Civil Disobedience"—which was very influential with the abolitionists, whose abstract morality Hawthorne opposed both directly in his campaign biography of Franklin Pierce and indirectly in his criticisms of reform efforts (past and present) in *The Scarlet Letter* and *The Blithedale Romance.*

7. Brook Thomas, *"The House of Seven Gables:* Reading the Romance of America," *PMLA* 97 (March 1982): 199, has also pointed out the critique of the classic "liberal" solution through the institution of government in *The House.*

8. Both Thomas, *"The House:* Reading," and E. Miller Burdick, "The

World as Specter: Hawthorne's Historical Art," *PMLA* 101 (March 1986): 218–32, also emphasize the way Hawthorne used history to counteract a "romantic" American tendency to forget the past.

9. At the conclusion of his introduction, Hawthorne thus celebrates the Whig defeat of the Democratic party—which deprived him of his patronage position. Participating in the spoils or rewards of political power did not bring him satisfaction or happiness as an individual. As he suggested even more clearly in *The House of Seven Gables,* the locus of both true community and happiness is private—not public.

10. Citations are from Nathaniel Hawthorne, *The Scarlet Letter* (Columbus: Ohio State University Press, 1962).

11. Richard H. Brodhead, *Hawthorne, Melville, and the Novel* (Chicago: University of Chicago Press, 1973), p. 44, has observed that "by choosing the punishment of Hester as his first scene, Hawthorne is able to reveal the Puritan community in what seems to him its most essential aspect." Terence Martin, *Nathaniel Hawthorne* (Boston: Twayne, 1983), p. 109, has also pointed out that by organizing the entire story around three scaffold scenes Hawthorne highlights the importance of the institution.

12. Hester's shame on the scaffold could thus be compared to Natty's humiliation in the stocks in Cooper's *The Pioneers.* Whereas Natty had Benjamin Pump to fight those tempted to taunt him, Hester has no friend to do battle for her.

13. Sacvan Bercovitch, *The Puritan Origins of the American Self* (New Haven, Conn.: Yale University Press, 1975), p. 23, has pointed out that among the Puritans "private insecurity [wa]s proportionate to public affirmation, just as, conversely, the force of I-ness [wa]s transparent in the violent vocabulary of self-abhorrence."

14. Sacvan Bercovitch, *The American Jeremiad* (Madison: University of Wisconsin Press, 1978), has documented the existence of such a tension or contradiction throughout Puritan thought.

15. Yvor Winters, "Maule's Curse, or Hawthorne and the Problem of Allegory," in *In Defense of Reason* (Denver: Alan Swallow, 1960), thus identifies Hawthorne too closely with the Puritans. Hyatt Waggoner, *Nathaniel Hawthorne: A Critical Study* (Cambridge, Mass.: Harvard University Press, 1963), comes closer to the truth when he observes, "The strongest way of putting the case for Hawthorne's 'Puritanism' is to say that he thought there were truths at the center of the Puritan faith that, when suitably translated, were still viable." Irving Howe, *Politics and the Novel* (New York: Vintage, 1957), p. 164, sees that Hawthorne transformed a dogma into an insight—to be defended on empirical, rather than revelatory, grounds.

16. Aristotle, *Politics* (Chicago: University of Chicago Press, 1984), passages 1253a20–30.

17. Allan Gardner Lloyd-Smith, *Even Tempered: Writing and Sexuality in Hawthorne's Fiction* (Totowa, N.J.: Barnes and Noble, 1984), pp. 9–30, has also pointed out the "doubled" meaning of the "sign of the Scarlet Letter."

18. The text does not therefore support A. N. Kaul, *The American Vision* (New Haven, Conn.: Yale University Press, 1963), pp. 185–86, when he suggests that Hawthorne endorsed Hester's plan. Nevertheless, it is true—as Joyce M. Warren, *The American Narcissus* (New Brunswick, N.J.: Rutgers University Press, 1984), pp. 189–211, maintains—that Hawthorne gives a very sympathetic picture of the problems that women face. Although Hawthorne did not share Rousseau's view of the essential goodness of human nature, he did thus share Rousseau's insight into the potentially tragic position of the intelligent woman. See, for example, Rousseau's discussion of the fate of the Sophie who reads Fenelon's *Telemachy* too intelligently in *Emile* (New York: Basic Books, 1979), ch. 5, as well as Sophie's own tragic fate in the unpublished conclusion. See Susan Okin, *Women in Western Political Thought* (Princeton, N.J.: Princeton University Press, 1979), pt. 3, pp. 167–94.

19. As Nina Baym has pointed out, Hawthorne's depiction of the Puritans was not historically accurate in all respects. "Head, Heart, and Unpardonable Sin," *New England Quarterly* 40 (March 1967): 31–47, and her "Passion and Authority in *The Scarlet Letter*," *New England Quarterly* 43 (1970): 209–30. Also Martin Green, *Re-appraisals: Some Commonsense Readings in American Literature* (New York: W. W. Norton, 1965), pp. 73–76.

20. According to Jacques Derrida, this misunderstanding has a very long and distinguished philosophic heritage—extending back at least to Plotinus's *Enneads,* if not to the origin of "metaphysics" in the works of Plato and Aristotle. See *Speech and Phenomena* (Evanston, Ill.: Northwestern University Press, 1974), pp. 13–14.

21. Sigmund Freud, *Civilization and Its Discontents* (London: Hogarth Press, 1946), p. 89.

22. Citations are from Nathaniel Hawthorne, *The Blithedale Romance and Fanshawe* (Columbus: Ohio State University Press, 1964).

23. Here again, Hawthorne anticipates Freud, who did not concern himself with the "economic criticisms of the communistic system" because he "recognized that psychologically it is founded on an untenable illusion." Freud, *Civilization,* p. 88.

24. In his preface, Hawthorne thus states that he is not debating the merits of any particular form of socialism any more than he is giving an historically accurate picture of the community at Brook Farm. He is using the outlines of the experiment in which he himself participated to raise a much more fundamental question about the character of human nature itself.

25. See Jonathan Beecher and Richard Bienveau, eds., *The Utopian Vision of Charles Fourier* (Boston: Beacon, 1971).

26. As Freud later observed, "[The] conflict between civilization and sexuality is caused by the circumstance that sexual love is a relationship between two people, in which a third can only be superfluous or disturbing, whereas civilization is founded on relations between larger groups of persons. When a love-relationship is at its height no room is left for any interest in the

surrounding world; the pair of lovers are sufficient unto themselves." *Civilization,* pp. 79–80.

27. Although most commentators see that Hawthorne is critical of utopian reform, they do not see the way in which the plot constitutes a comment on the setting. If the four major characters—united by familial relations, affection, common aspirations, and sexual attraction—cannot maintain a community based on love, the chances for the success of the larger experiment are surely slim. Kaul, *Vision,* p. 177, states that Hawthorne did not explicitly or externally criticize either Puritans or reformers so much as he depicted the internal contradictions or difficulties of their own enunciated principles, yet Kaul falsely concludes, p. 203, that Hawthorne affirmed the aims of Blithedale. According to Kaul, Hawthorne was simply showing the failure of these particular participants.

28. With regard to the Blithedale experiment as a whole, the narrator observes, "The presence of Zenobia caused our heroic enterprise to show like an illusion, masquerade, a pastoral, a counterfeit Arcadia, in which we grown-up men and women were making a play-day of the years that were given us to live in" (p. 21).

29. As Michael Davitt Bell, *The Development of the American Romance* (Chicago: University of Chicago, 1980), p. 183, has argued, the source of the failure of both the Blithedale social experiment and Coverdale's art is the same: a refusal to recognize the amoral, sometimes indecent, but always passionate character of its natural source.

30. Zenobia thus reveals the truth about Coverdale's "love" for Priscilla in the story she tells of a young man named Theodore who lost the woman he loved by refusing to kiss her before he lifted the veil and saw her face. Like Coverdale, Theodore was unwilling to risk himself and hence was incapable of loving another human being.

31. Zenobia's name itself has a threefold significance. Derived from the ancient Greek word for stranger or foreigner, her name indicates in the first place that she is an alien in the midst of the other reformers. Blithedale is supposed to be a community based on nature; but in fact, nature is a stranger there: Zenobia is not recognized for what she really is.

She is not recognized at least partly because she appears in several different guises, and so conceals herself. "Zenobia" is also admittedly a pseudonym; and the flowers with which she adorns herself are products of art—of the florist and the jeweler. Unlike the other Blithedalers, Zenobia knows that her own deepest desires are not completely decent and benevolent. She thus feels a need not only to conceal but also to beautify herself. Nature is the source of the need for art as well as of the desire for community, Hawthorne indicates. But to satisfy either of these natural desires, nature herself must be transformed. As a result of that transformation, nature becomes somewhat hidden and is liable, therefore, to be misunderstood.

Zenobia was, moreover, the name of an ancient queen. And with this historical precedent, Hawthorne points to the way he thinks that the natural equality of the sexes can be effectively recognized. Like her modern-day namesake, Queen Zenobia apparently believed that women were as capable of wielding public power as men. When her husband died, she not only took full control of the kingdom, but she also tried to create an eastern empire—free of Roman dominion. Defeated by the army that Aurelion sent, Zenobia nevertheless so impressed the emperor with her beauty and dignity when she was taken to Rome that he freed her and gave her an estate near Tivoli. Like nature, her presence or being was ultimately more politically powerful than either the rhetoric of equal rights or attempts to assert those rights with force.

32. See Nina Baym, *"The Blithedale Romance:* A Radical Reading," *Journal of English and German Philology* 67 (October 1968): 561; Hannah Arendt, *Totalitarianism* (New York: Harcourt, Brace, and World, 1951); Jeane Kirkpatrick, *Dictatorships and Double Standards* (New York: Simon and Schuster, 1980); and Michel Foucault, *Discipline and Punish: Birth of the Prison* (London: Allen Lane, 1977).

33. See John C. Hirsh, "The Politics of Blithedale," *Studies in Romanticism* 11 (Spring 1972): 141.

34. See Leo B. Levy, *"The Blithedale Romance:* Hawthorne's Voyage through Chaos," *Studies in Romanticism* 8 (Autumn 1968): 10.

35. Zenobia's speculations about Priscilla's past almost exactly parallel the description that Karl Marx gave of the life and death of a young milliner from London newspapers in *Capital* (London: Everyman, 1967), vol. 1, p. 257. But A. Lefcowitz and B. Lefcowitz, "Some Rents in the Veil: New Light on Priscilla and Zenobia in *The Blithedale Romance,"* *Nineteenth Century Fiction* 2 (December 1966): 263–75, go too far when they suggest that Priscilla's economic exploitation extends to prostitution. The little purses that Priscilla knits may have sexual innuendoes, but her "secret" is not her sexuality so much as her lack thereof. See Baym, "A Radical Reading," p. 561, who also argues that Zenobia represents a life force in contrast to the "artificial flower" that is Priscilla.

36. See Hawthorne, *Scarlet Letter,* pp. 165–66.

37. See Lloyd-Smith, *Even Tempered,* p. 50.

38. Letter to Madison, Paris, September 6, 1789, in J. P. Boyd et al., eds., *The Papers of Thomas Jefferson* (Princeton, N.J.: Princeton University Press, 1969), vol. 15.

39. Baym, *Career,* pp. 159–68, acknowledged the importance of Holgrave's art, but she failed to see the conversion or change that reading his story to Phoebe signaled in this Maule's understanding of the past. Holgrave explicitly denies himself the opportunity to take revenge on a member of the family that had wronged his. He has learned the evil consequences of mere retribution by reflecting on the history of his own family. Baym argued that Holgrave is frightened out of his radical political views by the night he spends in the living room with the dead judge. She ignored the import of two statements that she

herself quoted. According to Holgrave, "The presence of yonder dead man . . . made the universe . . . a scene of guilt *and retribution more dreadful than the guilt*" (p. 306; emphasis added). Baym speculated that Holgrave feels guilty—responsible for the death, insofar as he has wished ill to his hereditary oppressors. He seems, in fact, to be more impressed by the retribution or punishment incurred as a result of the repetition of hereditary crimes. He has already decided not to repeat those of his family. He makes it clear, moreover, what attracted him to Phoebe. She brought "hope, warmth, and joy." His is a positive choice. Baym was unwilling to accept the evident meaning of the plot, perhaps, because it ran counter to her own explicitly feminist politics.

40. If—as Austin Warren observes—*The House of Seven Gables* was Hawthorne's own favorite romance, it is probably because it came closest to revealing his own full understanding of himself, the significance of his art, and its proper relation to society. Austin Warren, "Introduction," to *Nathaniel Hawthorne: Representative Selections* (New York: American Book, 1934), pp. lxii–lxxiii. Critics generally agree that the novel has an autobiographical cast. See Crews, *Fathers*, p. 174. The marriage of the artist Holgrave to the descendant of a noble family parallels Hawthorne's own marriage to Sophie Peabody. ("Phoebe" was one of Hawthorne's favorite nicknames for his wife.) There is no one-to-one correspondence between Holgrave and Hawthorne, however, because Hawthorne himself came from an old and decayed aristocratic family like the Pyncheons. Sarah I. Davis, "The Bank and the Old Pyncheon Family," *Studies in the Novel* 16 (Summer 1984): 150–66, shows how closely Clifford and Judge Pyncheon resemble a member of Hawthorne's own family and an acquaintance of his.

41. Where Rudolph von Abele, *The Death of the Artist: A Study of Hawthorne's Disintegration* (The Hague: Martinus Nijhoff, 1955), p. 66, argues that Holgrave's conversion represents a "complicating of the theme of egalitarianism with art, and so producing the kind of muddle that Hawthorne's mind was always in about his respective loyalties to art and politics," I am attempting to show that it indicates exactly the political role that Hawthorne saw for his own art.

42. Alexis de Tocqueville, *Democracy in America* (Garden City, N.Y.: Doubleday, 1964), vol. 1, ch. 2.

43. Hawthorne explicitly compares the Blithedalers to the Puritans on pp. 13 and 117. Hollingsworth was the image of a Puritan judge—Coverdale comments—when he pronounced sentence on Zenobia and banished her from his company.

44. Harold Kaplan, *Democratic Humanism and American Literature* (Chicago: University of Chicago Press, 1972), p. 130, asserts that no one can understand Hawthorne's writing without taking into account the importance of sympathy. Kaplan links the need for sympathy with humans' imperfect knowledge and consequent need for society (comfort), but not with an accompanying sense of shame and the need to preserve the integrity of the individual by respecting his or her privacy.

5

Melville's Meditations

Only in passing had Hawthorne mentioned the indifference of nature as a whole to the suffering and survival of individuals. Herman Melville, however, made such cosmic indifference the theme of his metaphysical masterpiece. Nature as depicted in *Moby Dick* is ruled by the right of self-preservation, but the exercise of that right produces an unending "sharkish," "cannibalistic" struggle in which all must kill in order to live and are themselves finally killed. Like Nathaniel Hawthorne and unlike James Fenimore Cooper, Melville thus concluded that human beings cannot acquire the sympathetic support they so desperately desire merely by contemplating Creation.[1]

Unlike Hawthorne and more like Cooper, however, Melville suggested that human nature is fundamentally innocent—and hence good. To the extent that human beings merely struggle to survive like all other animals, they do not harm each other maliciously. The source of enmity is not to be found in their hearts—that is, their natural sentiments or inclinations—so much as in their heads—that is, certain mistaken ideas that they have acquired about nature. Melville's fictional accounts of a return to the state of nature were designed primarily to expose the faulty foundations of these pernicious ideas. Therefore, in contrast to the works of his predecessors, his novels are rather explicitly philosophical.

In a world permeated by strife—Melville showed—neither human life nor cosmos is entirely intelligible. Human beings are drawn together and united not merely through a calculation of their physical or economic interdependency, but ultimately through a shared appreciation of the spiritual courage that it takes even the lowliest man to live in the face of constant uncertainty and death. By depicting the lives of men who have withdrawn from the deceptive comfort and apparent security of their homes on land to brave the wild on the oceans, Melville thought that he could reveal the true foundations of human community. Unlike Hawthorne, he did not think that the return to nature represented a dangerous illusion. On the contrary—like Cooper—he thought that he could remind his compatriots of the true meaning of natural right by depicting such a return.[2]

In *Moby Dick* Melville showed that democracy requires a kind of metaphysical foundation in agnostic toleration. Whereas Captain Ahab's demand for reason in the world culminates in death and destruction, Ishmael's doubts enable him to perceive the source and value of human fellowship.

Because Ishmael's reflections seem to show that there is no intelligible order, most critics have concluded that Melville was a Nietzschean relativist.[3] There is an obvious difference, however. Melville explicitly celebrated the "democratic dignity" of humanity in *Moby Dick*;[4] Friedrich Nietzsche just as explicitly attacked all forms of egalitarianism, and urged the necessity of the emergence of a master race.[5] Melville's stance is more Rousseauian. Before Nietzsche, Jean Jacques Rousseau had also thought that it is impossible to prove the existence of an intelligible order on the basis of reason alone.[6] And in his autobiographical writings, Rousseau repeatedly raised Ahab's question about the cause, reason, and justice of individual (especially his own) suffering.[7] Like Rousseau and unlike Nietzsche, Melville tried both to find happiness and to found human community in the simple (natural) sentiments of the human heart.[8]

Like Cooper, Rousseau had suggested that citizens of a democracy need to accept a few basic precepts of a "natural" or "civil" religion. Unlike Cooper, however, Rousseau did not put forth such a doctrine in his own name. Nor did he suggest that such beliefs would occur "naturally" to an untutored individual. On the contrary—in a note to his "Discourse on the Origins of Inequality"—Rousseau explicitly stated that religious beliefs are only acquired by human beings living in civil society. One who lives all alone in the state of nature would know nothing of morality and God.[9] Because civilized human beings cannot literally return to that natural state once they have acquired reason and religion, they can only learn about it through thought— like Ishmael.

Melville made the political implications of his view of nature clearest in his final novella, *Billy Budd*. The fact that nature as a whole is (like

Billy) *alogos*—inarticulate, and hence never perfectly intelligible—
does not mean that human beings must maintain unreasonable, tradi-
tion-based orders contrary to their own commonly shared feelings
about what is right. In opposition to Thomas Paine's contentions in
The Rights of Man,[10] Melville held that human beings are not rebellious
by nature. And because they are not rebellious by nature, they do not
have to be forcefully controlled. Leadership and organization are
necessary to preserve human life and community, but that leadership
will not be successful unless based on an appreciation of the virtues of
common humanity. As a novelist, Melville sought—above all—to
foster such an appreciation.

Moby Dick

In *Moby Dick* Melville shows that neither humanity nor liberty is
menaced by hierarchical organization or economic dependency so
much as it is by intellectual servitude. To be free, it is necessary to
depart from "the lee shore"—that is, to question conventional Christian morality and the comforts of familiarity in the way that the
common sailor Ishmael does, but that the first mate Starbuck never
dares. The man who "braves the sea"—instead of clinging to land-
locked, particular beliefs and conventions—discovers the essential
equality of all creation. All are cannibals who destroy and are destroyed.

To be sure, human beings differ from one another in intellect, skill,
and conscience. Starbuck is better than Stubb or Flask in more than
position; Queequeg deserves more of the "lay" than Ishmael, for his
daring as well as his skill and experience. The nonelective authoritarian
structure of command on board the *Pequod* does not destroy democracy in its most essential sense, however, because all differences in
ability are recognized as valuable only insofar as they contribute to the
realization of common goals: survival and profit. The sailors do not
resent Ahab's command and the differential economic rewards that
they have been promised because they themselves, in effect, consented
to both. They are united by a sense of their interdependency and
common mortality. What causes their destruction is Ahab's demand
that he be personally recognized—his demand that his suffering be
justified and revenged in distinction from the common lot.[11]

Like sharks—Melville shows—men kill and are killed; but unlike
sharks, men can look ahead, so they are able both to act intentionally

and to fear death. In contrast to the rest of nature, human beings are conscious and caring. When they perceive the essential indifference of nature, they may thus rebel like Ahab. This rebellion on behalf of humanity—the demand that suffering have just cause, that the impersonal whole recognize the claims of individuality, that there be reason—is the greatest danger to democracy, because it arises out of and yet against the democracy of nature itself. Ahab is able to exercise autocratic authority and to divert the ship's entire resources to his own particular purpose not only by means of his conventional position and natural cunning, but also by enlisting the crew's sympathies with his desire for justice. They, too, wish savagely and naturally to strike back.

If nature be truly indifferent, however, there is no justice. As Hobbes argued in the *Leviathan,* in the state of nature there is only the natural right or liberty—which everyone has—to take whatever he or she needs for self-preservation. Justice is a matter of law, and there are no laws—strictly speaking—by nature.[12] As Ishmael puts it, justice is therefore man-made—a matter of convention, or "loose fish" and "fast fish."

> These two laws touching Fast-fish and Loose-Fish, I say, will on reflection, be found the fundamentals of all jurisdiction; for not withstanding its complicated tracery of sculpture, the Temple of the Law, like the Temple of the Philistines, has but two props. . . . Is it not a saying in every one's mouth, Possession is half of the law; that is, regardless of how the thing came into possession? But often possession is the whole law. . . . What are the rights of Man and the Liberties of the World but Loose-Fish? What all men's minds and opinions but Loose- Fish? (pp. 334–35)[13]

Unable to perceive the causes or reasons why things happen, human beings cannot achieve justice. They can maintain their liberty, however, by responding skeptically to anyone who would lead them on a crusade. If it be true that human beings are the only creatures who really care for others, then they need to cling to their sense of humanity and not allow it to be destroyed by prejudice or convention.

Ishmael's Rebellion

Unlike the emigrants to Blithedale, Ishmael does not withdraw from civil society and go to sea in order to escape conventional restraints or political and economic inequality. He will have to work to pay for his voyage, he acknowledges; but he reminds his readers how much better it is to be paid than to pay. To be sure, he will have to sweep down the decks at the order of some old hulk of a sea captain; but—he rationalizes—everyone else exists in a chain of command under God. "Who ain't a slave?" he asks. To be a captain, he would have to take responsibility for others, and—he reflects—"It is quite as much as I can do to take care of myself" (p. 14).

Ishmael is not sure, however, that there is a reason to take care of himself. The American polity and economy are both based on the right of self-preservation. But if human life has no value in itself—he recognizes—there is no reason to strive to preserve it. Ishmael goes to sea to find a reason to live; and his sea-born reflections thus raise questions about the very foundations of the American regime.[14]

Men have long associated the sea with thought and eternity, Ishmael reflects. But

> still deeper was the meaning of that story of Narcissus, who because he could not grasp the tormenting, mild image he saw in the fountain, plunged into it and was drowned. But that same image, we ourselves see in all rivers and oceans. It is the image of the ungraspable phantom of life; and this is the key to it all. (p. 14)

Human beings reasonably associate water with the source of life. The problem is that they tend to see only their own reflection in it. To discover what nature and life are really about, Ishmael must therefore explicitly look outside himself—to something different, to something nonhuman. Chief among the motives that have sent him on this ocean voyage—he reports—is curiosity about the whale itself. The very name of the sperm whale associates it with the source of life. But the whale is not simply attractive. Wanting to be reconciled to his world and to its inhabitants, Ishmael is prepared to take cognizance of its more terrible aspects. "Not ignoring what is good, I am quick to perceive a horror, and still could be social with it— would they let me—since it is well to be on friendly terms with all inhabitants of the places one lodges in" (p. 16).

By leaving civil society and venturing into the state of nature, Ishmael makes himself—at least potentially—a citizen of the world. His willingness not merely to tolerate—but to be sociable with—"horrors" is tested the very first night of the journey when, at Peter Coffin's inn, he finds himself housed with a savage.[15] Overcoming his startled fright at the sight of his tattooed yellow roommate, Ishmael reflects that the "man's a human being just as I am; he has just as much reason to fear me, as I have to be afraid of him" (p. 31). Next morning, Ishmael awakes to find his trust rewarded with a matrimonial hug from his sleeping bedmate.

Not only does Queequeg provide Ishmael with his first lesson regarding the community of humanity and the indifference of nature. The contrast between the cannibal's embrace and the sermon that Ishmael hears later that morning at the Whaleman's Chapel also brings out the unnatural inhumanity of certain Christian precepts and doctrines. Explicating the Biblical story of Jonah, Father Mapple appeals to his congregation: Men must not rebel against the commands of God; and to "obey God, we must disobey ourselves, wherein the hardness of obeying God consists" (p. 45). Christian interpretations of Scripture urge humans to distrust the very sentiments that would bring them together, for the sake of obeying some higher "Law."

Ishmael questions received religion in order to affirm the commonality of nature: He returns to the inn room and joins Queequeg in worshipping his pagan idol. And in the commonality of indifferent nature, he finds a certain peace. "No more my splintered heart and maddened hand were turned against the wolfish world. The soothing savage redeemed it. There he sat, his very indifference speaking a nature in which there lurked no civilized hypocrisies or bland conceits" (p. 53). Ishmael's faith in the humanity of his pagan friend is later externally confirmed when Queequeg not only exhibits his exceptional daring and physical prowess, but also—in effect—turns the other cheek by jumping overboard to save the young cabin boy who has been taking every opportunity to taunt him.

After witnessing this display of the savage's charity as well as great physical strength, Ishmael does not resent the inequality of their respective shares in the lay. The terms of their shipping aboard the *Pequod* does remind him, however, about the rigors of human existence in general. Human beings must not only earn their bread by the sweat of their brow; they must also risk their lives in attempting merely to preserve themselves. Like both Queequeg and Ishmael, humans are not ideally at home in the world; they are more like exiles.[16]

Human compassion and community seem to be grounded in a sense of mutual misery and mortality. On board the *Pequod*, Ishmael is led to reflect on the radical uncertainty and insecurity of human life after his first "lowering" in a whale-boat from the ship.

All men live enveloped in whale-lines. All are born with halters round their necks, but it is only when caught in the swift, sudden turn of death, that mortals realize the silent, subtle, ever-present perils of life.

Perceiving both the generality and the inescapability of the peril, Ishmael acquires a certain equanimity. Since death is possible at any time, and any place, it is irrational to be fearful or anxious. "If you be a philosopher," he concludes, "though seated in a whale-boat, you would not at heart feel one whit more of terror, than though seated before your evening fire with a poker and not a harpoon, by your side" (p. 241).

Living explicitly in the face of death even gives rise to a certain exhilaration. After the first lowering, Ishmael retires to write his will. And he reports, "After the ceremony was concluded, . . . I felt all the easier; . . . all the days I should now live would be as good as the days that Lazarus lived after his resurrection" (p. 197).

Human beings are not merely to be pitied. They can also be admired for the courage with which they face the ever present possibility of death. Their compassionate courage makes their suffering appear all the more irrational and unjustified, however. Both his insights into the human condition and his consequent questioning of received religion thus prepare Ishmael to raise his voice in the pagan crew's dedication to Captain Ahab's vengeful quest. Common sailors also wish to strike back at the mysterious supra- or sub-human—but, in either case, horrible—source of suffering that the white whale here represents.

Ahab's Leadership

As Melville shows in the course of the novel, Ahab's quest leads only to death and destruction. Human beings can find comfort and peace only in the company of others. As the voyage of the *Pequod* demonstrates, enduring human communities cannot be founded merely on mutual economic interest or antagonism to a common foe. Ahab represents a false—albeit, alluring—form of democratic leadership. Ishmael does not free himself from Ahab's pernicious influence by rebelling against the authority of the captain, however. He saves himself, eventually, by coming to a different understanding of humanity's place in the universe.[17]

Both leadership and freedom from domination are fundamentally matters of intellect, Melville indicates. The peg-legged Ahab commands his crew by virtue of the strength of his mind and will, as well as his autocratic powers as captain. His authority is therefore by no means simply conventional.

Ahab has risen to his position by means of natural endowments, both mental and physical. "He's a grand, ungodly, god-like man,

Captain Ahab; doesn't speak much; but, when he does speak, then you may well listen,'' one of the owners of the *Pequod* warns Ishmael. ''Ahab's above the common; Ahab's been in colleges, as well as 'mong the cannibals; been used to deeper wonders than the waves; fixed his fiery lance in mightier, stranger foes than whales. His lance! aye, the keenest and the surest that, out of our isle!'' (pp. 76–77).

Ahab's position is, however, merely that of foreman of a commercial enterprise. Ishmael reminds his readers that he has been describing only ''a poor old whale hunter . . . and, therefore, all outward majestical trappings and housings are denied [him]'' (p. 130). To the extent that Ahab's virtues are intellectual, they are not externally visible, in any case.

Ahab thus represents an emphatically democratic hero who has risen on the basis of his own deeds and talents, not so much to high social or political position as to nobility of soul. He is

> a man of greatly superior natural force, with a globular brain and a ponderous heart; who has also by the stillness and seclusion of many long night watches . . . been led to think untraditionally and independently.

Such a ''man makes one in a whole nation's census—a mighty pageant creature, formed for noble tragedies'' (p. 71). And by portraying the foreman of a commercial enterprise as great-souled as any Shakespearean king, Melville self-consciously glorifies the potential of democracy.[18]

> This august dignity I treat of, is not the dignity of kings and robes, but that abounding dignity which has no robed investiture. Thou shalt see it shining in the arm that wields a pick or drives a spike; that democratic dignity which, on all hands, radiates without end from God; Himself! . . . the center and circumference of all democracy! His omnipresence, our divine equality! (p. 104).[19]

On the Cannibalism of Nature and Herakleitan Strife

Ahab could not have enlisted the crew in his quest if he had not appealed to commonly held feelings and experiences. Ishmael makes the character of those experiences explicit in his own reflections. As men who have not only left civil society to brave the unknown dangers of the sea but who have also used their time at sea to think ''untraditionally and independently," Captain Ahab and the common sailor Ishmael have much in common. First and foremost, they understand the terrifying power of nature represented by the ocean.

> Though, to landsmen in general, the native inhabitants of the seas have been regarded with emotions unspeakably unsocial and repelling; though we know the sea to be an everlasting terra incognita . . ., though . . . the most terrific of all mortal disasters have immemorially and indiscriminately befallen tens and hundreds of thousands of those who have gone upon the waters; though but a moment's consideration will teach, that however baby man may brag of his science and skill . . . the sea will insult and murder him, and pulverize the stateliest, stiffest frigate he can make; nevertheless by the continual repetition of these very impressions, man has lost that sense of the full awfulness of the sea which aboriginally belongs to it. (p. 235).

In contrast to their land-loving compatriots—who have sought to secure their rights to life, liberty, and the pursuit of happiness by establishing a government—those who go to sea recognize the fundamental insecurity of life.

It is not simply a question of humanity versus nature, however. On the contrary, Ishmael quickly discovers that the sea is not just "a foe to man who is an alien to it." No, "it is also a fiend to its own offspring" (p. 235). "Consider once more," he urges his readers, "the universal cannibalism of the sea."

Human beings are not able to overcome the violent terrors of the deep—Ishmael discovers—because they themselves participate in them. By nature, human beings are all basically savages—even cannibals.

> Long exile from Christendom and civilization inevitably restores a man to that condition in which God placed him, i.e., what is called savagery. . . . I myself am a savage, owing no allegiance but to the kind of cannibals; and ready at any moment to rebel against him. (p. 232)

Nature is thus essentially the same in man and ocean.

If nature is indeed so forbidding, then why not strike out—like Ahab—and try to subdue it? To strike out seems to be in accord with nature, for the world described by Ishmael is characterized by Herakleitan opposition and strife: "There is no quality in this world that is not what it is merely by contrast. Nothing exists in itself" (p. 55).

Ahab appears to be speaking with the voice of nature when he responds to Starbuck's charge that it is blasphemy to take vengeance when the dumb brute (the whale) smote him from blind instinct:

> Talk not to me of blasphemy, man; I'd strike the sun if it insulted me. For could the sun do that, then I could do the other; since there is ever a sort of fair play herein, jealousy presiding over all creations. (p. 144)

But Ahab goes further than that, because he asserts, "But not my master, man, is even that fair play. Who's over me? Truth hath no confines."

Ahab seeks not simply to comprehend, but to conquer, with his mind. In this respect, he represents the dominant thrust of modern science, which explicitly seeks to relieve the human condition through a conquest of nature.[20] Like Descartes, Ahab suspects that his senses deceive him. "All visible objects, man, are but as pasteboard masks." It is all, indeed, the work of an "evil demon." For "in each event," Ahab thinks, "some unknown but still reasoning thing puts forth the mouldings of its features from behind the unreasoning mask." Where his mind fails him, Ahab would use his lance. "If man will strike, strike through the mask!" What Ahab hates above all is not the destructiveness or malice that he attributes to the white whale, but its inscrutability. He wants a reason for his suffering; where there is none, he pursues justice by wreaking vengeance on the agent.

Where Ishmael reads other men through his own feelings, Ahab reads the world as an image of his own mind. Reflecting on the head of the whale in a chapter that Melville has entitled "The Sphynx," the captain concludes, "O Nature, and O soul of man! how far beyond all utterance are your linked analogies! Not the smallest atom stirs or lives in matter, but has its cunning duplicate in mind" (p. 264). Ahab himself acts intentionally; and so he insists that there must be a hidden purpose in the world, as well. Suspecting in the end that he may be mistaken—and that his quest may be truly mad—Ahab nevertheless willfully persists. Although greatly moved by the compassion first extended by Starbuck and then more powerfully evoked by the idiot black boy Pip, Ahab turns his back on all humanity in his insistence on intelligent responsibility. He would die and take all his crew with him rather than admit the limits of his understanding. A strange version of equality among all creations! And yet, perhaps, not so strange. Representative of a fundamental tendency in democratic peoples, Ahab refuses to admit the existence of anybody or anything above or beyond him.[21]

The Solution Consists Not in Striking Out, but in Sticking Together

When the *Pequod* encounters other whalers, Ishmael is exposed to different interpretations or accounts, both of the character of the white whale and of the source of Ahab's power. And his later experiences on board the *Pequod* verify the truth of these alternative interpretations.

As a result of the *Pequod*'s first meeting—the society and conversation of the "gam" with a whaler called *Town-Ho*— Ishmael meets another captain who has lost a limb to Moby Dick. Rather than seek vengeance, this captain has tried to avoid further injuries to himself and his crew. Moreover, in the story told of Radney and Steelkilt, the white whale appears in the guise of an agent of justice. How can one creature be both malicious and just?

From his study of the physiognomy of the whale, Ishmael finally concludes that this embodiment of natural strife is neither good nor evil. It is beyond the compass of the human mind. Like Ahab, Ishmael observes that appearances are deceptive: Though the head of the whale is huge, its brain is nutlike. No inspection of the skeleton can give a sense of the size, beauty, or strength of the living whole. Eternally dumb, the whale will never tell the secrets of the deep. Ishmael's reflective investigations thus reveal that there is no Platonic parallel between the structure of the cosmos and the operations of the human mind—as Ahab is wont to believe. "Dissect him how I may, then, I but go skin deep; I know him not, and never will. But if I know not even the tail of this whale, how understand his head? Much more, how comprehend his face, when face he has none?" (p. 319). As the image of God or the whole, the whale remains unknowable. Like Ishmael, however, all human beings do feel "intimations" of the divine:

> Doubts of all things earthly and intimations of some things heavenly; this combination makes neither believers nor infidel, but makes a man who regards them both with equal eye. (p. 314)

Because human beings do not know, they can be misled. The *Pequod*'s second encounter with another whaler—the *Jeroboam*—shows Ishmael how a madman (crewman Gabriel) can acquire enormous influence over superstitious sailors through a combination of cunning and calculation. Ahab's ability to enlist his crew in his vengeful quest does not prove that quest to be sane or just. Fear and ignorance make men vulnerable to error.

Reflections of the kind that Ishmael engages in while on "the monkey rope," on the other hand, reveal the true position of human beings in the universe. It is a position of great danger: Human beings are mortal, and they are surrounded—like Queequeg—by both "sharks" and the erring knives of their "friends." But they are not necessarily alone. On the contrary, Ishmael reports,

> I saw that this situation of mine was the precise situation of every mortal that breathes; only, in most cases, he, one way or other has this Siamese connexion with a plurality of other mortals. If your banker breaks, you snap; if your apothecary by mistake sends you poison in your pills, you die. (p. 271)

A sense of their interdependence not only reminds human beings of the limits of their own power to control destiny, but also points them to the only possible source of support.

As the tragedy of Pip's insanity clearly demonstrates, humans can neither survive nor remain sane when isolated from others.[22] They can maintain their association and receive such support, however, only through a willingness to risk their own lives. Contrary to the argument in the Declaration of Independence—Melville insists—the desire for self-preservation alone does not suffice to succor the individual or to support community. People must learn to respect the needs of others and to acknowledge their own limitations.

Ishmael becomes fully reconciled with himself, others, and the world as he squeezes his shipmates' hands in the slippery sperm. At that magical moment—he reports—"I forgot all about our horrible oath; . . . I washed my hands and my heart of it; . . . I felt divinely free from all ill-will, or petulance, or malice, of any sort whatsoever" (p. 348). The feeling of complete unity with other human beings is as illusory as the pantheists' desire to be one with all creation. Yet, on the basis of repeated experiences, he concludes more sanely that human animosity and unhappiness are not necessary or fated. They result from man's unwillingness to learn from experience and to reduce his expectations.

> I have perceived that in all cases man must eventually lower, or at least shift, his conceit of attainable felicity; not placing it anywhere in the intellect or the fancy; but in the wife, the heart, the bed, the table, the saddle, the fireside, the country. (p. 349)

If it be true that human fellowship is good, then neither human beings nor their society needs to be fundamentally reformed. To live peacefully in association with others, people must simply lower their sights.

Ahab refuses to do so. He claims omnipotence to the point of abandoning the tools of science, and curses his need for the assistance of others in any form. "Oh, Life! Here I am, proud as a Greek god, and yet standing debtor to this blockhead for a bone to stand on! Cursed by that mortal inter-indebtedness which will not do away with ledgers" (pp. 391–92).

Salutary Doubts

Ishmael's sea-born meditations appear, thus, to have brought him in the end to the point where Starbuck began: courageous, but careful—attached primarily to wife and child. There is a fundamental difference between Starbuck and Ishmael, however; Starbuck is a believer, whereas Ishmael doubts. Ahab obtains ascendancy over his first mate not only because he can appeal to the young mate's pity—to his sense of suffering, and his own participation in it—but also because Starbuck's scruples prevent him from resisting. Just as he obeys the authority of the captain's orders, so Starbuck subscribes to a moral code that prohibits him from using the musket to stop Ahab from destroying ship and crew. "Thou art but too good a man, Starbuck," the captain states as he disarms his mate. In a world characterized by strife, pacifism is not a realistic option or effective response.[23]

Ishmael's doubts save him not only from the psychic subservience produced by Starbuck's scruples, but also from the enslaving effects of Ahab's cosmic rebellion. It is not simply the inscrutability, but—ultimately—the indifference of the universe, that enrages the captain. He demands recognition of, and a reason for, his suffering; he wants "the powers that be" to care.[24] As his tragedy reveals, though, the only beings who care about human beings are human beings themselves; and Ahab's insistence on cosmic recognition cuts him off from all compassion. The assertion of human will against the powers of nature might appear to be the greatest expression of human freedom. But Melville shows that, in demanding a purpose for their lives as individuals, human beings actually assert their sense of self-importance. They insist that the cosmos be formed in their own image. And this insistence leads not to liberty, but to the worst form of intellectual servitude. "What is it, what nameless, inscrutable, unearthly thing is it; what cozening, hidden lord and master, and cruel, remorseless emperor commands me," Ahab asks himself, "that against all natural lovings and longings, I so keep pushing?" It is his own intellectual pride that makes him refuse to trust his natural sentiments, yet he himself refuses to take responsibility. Something else—he insists—is in control. "But if the great sun move not of himself . . . nor one single star can revolve, but by some invisible power, how then can this one small heart beat; this one small brain think thoughts; unless God does that beating, does that thinking, does that living, and not I" (p. 445). Since he cannot discover the final cause, Ahab concludes that all is fated. The man whose mind would have penetrated the seas' deepest recesses thus ends by placing complete reliance on the unintelligible prophecies of the Parsee Fedullah. What is superstition—after all—but the projection of supernatural causes for events that human beings fail to comprehend.

The Role of the Novelist

In *Moby Dick* Melville suggests that democracy has a metaphysical foundation. To preserve their freedom, human beings must retain their doubts. The demand that there be a reason for human suffering culminates only in a fruitless, self-destructive attempt to master nature. In a world characterized by indifferent strife, comfort is not to be found in a divine purpose or order. It can be had only in the companionship of other courageous human beings.

Compassion alone is not enough, however. Only a critical mind can protect humans from the disastrous consequences of intellectual pride. Unfortunately, the mind only operates negatively; it creates doubts, but it cannot affirm. Democracy thus requires not only skepticism, but also poetic fiction; human beings need intimations of the divine. It is the novelist Melville who can show his readers not only the power and destructiveness, but also the brilliant beauty and energy, in the eternal Herakleitan play of opposites; it is the novelist who can dramatize the courage that it takes human beings to live in the midst of constant strife; it is the novelist—and not the philosopher—who can depict that immaculate manliness in the arm that wields a pike. As Ishmael's narrative reveals, the preservation of individual freedom and liberal political institutions depends not only on reason, but also on a continuing sense of the value, the beauty, and the dignity of humanity. By providing his readers with both, Melville is seeking to exercise a new kind of democratic intellectual leadership.[25]

Billy Budd

In *Billy Budd,* Melville dramatizes the inadequacy of two other accounts of the foundations of democratic civil society. He sets the story in the wake of the French Revolution—at a time of mutinies in the British navy, and a subsequent general fear for the preservation of the British constitution. More specifically, he tells the story in the context of the debate between the revolutionary ideology of Thomas Paine and the conservative outlook of Edmund Burke.[26] Melville uses Budd, in fact, as a natural standard by which to measure or test these two theories about human nature and its proper relation to the law.

Melville introduces Billy as an example of the phenomenon, "the handsome sailor"—a man who spontaneously and naturally attracts a following as a result of his physical beauty and strength. There is nothing intentional or intellectual about his preeminence. To make sure that readers perceive the universal and hence natural character of this phenomenon, moreover, Melville first presents them not with the blonde and Adam-like Billy, but with a huge black African capped by a Scotch Highland bonnet. Billy is young and innocent, as well as beautiful. Since he was a foundling, his names were all descriptive. Not only was he called "baby" as well as "beauty," but he was also a "bud" just coming into bloom. When Billy fails to resist his naval impressment, the narrator comments, "Like the animals, though no philosopher, he was, without knowing it, practically a fatalist" (p. 49).

> With little or no sharpness of faculty or any trace of the wisdom of the serpent, not yet quite a dove, he possessed that kind and degree of intelligence going along with the unconventional rectitude of a sound human creature, one to whom not yet has been proferred the questionable apple of knowledge. He was illiterate. . . . Of self-consciousness he seemed to have little or none.

In sum, "Billy in many respects was little more than a sort of upright barbarian" (p. 52).

The narrator concludes the description by commenting that—apparently corroborating the Biblical doctrine of humanity's fall—when "certain virtues pristine and unadulterate characterize anybody in the external uniform of civilization, they will upon scrutiny seem not to be derived from custom or convention, but rather to be . . . transmitted from a period prior to Cain's city and citified man" (p. 53). The corroboration of the doctrine of the fall is only apparent, however. Unlike Adam, Billy does not succumb to temptation; after his encounter with evil, he remains as much a "barbarian" and a "fatalist" as he was before. In Budd, Melville represents the natural—what was, prior to the city or civilization—in human beings; and his story reveals the vulnerability or inadequacy of nature—rather than the necessity or existence of original sin, as is often thought.[27] As in *Moby Dick,* Melville begins his story by repudiating the doctrine that human beings are inherently evil.

The merchant vessel that Billy first ships on is named the *Rights of Man,* after Paine's work. With the sailors all asserting and exercising their individual rights, life on board has been a "rat-pit of quarrels" until Billy arrives. Then, as the peace-loving captain who has not been able to keep order aboard reports, "Billy came, and it was like a Catholic priest striking peace in an Irish shindig. Not that he preached to them or did anything in particular; but a virtue went out of him, sugaring the sour ones" (p. 47). All the sailors willingly serve Billy— with one exception. Out of envy, Red Whiskers wants to pick a fight with the "sweet and pleasant fellow," as he mockingly calls Billy (in the very same terms that Claggart of the *Bellipotent* later uses). Billy tries to reason with him; but Red Whiskers continues the insults, whereupon Billy levels him with a blow. Ever after, Red Whiskers is one of his most loyal followers.

Using Billy as a touchstone, Melville suggests that Paine was wrong about both human nature and the foundations of government. Human beings do not naturally regard all others as equal; on the contrary, they spontaneously recognize the natural superiority or virtue of a man like Billy who does not himself seek preeminence, much less power. Leadership is neither unnatural, nor are people naturally or necessarily at odds. Not need or fear, but envy—or what Rousseau called amour propre—the desire to be recognized as better by one's fellows—leads human beings to hurt others.[28] Moreover, this desire for recognition is to be found only in citified people; it is associated with a kind of intelligence (present later in both Master- at-Arms Claggart and Captain Vere of the *Bellipotent*) that Billy lacks.[29] If envy is the source of contention, however, then neither reason nor consent will suffice to establish peace and order. Force is also necessary, although the order or hierarchy among human beings is not simply a product of force. Contrary to Paine, Melville suggests that people will not secure peace and order by asserting their rights. They need leadership, as well.

Revolution does not have its source in human nature. Billy accepts his impressment into service on the British warship, the *Bellipotent,* without demur. Melville speaks out against the thesis that human beings resist all authority and hierarchy by nature—not only through the plot, but also in the direct comments of the narrator. He describes the British navy as "the right arm of a power then but the sole free conservative one of the Old World" and the mutiny as "transmuting the flag of founded law and freedom defined into the enemy's red meteor of unbridled and unbounded revolt." In the British mutinies—the narrator observes—"reasonable discontent growing out of practical grievances in the fleet had been ignited into irrational combustion as by live cinders blown across the channel from France into flames" (p. 54). Insurrections and popular uprisings are caused by practical grievances created by oppressive government—not by a natural resistance to all order, or a natural irrationality. Order is restored to the British fleet—the narrator observes—not primarily with force, but through the loyal and voluntary cooperation of the greater part of the body of men. And the attachment of these men is secured—Melville reminds readers, using his description of Admiral Nelson—by the visible beauty and strength along with the fearless fatalism of the natural leader.

If Billy does represent what is natural, then neither Paine's doctrine of the rights of man nor the Burkean opposition to it is well founded.[30] If indeed human beings are not revolutionary by nature, then the attempt to found government and law on nature does not lead to disorder.[31] In fact, as Melville demonstrates through the arguments and actions of Captain Vere, it is the attempt to enforce order without reason—in violation of human beings' natural conscience and sentiments—that leads to the outbreak of mutiny and war.

Captain Vere opposes the new doctrines of natural right and then appeals to human reason, because he believes that they undermine civil order.

His settled convictions were as a dyke against those invading waters of novel opinion social, political, and otherwise, which carried away as in a torrent no few minds in those days, minds by nature not inferior to his own. While other members of that aristocracy to which by birth he belonged were incensed at the innovators mainly because their theories were inimical to the privileged classes, not alone Captain Vere disinterestedly opposed them because they seemed to him insusceptible of embodiment in lasting institutions, but at war with the peace of the world and the true welfare of mankind. (pp. 62–63)

Through the action of the story, Melville demonstrates that Vere is wrong. Nothing so threatens to arouse mutiny and disorder on board the *Bellipotent* as Vere's own determination to hang Billy immediately—against tradition, and against the conscience of everyone involved.

Captain Vere had been surprised when his master-at-arms Claggart accused Billy of treasonous insubordination. Sensing that Claggart was lying, Vere set up a private—and, as it happened a fatal— confrontation, to test his officer's word. Although he intuited Billy's innocence, Vere did not perceive the broader significance of the young sailor's defective *logos*—which made it impossible for Billy to plot or scheme. Billy's stammer represented not only a physical but also a mental inability to articulate his own defense. Earlier on, Vere and his boarding lieutenant had interpreted Billy's parting comment on his impressment—"and good-by to you too, old *Rights of Man*"—as a satiric sally. But the narrator commented that it could hardly have been so by intention because Budd lacks the "sinister dexterity. . . . To deal in double meanings and insinuation of any sort was quite foreign to his nature" (p. 49). He could not see beneath the surface. Despite his experience with Red Whiskers, Billy could not understand why the Dansker (salty, old Danish crewman) concluded that "Jemmy Legs" (Claggart) was down on him, because the master-at-arms had called him a "sweet and pleasant fellow." Had the legalistic confrontation proceeded any further, Claggart would have successfully implicated Billy, because the sailor could not have explained to Vere why he failed to report the proffered bribe and planned rebellion.[32] Billy thus preserved his innocence—ironically—by striking out and killing Claggart. He also prevented Vere (as well as the general reader) from perceiving the broader significance of his one natural defect.

Billy's inability to speak on his own behalf under conditions of stress is connected not only with a rational, but also with a social or moral, fault. Like Rousseau's natural man, Billy has no particular or enduring ties; he has no sense of obligation to anyone or anything else. Like the cosmos that Melville depicted in *Moby Dick,* human beings are by nature indifferent. Although his former shipmates regarded his departure "sorrowfully," Billy himself left the *Rights of Man* "with the gayety of high health, youth, and a free heart" (p. 49). He expressed no regret at leaving his friends. Later witnessing a flogging aboard the *Bellipotent,* he becomes extremely punctilious in duty—not from loyalty to the king (or the captain), however, but simply to avoid the pain of punishment.

Billy is somewhat asocial because he is somewhat *alogos*. But Melville shows that Billy cannot preserve himself on the basis of his physical prowess alone. He needs the help of others, but he fails to recognize his dependence until it is too late. Even then, his faith in Vere is somewhat misplaced.

By dramatizing the defenselessness of uneducated human nature confronted with the powers of reason, Melville raises questions about the adequacy of such innocence as a definition of human excellence. "One person excepted," the narrator concludes, "the master-at-arms was perhaps the only man in the ship intellectually capable of adequately appreciating the moral phenomenon presented in Billy Budd" (p. 78). And Claggart's view of Billy—which the narrator thus indirectly invites the reader to share—is characterized by a fundamental duality. On the one hand, the master-at-arms scorns innocence. For one who knows no temptation, there is no choice, achievement, or virtue in being good. "Yet in an aesthetic way"—the narrator reports—Claggart "saw the charm of it, the courageous free-and-easy temper of it, and fain would have shared it, but he despaired of it" (p. 78).

If Claggart does understand the "moral phenomenon" that Billy represents, then is his persecution of Billy justified? Not according to the narrator, who carefully distinguishes Claggart's insight from his passion—as he also distinguishes Claggart's passion from his intellect, which is in service to his "natural depravity." Claggart is perverse or depraved because his pride leads him to hate and destroy what he is not, even when he himself recognizes that it is both natural and good.[33]

Comprehending the limits of Budd's virtue, the Dansker merely watches and philosophically reflects on Billy's seemingly inevitable demise. He is surely the "one person excepted" who is also capable of understanding the "moral phenomenon presented in Billy Budd." And he looks at Billy with "an expression of speculative query as to what might eventually befall a nature like that, dropped into a world not without some mantraps and against whose subtleties simple courage . . . is of little avail; and where such innocence as man is capable of does yet in a moral emergency not always sharpen the faculties or enlighten the will" (p. 70).[34]

Are despair and resignation the only possible responses to an insight into humanity's lost primal innocence?[35] Or can this natural virtue be transformed somehow so as to be preserved in civil society? Vere thinks that the tragic destruction of natural goodness is necessary. Through the plot, Melville demonstrates that it is not.

Although Vere decrees Billy's striking Claggart dead to be the work of "an angel of God," the captain concludes that "the angel must hang" (p. 101). He assures both Billy and his own officers that he knows the young sailor had no intention of killing an officer. Nevertheless, the captain decides that he must punish Billy to maintain law and order. His long-settled convictions concerning the tension between nature and convention have made him think that such tragic injustice is inevitable.

Vere thus questions the drumhead court that he has called, and then provides his own answers.

> How can we adjudge to summary and shameful death a fellow-creature innocent before God, and whom we feel to be so? I too feel that. . . . It is Nature. But do these buttons that we wear attest that our allegiance is to Nature? No, to the King. Though the ocean, which is inviolate Nature primeval, though this be the element where we move and have our being as sailors, yet as the King's officers lies our duty in a sphere correspondingly natural? So little is that true, that in receiving our commissions we in the most important regards ceased to be natural free agents. (p. 110)

Whatever their feelings or conscience tell them—Vere concludes—they must enforce the law. He explicitly chooses to follow conventionally instituted authority in opposition to his own judgment with regard to the facts of the case and his natural feelings. His study of history has convinced the captain that civil authority cannot be maintained on a natural foundation.

On leaving the captain's cabin, the surgeon points out two problematic aspects of Vere's judgment. In the first place, the great defender of law and order is not himself abiding by accepted procedure. According to traditional usage, Vere should have locked Billy up and then taken him ashore for trial, or to the fleet admiral. Stirred by the exceptional circumstances, Vere has acted more harshly and expeditiously than an officer would customarily. Second, the surgeon remarks on the "unwonted agitation of Captain Vere and his excited exclamations so at variance with his normal manner. Was he unhinged?" (pp. 101–2). The surgeon cannot prove that this is the case. Indeed, none of the inferior officers can resist Vere, although they are as convinced as Vere and the common sailors that Billy is innocent. As the surgeon points out, however, Vere had to interfere in the trial in an extraordinary manner to get the result that he was seeking. He became excited because he was seeing his theories realized in practice.

Vere produces a tragedy because he considers human life to be tragic—not because he has no choice. Melville brings out the irrationality of Vere's judgment in the scene on the deck at the time of Billy's hanging. As the young sailor rises to walk the plank, the men assembled to witness the punishment begin to murmur. Had Billy cried out, "I'm innocent"—rather than "God bless Captain Vere"— the results would have been quite different. The men would have revolted and seized power from the officers, rather than repeat Billy's blessing. Only Billy's innocent trust in the benign wisdom of his superior saves Vere from death and ignominy.[36] Vere is thus protected by the natural trust and pacifism that he himself denies in both theory and practice.

The narrative is thus highly ironic, as many commentators have observed. If human beings are as naturally resistant to order or as mutinous as Vere believes, then he surely would have failed to keep order on his ship. If they are not so irrational or revolutionary as he imagines, however, then his indomitable enforcement of unreasoning discipline is not necessary or justified. On the contrary, it constitutes the sort of abuse that brings about the insurrection he so fears.

Should we conclude then that Melville damns the intellect as the locus of perversity and evil (depicted in Claggart and Ahab) or as the agent of a tragic but necessary destruction of innocence (shown by Vere)? Not—I think—in quite such simple terms. Melville's story does suggest that two of the major modern philosophic understandings of the relation between nature and convention are incorrect because they are based on an erroneous view of nature. Represented by Billy, human nature is innocent, unconcerned with the opinions and welfare of others, amoral, and physically strong. Nature is also vulnerable—but not to envy or evil per se. Billy struck down both Red Whiskers and Claggart with his fist. Although he might not have recognized evil for what it was because he did not participate in it, Billy was yet able to defend himself against it. It turns out to be the man of good intentions but mistaken ideas about human nature who victimizes Billy in the end (just as it is Ahab's demand for justice that ultimately destroys his crew).

Like Rousseau, Melville shows that natural innocence cannot be preserved in society. It can be recognized and improved upon, however, through art. Vere might represent a "tragic hero," in Aristotle's sense of the term.[37] Vere does make a serious error in judgment, but erroneous ideas can be corrected; neither they nor their consequences are necessarily inescapable. By depicting the beauty of man's original nature, the novelist remedies Billy's one fatal defect: his inability to speak on his own behalf. As Aristotle argued, art cannot merely imitate, but should bring to completion what is only potential or implicit in nature.

By showing that human nature is good but vulnerable, in *Billy Budd* Melville was able to accomplish two related goals. In the first place, he could save common men from the destructive effects of the intellectual errors of their superiors, by revealing them to be errors. At the same time, he could show that leadership is both natural and necessary, and so undermine the ideology of rebellion. Because common people are not able to defend their own rights without organization, some form of hierarchy must be instituted. In order to be just, however, that hierarchy must be based on a true sense of nature.

At the end of the novel, Melville transcribes a song in which the common sailors express both their conviction that Billy was innocent and their passive belief that there must be some reason that he had to die. The common sailors retain a truer sense of justice than their officers, because their natural sentiments are less distorted by philosophical reflections. "Gifted, as some sailors are, with an artless poetic temperament" (p. 131), they intuit the truth. They are not able to act on the basis of their intuitions, however. They do not rebel against unjust authority, because—like Billy—they are not able to articulate the reasons why their superiors are wrong. They need the philosophical fiction of Melville to show that their oppressors are acting on the basis of a mistaken view of human nature.

Just as human nature requires artful defense to preserve its goodness in the face of its philosophical detractors, so do the common people need artful and intelligent leadership to secure their rights. Like Billy— Melville shows—the mutinous sailors on the *Nore,* the quarrelsome merchantmen on the *Rights of Man,* and the impressed servants on the *Bellipotent* were unable to defend themselves. They could rebel, fight, and destroy; but they could not organize or establish peace. As a "natural" leader, the handsome Billy attracted a spontaneous following, and so temporarily brought peace to the "rat-pit of quarrels" aboard the *Rights.* But lacking foresight, Billy also lacked a fear of death; therefore, he did not resist Vere or lead a justified rebellion against the oppressive and illegal use of power. Natural beauty and justice need to be supplemented by art and intelligence. And Melville presents his readers with the image of just such a "civilized" leader, in Admiral Nelson.

Like the natural leader—the handsome sailor—Nelson flaunts his person and his daring. But it is his clothes rather than physique that dazzle, and his fortitude rather than brute strength that impresses his men. Although he accepts danger and death without complaint, Nelson demonstrates foresight, as well: He writes a will before Trafalgar.

Reason has a role in leading men, and leadership is necessary to defend freedom under law.

Melville does not praise Nelson himself—with his obvious desire for glory—so much as his ability to execute an essential function successfully. Most of the novelist's praise goes to the common man.[38]

Captain Vere dies alone, unmourned and unsung. Not so, Billy Budd.[39] Unlike the skeptical surgeon, the common sailors who compose "Billy in the Darbies" do recognize the exceptional; they are able to admire and to admit what they do not understand. They are poets of sorts; and their account of Billy's death is truer than the official naval chronicle, which gives the facts of the case, crudely (as Vere himself acted on them, against his own better judgment of the respective characters of the men involved): Billy, a rebellious villain, killed an officer who had been conscientiously attending to his duty.

The "common" sense that Vere possesses and that enables him—like his men—to perceive truth and falsity in human character is better than his educated theory. Indeed, it is just this appreciation of our common nature—including, preeminently, the sailors' stoical acceptance of the inevitability of death—that Melville embodies in *Billy Budd*.

Three Versions of Rousseauian Politics

Usually, Melville's writing is associated with Hawthorne's "blackness"; however—like Cooper and unlike Hawthorne—in both *Moby Dick* and *Billy Budd* Melville portrayed human nature as being essentially good. Like Cooper, Melville saw that this natural goodness is vulnerable to manipulation and corruption. Also like Cooper, Melville thus showed that human beings need legal protection. (If Vere had abided by the specified procedures and had testified in court to his own belief in Billy's innocence, Billy would probably not have been hanged.) Further like Cooper, Melville demonstrated that laws work justice only when based on an insight into humanity's natural goodness. Unfortunately—as Melville recognized— being an internal rather than an external quality, this goodness usually remains invisible because human nature qua nature is—like Billy—inarticulate. It requires an emphatically educated, civilized writer of fiction to bring the natural goodness of human beings into view, and thus to reveal the true foundations of democracy.

There are, however, important differences between Cooper's and

Melville's understandings of the various threats to democracy and of the poet's role in counteracting them. In the first place, the two novelists had a decidedly different understanding of the proper form of poetic public teaching. Cooper believed that, in a democracy, it is necessary to convince the people as well as their leaders of the intrinsic goodness of human nature. Since religion had traditionally served as the major conduit of popular morality, not only did Cooper write for a broader, less philosophically (mis)educated audience, but he also sought to cast his teaching rather explicitly in the form of a natural religion. Where Cooper caused his protagonist to preach, Melville attempted to link democratic politics to philosophical skepticism. Like Hawthorne, Melville showed not only that the cosmos is fundamentally unintelligible (as Rousseau had also argued), but also that it is basically indifferent to human concerns.

Cooper, Hawthorne, and Melville all stressed the limits of the human intellect. However, Cooper and Hawthorne were content to illustrate the evil consequences of intellectual pride, which makes people unconscious—if not indifferent—to the suffering that their experiments occasion.[40] Melville sought to show that the doctrines of specific philosophers like Paine and Burke had problematic foundations, because he thought that these false views of human nature were the cause of the great political turmoil of the nineteenth century. By misleading leaders—Melville suggested—these philosophers had not merely denigrated humanity, but also caused the common people a great deal of unnecessary suffering. In defending people from the destructive effects of philosophically (mis)shaped politics, Melville's own fiction—rather ironically—became increasingly philosophic and, so, increasingly unpopular. If the major cause of oppression were to be found in the miseducation of leaders, however, Melville could still succeed in his mission by reaching a rather restricted audience.

The view of human nature that Melville presented also differed in an essential respect from that presented by Rousseau, Cooper, and Hawthorne. All these authors recognized that conflict arises from the competing requirements for self-preservation of the various species. According to Rousseau, Cooper, and Hawthorne, such conflict becomes invidious only as a result of a peculiarly human desire for distinction that is associated with the intellect or imagination, but rooted in human sexuality. And because the desire for distinction is rooted in human sexuality, it cannot be eradicated without destroying the race. This divisive desire can be moderated, however; human beings can live moderately satisfying lives (these authors suggested), but only in the context of the private family.[41] Melville associated the desire for distinction both with intellectual arrogance (as in Ahab and Vere) and with the desire for popular adulation (as in Nelson). He believed that this desire could be effectively checked and redirected in a politically salutary direction by a literary art that would reveal the fundamental good sense of the common people; and so, he made an implicit case for the rationality of seeking fame by leading—that is, serving—them. Despite his own reputed blackness, Melville's vision is thus fundamentally more optimistic about the possibilities of democratic public life than that of his predecessors.

By depicting human beings outside the bounds of civil society—and so, metaphorically, in the state of nature—aboard ship where no women were present, however, Melville abstracted from what is potentially the cause of the most severe human conflict. At the very least—the comparison with Rousseau, Cooper, and Hawthorne suggests—Melville's picture of the courageous fellowship of men self-consciously confronting death together does not constitute a full view of the human condition, because sexual differences and the consequences of sexual attraction certainly are natural.[42]

Notes

1. Melville explicitly associated himself with Hawthorne's "blackness" in his famous review of the *Mosses*. See Herman Melville, "Hawthorne and his *Mosses*,"*Literary World,* August 17 and 24, 1850.

2. Michael Rogin, *Subversive Genealogy* (New York: Knopf, 1975), has thoroughly documented Cooper's influence on Melville.

3. Harold Beaver has observed in "Herman Melville: Prophetic Mariner," Richard Gray, ed., *American Literature: New Readings* (Totowa, N.J.: Barnes and Noble, 1983), p. 66: "For the truth is that our contemporary grasp of Melville is partly dependent on our earlier apprenticeship to Baudelaire, say, or Nietzsche." Laurence Thompson, *Melville's Quarrel with God* (Princeton, N.J.: Princeton University Press, 1952), was first to give such a reading.

4. Ray B. Browne, *Melville's Drive to Humanism* (Lafayette, Ind.: Purdue University Studies, 1971); Harold Kaplan, *Democratic Humanism and American Literature* (Chicago: University of Chicago Press, 1972), pp. 159–97; and Joyce Adler, *War in Melville's Imagination* (New York: New York University Press, 1981), all emphasize Melville's egalitarian humanism.

5. If there be no natural or divine order—Nietzsche observed—then noth-

ing has any inherent value. The only way in which things (and, most importantly, human life itself) can acquire value, therefore, is for some human beings self-consciously to impose their values on others—the way philosophers had unconsciously projected their own deepest desires onto the universe as a whole, in the past. See *Beyond Good and Evil* (New York: Vintage, 1967), esp. pts. 5, 7, 9, and *Genealogy of Morals* (New York: Vintage, 1968).

6. See "The Creed of the Savoyard Priest" in Jean Jacques Rousseau, *Emile* (New York: Basic Books, 1979).

7. Jean Jacques Rousseau, *The Confessions* (London: Penguin, 1953), and *Reveries of a Solitary Walker* (New York: New York University Press, 1979).

8. Since Rousseau himself was not an altogether consistent thinker— his doctrines have been argued both to undermine all political order and to initiate totalitarian dictatorships—his teachings could be adapted by American novelists in rather different ways. After examining two of Melville's works in detail, at the conclusion of this essay I will therefore compare and contrast Melville's Rousseauian vision with those of both his predecessors. Although Hawthorne did not accept the fundamental Rousseauian premise that human beings are innocent by nature, the conclusion he came to about the locus of human happiness in middle-class marriage very much resembled Rousseau's practical recommendation for most individuals, given in the *Emile*. On Melville's familiarity with Rousseau, see Merton J. Sealts, *Melville's Reading* (Columbia: University of South Carolina Press, 1988).

9. Jean Jacques Rousseau, "Discourse on the Origins of Inequality," note (i), in *The First and Second Discourses* (New York: St. Martin's Press, 1964).

10. Thomas Paine, *The Rights of Man and Other Writings* (London: Heron, 1970).

11. Human beings have different talents by nature—Rousseau admitted at the beginning of his "Discourse on Inequality"—but these natural inequalities do not develop and thus have no relevance or importance outside of civil society. So long as human beings live in solitude, they are therefore naturally equal. Even when they come to live together, the development of different talents and economic interdependence per se does not fundamentally threaten their liberty or equality. Human beings lose both only when they come to define themselves solely in terms of their value in the eyes of others.

12. Thomas Hobbes, *The Leviathan* (Indianapolis: Bobbs-Merrill, 1958), chs. 14 and 15.

13. Textual citations are from Herman Melville, *Moby Dick* (New York: Norton, 1967).

14. Edgar Dryden, *Melville's Thematics of Form* (Baltimore: Johns Hopkins University Press, 1968), pp. 85–7, has pointed out that the narrator's tone in the first chapter of *Moby Dick* does not seem bitter or angry. Dryden takes the choice of the name "Ishmael" to suggest not alienation from society, therefore, but a self-conscious literary freedom from fact. Freedom and alienation are often joined, however. As Ishmael's departure shows, he *was* alienated; he

has returned to tell how he conquered despair and anger. The difference between his postjourney and prejourney perspectives gives an ironic tone to the introduction.

15. Randall Bohrer, "Cannibalism and Cosmology in *Moby Dick*," *Studies in Romanticism* 22 (Spring 1983): 65–92, has pointed out the parallel between the microcosm—the cannibal Queequeg with his cosmological tattoos—and the "cannibalistic" whole. Just as Ishmael overcomes his fear of Queequeg by suspending his particularistic prejudices, so he eventually overcomes his terror of the "sharkish" strife characteristic of the cosmos by giving up an Ahab-like demand for special dispensation or place.

16. By choosing the name of Ishmael, the narrator indicates not only that he is alienated, but also that the alienation is not simply desired or self-willed. Queequeg is also an exile, although by his own choice; having left his native land to explore the ways of other men, he feels he has become so corrupted by the Christians that he cannot return. Unlike his fellow cannibals, he is now somewhat conscious of the estrangement of man from world. Thus he reflects at the end of Chapter 66: "Queequeg no care what god made him shark . . . wedder Fejee god or Nantucket god; but de god wat made shark must be one damn Ingin" (p. 257).

17. Mark T. Patterson, "Democratic Leadership and Narrative Authority in *Moby Dick*," *Studies in the Novel* 16 (Fall 1984): 285–95, has also compared Ahab's authority—based on his position and an appeal to his men's resentment of their suffering—to Ishmael's authority as a didactic narrator. But, he argues that there is something incomplete about both their quests.

18. Melville stylistically underlines the link between Ahab's story and classical drama by organizing most of the chapters that deal specifically with Ahab's quest in the form of stage directions—for example, "Enter Ahab, To Him, Stubb" or "Midnight, on the Forecastle." F. O. Matthiessen, *American Renaissance* (New York: Oxford University Press, 1941), pp. 423–31, has emphasized Melville's use of Shakespearean language. Ahab is very explicitly the hero of a tragedy that readers are meant to watch and reflect on, with the assistance and in the context of Ishmael's more passive meditations. Those who have emphasized the tragedy—see, for example, William Ellery Sedgwick, *Tragedy of Mind* (Cambridge, Mass.: Harvard University Press, 1948)—have tended not to recognize the way Melville explicitly sets that tragedy into the frame provided by Ishmael's reflections. Alfred A. Kazin did so, however, in his introduction to the Riverside edition of *Moby Dick*, reprinted in Richard Chase, *Melville* (Englewood Cliffs, N.J.: Prentice-Hall, 1962), pp. 39–48.

19. Melville's statement here ought to be compared with Alexis de Tocqueville's argument in *Democracy in America,* (Garden City, N.Y.: Doubleday, 1964), vol. 1, ch. 9, concerning the compatibility of generalized Christian beliefs with democratic social conditions: All human beings are equal before or under God. Insisting that Melville was a Nietzschean, Laurence Thompson, *Melville's Quarrel with God* (Princeton, N.J.: Princeton University Press, 1952), takes all such statements to be ironic.

20. See René Descartes, *Discourse on Method* (Indianapolis: Bobbs-Merrill, 1950).

21. If modern democrats do not preserve the basic tenets of the religious faith that they have inherited from earlier times—Tocqueville argued in *Democracy*—their antagonism to authority would result in the loss of faith and morality both. In his attempt to conquer the universe with his mind, and in his consequent loss of all sense of humanity, Ahab embodies the fundamental thrust of Western metaphysics, as Martin Heidegger later analyzed it in *The Question Concerning Technology* (New York: Harper, 1977).

22. Afraid of the whirring whale line, Pip jumped overboard at each lowering and was finally left far behind by all the boats. By the time they returned and found him, he had lost his mind.

23. John Berstein, *Pacifism and Rebellion in the Writings of Herman Melville* (The Hague: Mouton, 1964), thus misconstrued the alternatives that Melville is investigating. Adler, *War,* has documented the pervasiveness of conflict or "war" in human relations as Melville portrays them, and hence the need for order to be enforced. But she did not connect the human to the cosmic situation as Melville portrays it.

24. Sensing the futility, Ahab nevertheless persists in his opposition. Thus, he shouts into the storm: "No fearless fool now confronts thee. I own thy speechless, placeless power; but to the last gasp of my earthquake life will dispute its unconditional, unintegral mastery in me. In the midst of the personified impersonal, a personality stands here" (p. 417).

25. Rowland A. Sherrill, *The Prophetic Melville* (Athens; University of Georgia Press, 1979), p. 237, has emphasized the didactic character of Melville's work, although Sherrill concluded that Melville came to doubt whether his work could have this desired effect.

26. Ray B. Browne, *"Billy Budd:* Gospel of Democracy," *Nineteenth Century Fiction* 17 (March 1963):321–38, has documented the extensive public attention to both Paine and Burke at the time Melville was writing *Billy Budd*. Browne did not perceive Melville's decided criticism of Paine, however. Textual citations are from Herman Melville, *Billy Budd* (Chicago: University of Chicago Press, 1962).

27. Newton Arvin, *Herman Melville* (Westport, Conn.: Greenwood, 1972); and Nathalia Wright, *Melville's Use of the Bible* (New Haven, Conn.: Yale University Press, 1957). Thomas Scorza, *In the Days before Steamships* (De Kalb: Northern Illinois Press, 1979), and John Noone, *"Billy Budd:* Two Concepts of Nature," *American Literature,* 19 (November 1957):249–62, were thus correct to see Billy as essentially a Rousseauian natural man. Noone was incorrect, however, when he identified the alternative to Billy as Claggart or Hobbes. The narrator explicitly describes Claggart in Platonic terms of "natural depravity." For Hobbes, good and evil represented merely subjective attractions and aversions in the natural condition, before humans passed laws declaring what is just and unjust. There is no such thing as natural depravity,

therefore, according to Hobbes. (Nor was there for Rousseau, who considered depravity to be a product of civilization.)

28. Rousseau, "Discourse on Inequality," note (o).

29. C. N. Manlove, "An Organic Hesitancy: Theme and Style in *Billy Budd*," in Faith Pullin, ed., *New Perspectives on Melville* (Kent, Ohio: Kent State University Press, 1978), pp. 274–75, emphasizes both the battle between nature and civilization and the fact that evil (Claggart) can be aligned with civilization (Vere). This notion is essentially Rousseauian, although—for Rousseau as for Melville—civilization does not have to be evil. See Jean Jacques Rousseau, *On the Social Contract* (Indianapolis: Hackett, 1983).

30. See Edmund Burke, *Reflections on the Revolution in France* (Indianapolis: Hackett, 1987).

31. The "testament of resistance" reading of *Billy Budd* is contradicted by the signal fact that neither Billy nor the sailors aboard the *Bellipotent* actually resist or rebel. Like the inferior members of the drumhead court, the common sailors respond to character (leadership) and to accustomed order (the drums). See Phil Witham, *"Billy Budd:* Testament of Resistance," *Modern Language Quarterly* 20 (June 1959):115–27.

32. Scorza, *Before Steamships,* pointed out that, although most readers have concentrated on Vere's decision to hang Billy, his previous determination to apply legal procedure to ferret out the truth is what actually provokes the tragedy. This reliance on legal procedure characterizes Vere, I agree; he is blind to the presuppositions of the law, or the need for the law to find a foundation and justification in either nature or divine revelation. Scorza concluded that Vere's resulting decision to hang Billy is justified. I disagree, for reasons spelled out in the text.

33. In his violent reaction to that which his reason cannot entirely decipher or conquer, Claggart—ironically—resembles Billy. Both are more natural than Vere. Vere is the emphatically moral man, and morality is not quite or simply natural, as Billy demonstrates. The quotation from Aristotle's *Politics* that Rousseau used on the frontispiece to his "Discourse on Inequality" is relevant here: *Non in depravatis, sed in his quae bene secundum naturam se habeant, considerandum est quid sit naturale* ("Not in corrupt things, but in those which are well ordered in accordance with nature, should one consider that which is natural"). Unlike Vere, Claggart appreciates the significance of Billy's innocence—and perversely hates it because it represents not merely a, but *the,* challenge to his own particular area of excellence to the intellect.

34. There is a strong parallel between the active Ahab and Vere—who make decisions on the basis of their reason, against their better feelings—on the one hand, and the reflective Ishmael and Dansker, on the other. The Dansker merely watches silently, however; Ishmael—like the poet himself—returns to tell his tale. Understanding enables human beings to live with themselves and the world; it does not change the world or the humans in it, according to Melville.

35. Dennis Grunes, "Preinterpretation and *Billy Budd,*" *Essays in Literature* 13 (Spring 1986):106–13, also points out the way in which Melville undermines a purely positive view of every one of the characters—Billy, Vere, Claggart, or the Dansker—but he argues that Melville does this in order to question the existence of any sort of wisdom and to destroy the tyranny of any one viewpoint over another.

36. The narrator's description of this crucial moment is worth rereading with care: " 'God bless Captain Vere!' *Syllables so unanticipate* coming from one with the ignominious hemp about his neck . . . *had a phenomenal effect,* not unenhanced by the rare personal beauty of the young sailor spiritualized now through late experiences. . . . Without volition as it were, as if indeed the ship's populace were but the vehicles of some vocal current electric, with one voice from alow and aloft came a resonant sympathetic echo—'God Bless Captain Vere'! And yet at that instant Billy alone must have been in their hearts, even as he was in their eyes" (p. 123; emphasis added).

37. Aristotle, *Poetics* (Cambridge, Mass.: Harvard University Press, 1926), passages 1453a5–10. Richard Harter Fogle, *"Billy Budd*—Acceptance or Irony," *Tulane Studies in English* 8 (1958):107–13, has also pointed out the classically tragic elements of the plot.

38. Scorza's reading of *Billy Budd (Before Steamships)* as a return to a prephilosophic understanding of the relation among poetry, philosophy, and politics thus has two difficulties. First, he ignores the importance of philosophic reflection or skepticism in Melville's fiction—not only as an expression of but also as a necessary foundation for individual freedom, as Ishmael's experience reveals. That is, Scorza ignores Melville's philosophic concerns in his interpretation of Melville's politics. Second, Aristophanes—whom Scorza takes as representative and embodiment of the older view with which he identifies Melville—was a strong conservative with sympathies for the older aristocratic order. Aristophanes also emphatically taught the need for piety. Melville was emphatically—ruthlessly—democratic. He was skeptical about what human beings can know, but he never suggested that political order requires myths about the gods. On the contrary, he presented doubts about the deity very sympathetically.

39. This evident fact in the text seems to contradict commentators like Milton R. Stern, *The Fine Hammered Steel of Herman Melville* (Urbana: University of Illinois Press, 1957), who identify Melville's position with that of Vere. In *Billy Budd,* the narrator explicitly suggests that it is the poet's special function to immortalize great men: "The poet but embodies in verse those exaltations of sentiment that a nature like Nelson, the opportunity being given, vitalizes into acts" (p. 58). Again, there is irony here. The narrator speaks specifically of great epics and dramas, while Melville has written an inside narrative in which he explicitly states that Billy "is not presented as a conventional hero, but also that the story in which he is the main figure is no romance" (p. 53). Because Melville seeks to elevate the experience or senti-

ments of the common man—to glorify the human, rather than the heroic—he cannot use any of the classical forms.

40. Hawthorne enunciated this theme more clearly in "The Birthmark" and "Rappacini's Daughter" than he did in his full-scale romances. *Complete Short Stories* (Garden City, N.Y.: Hanover House, 1959).

41. Although Hawthorne did not accept the fundamentally Rousseauian premise that human beings are innocent—if not good—by nature, his conclusion about the locus of human happiness in the middle-class family very much resembled Rousseau's practical recommendation concerning the way most human beings should live. Rousseau, *Emile*.

42. Here again, Melville also differed significantly from Nietzsche who used the difference between the sexes to indicate a natural foundation for aristocratic distinctions. *Beyond Good and Evil,* aphorisms 232–39. Attempting to make Nietzsche completely relativistic (and so, more egalitarian), Jacques Derrida has thus "de-constructed" Nietzsche's view of "woman" in *Spurs: Nietzsche Styles* (Chicago: University of Chicago Press, 1978).

6

Twain's Comic Critique

Mark Twain's *Adventures of Huckleberry Finn* marked a new beginning in American literature.[1] The story of Huck and Jim's trip down the river replaced Cooper's Leatherstocking tales as *the* depiction of a return to the state of nature. Both Hemingway and Faulkner traced the origins of their own work to Twain's novel.[2]

This new beginning marked a crisis in "natural rights" or "state of nature" thinking, however. By showing not only that Huck flees civil society in search of his freedom but also that he must return to free his friend Jim, Twain in effect ratified the reasoning of the social contract theorists. Natural rights or liberties were not secure in the state of nature; they could only be guaranteed through the institution of government and laws. But in his novel Twain also demonstrated that such reasoning had not and was never apt to persuade human beings, in general—and Americans, in particular. It went counter to their strongest desires.

Twain himself thus took a different rhetorical tack. Rather than merely present a romantic picture of the naive goodness that individuals like Natty and Huck display in the state of nature—in contrast to the evil effects that the desire for distinction works in civil society— Twain combined such a picture with ridicule of aristocratic pretensions. Instead of opposing popular passions directly with reason or preaching—like Cooper—Twain thus appealed to egalitarian democratic prejudices. Not surprisingly, perhaps, his work has had more enduring success with both popular audiences and literary critics.

Adventures of Huckleberry Finn

At first glance, Huck's life on the river appears idyllic. Having evaded the supervision of both guardian and father, Huck can do as he pleases; and living outside both legal and moral conventions, the boy befriends a runaway slave. As Huck and Jim float down the river, most readers come to admire the ease and excitement of their existence much less than the naive moral sense that leads Huck finally to declare he would literally be damned rather than see his black companion reenslaved. Like Natty Bumppo and Billy Budd, Huck clearly embodies the goodness of natural sentiment. Like the works of both Cooper and Melville that incorporate the same theme, however, Twain's novel also shows that good sentiments do not suffice to secure either liberty or humanity.

Impressed by the independent spirit and resourceful intelligence that Huck displays on the river, readers are often dismayed to see him revert to his old habits and meekly follow Tom Sawyer as soon as he rejoins civil society.[3] Was the amity and ease of Huck and Jim's life in the state of nature merely illusory? That seems to be Twain's point when he shows that Huck must return to civil society if he is really to free Jim. On reflection, we realize that the runaway slave could not possibly have secured his freedom simply by floating down the Mississippi (right into slave territory). Even the white orphan Huck proves unable to maintain his independence from the force-based domination of adults when the "Duke" and the "Dauphin" board his raft.

Huck has to return to civil society—Twain insists—because the force and fraud that characterize relations among human beings in the state of nature make it impossible to secure anyone's right to life, liberty, or the pursuit of happiness outside the protection of the law. Jim does acquire his freedom at the end of the novel, but only through the operation of two forces that Huck despises: religion (in the form of Miss Watson's conscience) and law (in the form of her legal will).

Huck's return is as necessary artistically as it is thematically. Because Twain wrote part of the novel, put it down, and then completed it several years later, some critics have argued that it constitutes a picaresque series of loosely related incidents without much internal order or coherence.[4] They have failed to note the implications of Twain's beginning with Huck not merely as narrator, but as author. For Huck to write and publish his story, he would *have* to return. Twain may have taken some time to figure out exactly how to engineer the ending, but such a conclusion was artistically required from the very beginning of the manuscript.[5]

Twain's Corrections of Cooper

Both the unity and the thematic significance of the structure of the novel come out if we view *Huck Finn* in light of Twain's critique of Cooper. Not content to destroy the reputation of "the American Scott" with his list of "Fenimore Cooper's Literary Offenses," Twain tried to remedy all the defects that he found in *The Deerslayer* in his own version of the return to nature.[6] According to Twain, Cooper's first and worst fault lay in the faulty organization of his tale, which did not—in Aristotelian terms—have a clear beginning, middle, and end. *Adventures of Huckleberry Finn* clearly does: It begins with Huck's withdrawal from civil society on the banks of the river, has its center and climax during his trip down the Mississippi, and concludes back in civil society on the river bank at the Phelps farm. Twain also corrected the inauthenticity and inconsistency in Cooper's dialogues and dialects, as he reminds his readers in the opening "Explanatory." Unlike his predecessor, Twain did not describe any physically impossible relations among streams, woods, and houseboats (or rafts).

Twain's novel is more realistic not only in its careful depiction of speech and setting, but also in story line. Human beings would not live long or well—Twain recognizes—in isolation from others. Cooper's hero was self-sufficient; Twain's clearly is not. A young boy is a more credible spokesman for untouched nature than a mature woodsman, as Cooper himself came to realize; but a boy is also physically vulnerable and weak.

Cooper himself preached the need for law and order, especially with respect to property rights; but his hero brought the legitimacy of those selfsame laws into question by fleeing the settlements. In *Adventures of Huckleberry Finn* Twain also raises questions about the justice of property rights, by presenting the dehumanizing effects of slavery. Nevertheless, his story shows that there is no security of life or liberty without legal protection. Unlike Natty, neither Huck nor Jim attains freedom through flight.

Both Natty and his creator moralized, moreover; Twain and his hero explicitly do not. Human beings resist moral suasion, Twain reminds his readers in Huck's reaction to Miss Watson. And by making Huck the narrator of his own story, Twain achieves significant rhetorical advantages. Whereas Natty preached, Huck confesses that he has a bad conscience. Twain stresses the nondidactic character of his novel by adding a prefatory warning: "Persons attempting to find a motive in this narrative will be prosecuted; persons attempting to find a moral in it will be banished; persons attempting to find a plot in it will be shot."

To be sure, Twain's disclaimer has to be read somewhat ironically. In the first place, he lacks the power or authority to carry out his threats, as he himself implies by signing the notice "by order of the author, per G. G., Chief of Ordnance." Whether "plot" simply means "story" or the more sinister "conspiracy," moreover, plots certainly do abound—both in the form of a clear story line and as schemes to fool parents and to free Jim.

"Humor must not *professedly* teach or *professedly* preach," Twain wrote in his *Autobiography,* "but it must do both if it is to live forever." And he admitted, "I have always preached. . . . If the humor came of its own accord uninvited I have allowed it a place in my sermon, but I was not writing the sermon for the sake of the humor. I should have written the sermon just the same."[7] He simply presented his own teaching indirectly and ironically.

The Difference Between Narrator and Author

There is a difference between narrator and creator, Twain reminds his readers both through his prefatory notes by "the author" and in Huck's self-introduction.

> You don't know about me without you have read a book by the name of *The Adventures of Tom Sawyer;* but that ain't no matter. That book was made by Mr. Mark Twain, and he told the truth, mainly. There was things which he stretched, but mainly he told the truth. That is nothing. I never seen anybody but lied one time or another, without it was Aunt Polly, or the widow, or maybe Mary. (p. 3)[8]

Unlike the author (who is writing fiction under a pseudonym), Huck suggests that he—the narrator—is telling the whole truth, and nothing but.[9] As Huck recounts his adventures, it becomes ever more clear over the course of the novel that he lies constantly. He regularly "takes in" his interlocuters by appealing to their compassion for a poor, weak orphan. Does he try to take in his readers the same way?

Describing his inner debates with his conscience, Huck's narrative voice is so appealing that readers rarely stop to reflect on the reasons this almost illiterate boy—who tried to rid himself of all civic identity in order to be free—has now decided to write and publish his story. Does he want fame? At the end of his adventures, Huck assumes the identity of Tom Sawyer easily and gladly; and certainly—in both novels—Tom has openly sought glory.[10] Is Huck attempting to justify himself and his actions to the good citizens of St. Petersburg? Maybe by showing that he himself has simply been trying to escape life-threatening beatings from his father, and that Jim has really been legally free all along, Huck can establish his innocence, reenter society, and be rid of the loneliness that constantly plagues him.

And so, not only is there a difference between author and narrator, but the narrator is also unreliable. To determine what Twain is doing in presenting Huck's adventures, readers cannot rely on the explicit statements of any of his fictional characters. We have to attend, rather, to what Twain describes as happening to those characters—that is, to the plot.[11] And imbedded in the plot of *Huck Finn,* Twain has left us a truly ironic teaching.

Through Huck and Jim's famous friendship, Twain shows that human beings are by nature free and equal; but, through the course of the friends' adventures, Twain shows that these natural rights must be secured by law. The principles of the Declaration of Independence are true, to be sure; but Twain also demonstrates that—like Huck—Americans generally do not understand them. And if Americans do not understand them, the Declaration's principles will never govern their lives.

Huck's Adventures in the State of Nature

Huck would appear particularly well suited to reveal the true relation between nature and convention, because he has grown up as an orphan and outcast—free from the pretenses and pretensions of polite society. As he explains at the beginning of his story, after Huck saved the Widow Douglas's life she gratefully "took me for her son, and allowed she would sivilize me; but it was rough living in the house all the time, considering how dismal regular and decent the Widow was in all her ways; and so when I couldn't stand it no longer I lit out" (p. 4). But when Tom Sawyer tells Huck that he cannot join the gang unless he returns to the Widow's, Huck immediately goes back. In Huck, Twain thus depicts both the forces that lead human beings to resist conventional restraints, and those that make them voluntarily submit.[12]

Huck wants to escape because he finds the physical constraints imposed by conventional manners and morality uncomfortable. Unlike both Natty in *The Pioneers* and the emigrants to Blithedale, Huck does not resist on principle.[13] Although he knows that Miss Watson's religion runs counter to his own desires, for example, he never concludes that her lessons are wrong. On the contrary (and in contrast to the reader), Huck simply believes that he himself and his wishes are "low down." Thus, at the Widow Douglas's, Huck is content to slip out at night and merely playact outlaw.

Nevertheless, the tricks that Huck and Tom play on Jim—and the gang of "robbers" that Tom organizes in Chapter Two—comically foreshadow the black humor of their attempt to steal the slave at the end. Tom begins by wanting to tie up Jim in his sleep—that is, to make him a prisoner; but Huck persuades Tom merely to trick Jim into thinking that witches have taken his hat. Even this apparently harmless trick has its questionable consequences, for—as Huck observes—"Jim was most ruined for a servant, because he got stuck upon account of having seen the devil and been rode by witches" (p. 11). There is a fundamental tension—Twain indicates from the very beginning—between the boys' desire to have fun and the requirements of social order.

That tension cannot be accurately described simply in terms of nature and convention, however, because—unlike Huck—Tom's desires are explicitly cast in "conventional" terms. As his long-standing friendship with Huck indicates, Tom does not simply accept and obey conventional authority. Unlike Huck, however, Tom is concerned about his reputation, and thus about keeping up appearances. He displays his own curious mixture of conventional morality and immorality when he first insists on leaving a nickel to pay for the candles that they have taken from Jim's table, and then goes on to organize a gang of "murderers and robbers." Tom is not worried about acting dishonestly, but about acting basely. "We ain't burglars," Tom later explains to his cohort. "That ain't no sort of style. . . . We stop stages and carriages on the road, with masks on, and kill the people and take their watches and money. . . . I've seen it in books; and so of course that's what we've got to do" (pp. 13–14). Although neither the legal nor the religious injunctions against killing and stealing have much weight in Tom's estimation, he does clearly recognize a kind of authority—in the form of the romantic novels that he reads. He wishes to achieve the glory of the heroes for himself; above all, he wants to be envied for his daring exploits. This same desire later leads him to perpetuate Jim's incarceration, to prolong the pleasure of saving him "by the book."

Some human beings like to pretend that they are better than others, and thus rightfully above the law. But—Twain also shows us—most are endowed with a good bit of natural skepticism, as well. Like the rest of Tom's followers, Huck eventually quits the gang.

> We played robber now and then about a month, and then I resigned. All the boys did. We hadn't robbed nobody, hadn't killed any people, but only just pretended. . . . So then I judged that all that stuff was only just one of Tom Sawyer's lies. I reckoned he believed in the A-rabs and the elephants, but as for me I think different. It had all the marks of a Sunday-school. (pp. 18–22)

In contrast to Tom, Huck is something of a pragmatic empiricist. Just as he once tested Miss Watson's claim that God helps those who pray—by trying for fishhooks—so he rejects Tom's claim that there were "di'monds, A-rabs, and elephants" at the Sunday school picnic that the boys invaded. Huck had not seen any; and he saw no profit in the pretense.[14]

At first sight, Huck and Tom appear to be markedly different. Tom's antics parody aristocratic romances; Huck speaks for down-to-earth democratic skepticism. Nevertheless, Tom retains a great deal of influence over Huck. To discover the source of this influence might, therefore, be to discover what Twain considered to be the natural roots of civilization.

Although Huck remains skeptical about the pretenses and pretensions of polite society, he never actually rebels against it. On the contrary—he admits—the longer he stays at the Widow's, the less uncomfortable he finds "sivilization." When he does leave his foster home, it is not of his own volition. Hearing that Huck has not only acquired a fortune but is also attending school, his natural father comes back to get some of the money and to prevent his son's making himself better than his forebears by acquiring an education.

And in Pap, Twain shows how ugly the apparently natural inclination to escape conventional restraints can look in adults. Pap is dirty, a gambler, and a violent drunk. Nor can he be reformed. Rather than give Judge Thatcher or the widow legal custody of the boy, the new judge thinks that he ought to try to preserve the natural family. So he takes Pap home and gets him to sign a temperance pledge. Feeling a thirst in the middle of the night, Pap climbs down from his bedroom window and trades his new suit of clothes for a gallon of whiskey. Pap thus resists civilization the same way Huck did at the Widow's. The judge concludes that the only way the old man would be reformed is with a shotgun.

As Twain shows again later during the course of Huck's adventures, Americans generally tend to vacillate between an overly sentimentalized view of nature and the use of unadulterated force. As a result— like the new judge—they ironically missed both the basis and function of law.

What may look innocent in young boys does not appear equally harmless or tolerable in their elders. And in adults—Twain shows—the desire to escape conventional restraints has clear political implications.

Whenever Pap got drunk—Huck reports—he almost always "went for the govment." Pap blames the "govment" for virtually all his misfortunes.

> Here's the law a-standing ready to take a man's son away from him—a man's own son, which he has had all the trouble and all the anxiety and all the expense of raising. That ain't all, nuther. The law backs that old Judge Thatcher up and helps him to keep me out o' my property. [It] takes a man worth six thousand dollars and up-ards and jams him into an old trap of a cabin like this, and lets him go round in clothes that ain't fitten for a hog. (p. 37)

By blaming external authorities for his misfortunes, Pap has absolved himself of all responsibility.

Rather than make him sympathetic to the plight of the oppressed, Pap's own miserable condition makes him all the more insistent that others should be even worse off. "A man can't get his rights in a govment like this," he concludes. "Sometimes I've a mighty notion to just leave the country for good and all." And when he hears about "a free nigger there from Ohio . . . a pr'fessor in a college [who] could vote," Pap decides never to participate actively in the polity again. Poor whites at the bottom of the nineteenth-century social ladder wanted to see the newly liberated blacks kept below them. The desire to escape conventional restraints and consequent social distinctions is not necessarily accompanied by a recognition of the natural equality of all human beings.

When his desires are frustrated in court, Pap seizes Huck and takes him across the river and beyond the jurisdiction of Missouri law, to "show who was Huck Finn's boss." Living outside of town with his natural parent rather than a court-appointed guardian, Huck finds himself living closer to nature than when he was with the Widow Douglas. Although he easily returns to the irregular hours and dirty clothes of the "uncivilized" way with Pap, his life is actually not any better than it had been at the Widow's; he still cannot do as he pleases. Whenever Pap goes into town, he locks Huck in the cabin, stays away for days at a stretch, and then whips the boy when he gets back. By moving outside civil society, Huck has not found freedom so much as he has become the subject of force.[15]

Lonely and restless, Huck again decides to escape. Faking evidence of his own murder, he loads a canoe with supplies from the cabin and rows to an uninhabited island in the middle of the river. Once Huck is legally "dead," he will obviously no longer be a part of—nor regulated by—civil society. Having no social identity at all, he will now be really free to live not merely in—but according to—nature.

Thus, Huck's experience on Jackson's Island and his subsequent flight down the river rather clearly constitute a fictional portrait of human life in the state of nature. And in the state of nature—Twain shows—life is not altogether humanly satisfying.

Human beings might naturally dislike external constraints, but they are also naturally sociable. Once he has explored the island from top to bottom—Huck becomes lonely and bored. He is therefore delighted to find Jim.

Jim is equally delighted to meet Huck. Not only do human beings not live well or happily all by themselves in the woods; in the absence of all civilization, they may not even survive. Strawberries do not constitute a satisfying diet for a grown man, the black has found. Because he left in a hurry, Jim has no equipment with him; and he cannot catch fish, mud turtles, or birds with his bare hands. He is thus extremely glad to hear that Huck has brought a gun, fishhooks, and a frying pan with him.

Living all by himself in the state of nature, Huck has acquired a certain kind of freedom. What people think no longer matters. Hearing that Jim has run off, Huck declares. "People would call me a low-down Abolitionist and despise me for keeping mum—but that don't make no difference. I ain't a-going to tell, and I ain't a-going back there, anyways" (p. 60). Having cast off his civic identity, he has no reason to be concerned about conventional law or morality.

Jim's motive for fleeing thus stands in dramatic contrast to Huck's. Whereas Huck is leaving his family—both adopted and natural—Jim is running because he wants to preserve his. Having overheard Miss Watson consider selling him down river, the black man decided to escape and find his way up the Ohio to a free state where he can earn enough money to buy back his wife and children, and so reunite them.

But Jim's problem points up an ironic aspect of Huck's fate, as well. The most natural form of association—the family itself—has to be protected and régulated by law. Huck did not leave the widow's house willingly; he was forcibly stolen by a man who hoped to make money by gaining possession and control of the youth.[16] Natural ties do not protect children from violence at the hands of greedy adults any more than the precepts of their religion have prevented Christians from enslaving others for profit.[17] Neither sentiment nor religion is a satisfactory or effective substitute for legal protection. Both Huck and Jim have withdrawn from civil society and returned to the state of nature because the law failed to secure their natural rights to life, liberty, and the pursuit of happiness. But when the friends board a wrecked houseboat and find a man (who turns out to be Huck's Pap) shot in the back, Twain reminds his readers that—as Hobbes argued—life in the state of nature is "solitary, poor, nasty, brutish, and short."[18]

Life in the state of nature does not only consist of the struggle for self-preservation, however. As Hobbes also argued, there is a kind of natural religion, as well.[19] Although neither Huck nor Jim is religious in any conventional sense, they are both full of superstition. But—as Huck observes when Jim lists all the things that they should and should not do in setting up camp—the "signs" are almost all about bad luck. When Huck asks if there are any good-luck signs, the black responds, "Mighty few—an' *dey* ain't no use to a body. What you want to know when good luck's a-comin' for? Want to keep it off?" (p. 64; emphasis in original). Such natural "religion" is based primarily on fear and aversion, rather than hope or attraction. The pragmatic reasoning that led Huck to doubt both Miss Watson's lessons and Tom Sawyer's "di'monds" gives credence to signs. When Huck tested prayers by asking for fishhooks and tried rubbing a brass lamp to arouse genies, he did not get the desired results; and the spiritual goods promised instead did not sound all that attractive. Unlike Christianity—which promises future rewards—signs warn of impending misfortune; and there are always enough ups and downs in human life to verify a general prediction of bad luck.

The real source of danger that the two friends face is not devils, however, but other human beings. They simply cannot leave each other alone. Twain shows that—even when humans do not associate from need—they do so for pleasure, for gain, or out of sheer curiosity. As soon as they are comfortably settled into camp, Huck decides to trick Jim by putting a dead rattlesnake in his bed. Huck is truly sorry when the dead snake's mate joins it and bites Jim; but as soon as Jim recovers from the snakebite, Huck becomes bored again. He decides to go back to society on the banks of the river to discover what is going on! His attachment to their idyllic life in the state of nature surely does not last long!

Human beings do not only seek the company of others; but also, once civilized—Twain reminds his readers—they do not willingly allow others (especially valuable laborers like Jim) to withdraw at will. Disguised as "George" alias "Sarah Williams," Huck discovers that a group of men will soon be searching the island for Jim in order to obtain the reward. Huck rushes back, and he and Jim take off down the river on their raft.

Huck's actions are not determined simply by the need to secure Jim's safety, however. On the contrary—in opposition to Jim's outspoken fears—Huck insists on boarding a wrecked steamboat that they sight farther down the river, just because Tom Sawyer would have. "He'd call it an adventure . . . and he'd land on that wreck if it was his last act" (p. 92). It threatens to be Huck's "last act," indeed; he discovers that there are two murderers aboard, that the wreck will break up in two hours, and that their raft has gone off. (For the second time, Twain reminds his readers how dangerous Tom Sawyer-type adventures really are.)[20]

In copying Tom, Huck has made himself the leader.[21] His desires—not Jim's—determine their course of action. But unlike Tom, Huck does not seem to care about reputation or status. And in what follows, Twain gives his readers their first glimpse of Huck's peculiar virtue—and vice.

A fugitive from the law himself, Huck tends to feel that all criminals are his fellows. Once he and Jim are safely off the wreck, Huck thus begins "to think how dreadful it was, even for murderers, to be in such a fix. I says to myself, there ain't no telling but I might come to be a murderer myself yet, and then how would I like it?" (p. 99).

Like Rousseau's natural man, Huck is concerned first and foremost about his own self-preservation. Once this concern is satisfied, he has compassion for the sufferings of others. Through the narration of Huck's adventures, however, Twain demonstrates that such Rousseauian compassion is no substitute for regulation by law.

Huck's compassion makes him the hero of this narrative. And the compassionate nature of their association makes Huck and Jim's friendship look superior to the various forms of civil society that they encounter on the riverbanks. Nevertheless, Twain also shows that Huck himself does not appreciate the value of his own naive feelings.

Nor is compassion sufficient to protect the two friends from the self-interested schemes of others.

After they are separated and lost from each other in a fog at night, Jim's expression of relief at finding Huck safe causes the young white boy to be ashamed of trying to trick his grown-up black friend into thinking that he had been beside him all along. "It was fifteen minutes before I could work myself up to go and humble myself to a nigger," Huck admits, "but I do it, and I warn't ever sorry for it afterward, neither. I didn't do him no' more mean tricks, and I wouldn't done that one if I'd a knowed it wuld make him feel that way" (p. 119).

Huck's compassion enables him to overcome conventional differences in his personal relations, although he never changes his conventional opinions about the natural and proper differences between the races.[22] Indeed, Twain indicates in the conversation preceding their separation in the fog (which is perhaps, thus, also an intellectual haze) that neither Huck nor Jim understands the relation between nature and convention.

Believing that human beings are all basically the same, Jim is amazed to learn not only that the French "dolphin" may have come to America, but also that he speaks a language Jim would not understand. "Lookey here, Jim," Huck responds, "does a cat talk like we do? . . . Does a cow? . . . It's natural and right for them to talk different from each other, ain't it?" "Course," said Jim, but "is a cat a man, Huck?" (pp. 109–10). Where Jim fails to understand the way convention can intervene in the communication of feeling and meaning from one human being to another, Huck fails to recognize the difference between conventional and natural distinctions.[23]

Understanding humanity as one big family, Jim does not see the way in which generational and family differences can create divisions among human beings. Throughout the adventures of the white boy and the black man on the river, Twain ironically reminds his readers that both slavery and aristocracy were justified by claims about differences of birth, generation, and family (in the form of tribe or race). The family may be a natural form of association, but the family can nevertheless become tyrannical (as in Pap's relation to Huck) or a source of warfare (as Twain subsequently shows in the Grangerford-Shepherdson feud). Natural attachments alone do not produce peace and harmony, because these same attachments lead people to prefer their own to the rights of others. (The Grangerford-Shepherdson feud begins when the losing party in a court case refuses to accept the verdict, and his family backs him up.) Human beings must recognize a common authority, if they would live in peace. The family itself has a legal foundation as Twain also reminds his readers (by leaving only two survivors of the feud—Harley and Sophia—who run off to get married!).[24] Jim's own family has been sundered precisely because the law gives no protection to him and his people.

If Jim does not understand the way in which nature must be supplemented by convention, Huck does not understand the way in which nature can be used to question the legitimacy of unjust laws. When Jim objects to King Solomon's proposal about cutting the baby in half and dividing him between the two women who were claiming to be his mother, Huck ironically retorts that Jim does not see the "pint." The point is that Solomon was testing the truth of the claims through an appeal to natural feeling. Yet Twain repeatedly shows that Huck himself never recognizes how his own feelings and personal attachments might be used to test the truth of others' claims. Whatever Miss Watson and others—preeminently, Tom Sawyer—say is right, Huck takes to *be* right, respectable, and religious. Huck acts on the basis of his feelings; but when his own feelings or experience contradict socially approved norms, Huck simply concludes that he and his feelings are bad. As a result, he never learns from experience. Although he himself implicitly recognizes Jim's status as a fellow human being when he swallows his pride and apologizes to a "nigger," Huck continues to regard Jim as rightfully Miss Watson's property, and himself as wrong in assisting the slave to freedom. At the end of his adventures, moreover, Huck is determined to light out again for the territories, where he will surely encounter more force and fraud in the state of nature.

As a natural man, Huck lacks self-consciousness.[25] He does not recognize the goodness of his own nature, because people come to recognize the goodness of nature only in contrast to the pretensions of society. But through the course of the novel, the contrast becomes evident enough to the reader.

Twain brings the opposition between nature and convention to a climax when—having, in the fog, floated right past Cairo (and all hope of Jim's attaining freedom by going east to Ohio)—Huck confronts the slave hunters the next morning. Torn between his "conscience" and his pleasure, Huck chooses the latter, and he lies in order to save Jim.

They went off and I got aboard the raft, feeling bad and low, because I knowed very well I had done wrong, and I see it warn't no use for me to try to learn to do right. . . . Then I thought a minute, and says to myself, hold on; s'pose you'd 'a' done right and give Jim up, would you felt better? . . . No, says I. . . . Well, then, . . . what's the use you learning to do right when it's troublesome to do right and ain't no trouble to do wrong and the wages is just the same? (pp. 143–44)

Legally Jim is Miss Watson's property. Since Huck recognizes no standard or right but convention, he thinks that he has done something wrong. The reader, on the other hand, sees that Huck has acted correctly.[26] Nature is good, and laws that do not respect natural standards of right are wrong.

But how—we ought to ask—can such good and natural sentiments be overtaken by such evil and unnatural conventions, like slavery? Twain provides an answer in Huck's subsequent adventures.

Since Huck withdrew from the protection of the law by faking his death, he has repeatedly found it necessary to appeal to the compassion of the inhabitants of the riverbanks. As Huck's conversations—first with ferryman, and later the slave hunters—reveal, human beings feel compassion for others only when they have no reason to fear for themselves. Compassion is limited not only by personal fear and greed, but also by convention. Human beings have sympathy only for fellow creatures whom they believe are fundamentally like themselves. In Twain's South, "niggers" do not count. Even Huck, when he arrives at the Phelps farm in the guise of Tom Sawyer, reports that no one was hurt in the supposed ferry crash. It only "killed a nigger" (p. 317). Although Aunt Sally Phelps is kind, she does not demur.[27]

When Huck and Jim are forced back into civil society on the banks of the river, Twain shows (as Rousseau had also argued) that in civil society people's natural compassion is almost entirely overcome by their concern for social standing or status—that is, their amour propre. As Huck himself assumes various disguises, so Twain suggests that human "nature" itself is somewhat malleable.[28]

Huck and Jim are first forced off the river when a steamboat rams into the raft. (The civilized arts or technology serve to destroy as well as to preserve human life. How they are used depends on the human beings using them.)

Swimming ashore, Huck finds himself in the midst of a bloody family feud. Despite their chipped plaster ornaments and oilcloth tablecovers, Huck takes the Grangerfords for aristocrats; and—like their feudal Scottish ancestors—these "aristocrats" prefer clan loyalty to civil justice. Although their living room is decorated with pictures of heroes of the American Revolution—including one entitled the "Signing of the Declaration''—the Grangerfords obviously have not absorbed the principles announced in that document. They own many slaves. Rather than look to the government to secure their rights, moreover, they take the law into their own hands.

Neither manners nor morals suffice to end violent competition—Twain shows—where there is no respect for law. Although both the Grangerfords and the Shepherdsons claim to be Christian—and praise the minister's sermon on turning the other cheek—they take their guns when they go to church on Sunday. They only respect people who are willing to risk their lives in order to maintain their honor. Rather than lay down their arms and celebrate the union of two noble families when Sophie (''wise'') Grangerford was off to marry Harley Shepherdson, each family tries not only to prevent the marriage, but also to destroy the other family entirely.

And there is little respect for law in the towns that Huck visits on the banks of the river. To respect the law, people must believe that it is right. But in the pre-Civil War South, preeminence and ''right'' are based on force.

Escaping from the aristocratic bloodbath, Huck and Jim have one of their most idyllic moments on the river. The idyll is cut short, however, when Huck picks up two other men who are running away from the law. Compassion in itself does not discriminate sufficiently among its beneficiaries, Twain dramatically emphasizes. Once on the raft, the two fugitives pretend to be dethroned royalty, and they make both the boy and the black man their servants. As a result, the two friends have an opportunity to experience the effects of the aristocratic pretensions that they have previously only read about.

Even though Huck has no illusions about the fraudulent character of his new guests' claims to be a ''duke'' and the lost French ''dauphin,'' he acquiesces in their pretensions and allows them to rule on the raft. ''If they wanted us to call them kings and dukes,'' he explains, ''I hadn't no objections, 'long as it would keep peace in the family.'' Clearly, Huck has no notion of the real basis of family life or natural association. How can he—having had a father like Pap? ''If I never learnt nothing else out of Pap,'' Huck reflects, ''I learnt that the best way to get along with his kind of people is to let them have their own way'' (p. 189).

The purported lesson is erroneous, however. Letting Pap have his own way eventually resulted in his being shot in the back by some fellow gamblers. By showing street bums in an ''Arkansaw'' town setting fire to stray dogs, Twain reminds his readers that unregulated human beings can be extremely cruel—if merely to alleviate the boredom of their own miserable existence. Indeed the situation that Twain describes in the town of Bricksville shows that there can be no justice unless decent citizens band together and resist those who would use force to have their own way.

After Colonel Sherburn shoots a harmless old drunk down in cold blood, a mob gathers at his doorstep. Sherburn defies them to lynch him in broad daylight. There is no real man among you, he taunts, as the crowd gradually withdraws. Blacks were not the only people read out of the race in the Old South. Where violence rules, human kindness appears to be mere weakness. "Men"—as Sherburn understands them— enforce their will on others, and so prove their right to rule. They are the true masters.[29] Perceiving their vulnerability as individuals, the others act only anonymously—masked, in a crowd, at night. As a result—as Sherburn points out—legal order dissolves. "Why don't your juries hang murderers?" he asks. And then answers, "Because they're afraid the man's friends will shoot them in the back, in the dark—and that's just what they would do" (p. 217).

There is no rule of law in the American South that Twain is depicting, because the people themselves are not willing to enforce or obey it. Feeling themselves weak and vulnerable, they are content— like Huck—to sneak out nights and play dirty tricks, rather than stand up for their own or anybody else's rights.

Human beings may dislike external controls, but—like Melville— Twain also indicates that they are not naturally rebellious. Until the kindness of the Wilks's daughters awakens his compassionate conscience, Huck does nothing to resist the two oppressive rapscallions on his raft. He had no choice, he later explains to Mary Jane. He was but a boy, and they were two men. If he had left the raft to seek assistance, he would have been—in effect—turning Jim in.

Living outside the law himself, Huck cannot appeal to its protection. Like Cooper, Twain reminds his readers that, without legal protection, the weak become victims of the strong.

Wishing to escape all forms of external restraint, Huck himself does not really see any difference between legitimate and illegitimate government—between law and force. To him, they all seem equally to impinge on his freedom.

> What was the use to tell Jim these warn't real kings and dukes. It wouldn't 'a' done no good; and, besides, it was just as I said: you couldn't tell them from the real kind. (pp. 228–29)

Having typically American democratic prejudices, Huck regards all claims to rule by right of birth as mere pretension. Like the "aristocratic" Grangerfords, however, he shows absolutely no understanding of the reasons why his forefathers rebelled against their European monarch.

> You don't know kings, Jim, but I know them; and this old rip of ourn is one of the cleanest I've struck in history. Well, Henry he takes a notion he wants to get up some trouble with this country. How does he go at it—give notice?—give the country a show? No. All of a sudden he heaves all the tea in Boston Harbor overboard, and whacks out a declaration of independence, and dares them to come on.

So little does Huck understand the principles by which democracy is superior to aristocracy that he denies natural equality. Hearing Jim moaning for his lost family, Huck observes, "I do believe he cared just as much for his people as white folks does for their'n. It don't seem natural, but I reckon it's so" (p. 229).

Human beings do not like to admit that others are better than they are, but they take great pleasure in feeling superior themselves. As Huck discovers at the circus before their "Shakespearean" performance, there is little more amusing than seeing someone else taken in. Likewise, there is little more painful than being taken in oneself, and so looking foolish before others.

Those who do not openly desire distinction nevertheless fear ridicule. Indeed—Twain indicates—people fear ridicule second only to physical violence. When the duke and dauphin swindle the inhabitants of Bricksville with a brief—somewhat obscene—performance of *The Royal Nonesuch,* no one in the audience suggests taking them to court. Rather than become laughingstocks themselves, they decide to help the frauds take in the whole town. Then everyone will join in—as a mob—to take action against the imposters.

The people of Bricksville do not like conventional constraints any more than Huck does; they (or the menfolk, anyway) attend the performance in droves only after the Duke has added one line to the promotional advertisement: No women and children allowed. Huck's desire to escape the confines of law and morality is all too common; but in adults, it does not look quite so innocent. In fact, it is not.

When the Duke and Dauphin then attempt to impersonate Peter Wilks's British brother and nephew in order to inherit the Wilks's estate, Twain demonstrates how grief and compassion can also lead people to deceive themselves—almost willfully. An old friend of the Wilks family shouts out that the two imposters are frauds; but both the daughters and the townsmen want to believe the strangers. Only when the real relatives arrive—and there is a lawyer-led investigation of the claims of both parties—does the truth come out.

Twain's Ironic Lesson at the End

All of Huck's adventures on the banks of the river—his experiences with the family feud, mob justice, the contest over the Wilks will, and the final abortive attempt to free Jim—should have convinced him (as well as Twain's readers) that law is the only effective way to settle conflicts and end disputes. Yet in all four instances, Twain portrays the law as being undermined by a natural aversion—represented by Huck—to any externally imposed restraints.

Huck himself does not draw the clear lesson of his story. On the contrary, he continues to act in defiance of his own conventional opinions and on the basis of his feelings. After the Duke and Dauphin lose all their money while attempting to defraud the Wilks's daughters, they turn Jim in for part of the reward. Torn again between his "conscience" and his attachment to his friend, Huck resolves to be "damned" and to steal Jim. His plan is to

> find . . . Jim. . . . Then get up my canoe . . . and fetch my raft over from the island. Then the first dark night that comes, . . . shove off down the river on the raft, with Jim, hiding daytimes and running nights, the way me and Jim used to do before. (p. 333)

Huck certainly has not learned that slavery is wrong, nor that he cannot attain freedom through flight. He simply wants to go on having adventures.

The extent to which Huck's adventures have not changed him is underlined when the boy meekly follows his friend Tom Sawyer again, once he has returned to civil society. Indeed, by having Huck impersonate Tom, Twain seems to say that the two boys are—at some level—basically interchangeable.

Discovering that Jim is being held at the Phelps farm, Huck is amazed at his good fortune when the woman there greets him as "Tom Sawyer." What easier disguise for Huck to assume! To impersonate Tom, Huck must secure his old friend's cooperation. But when Tom agrees not only keep mum but even to help steal Jim, Huck admits that "Tom Sawyer fell, considerable, in my estimation. Only I couldn't believe it" (p. 324). A respectable member of civil society like Tom would not really help free a slave.

Huck lets Tom prolong the escape by insisting Jim do all the things Tom has read that princely prisoners always do, because Huck believes that Tom is better than he. Tom is better because he knows how to do things right—that is, with style. For Huck, Tom has the same kind of authority that the romances have for Tom; he represents the most desirable form of life. Huck can play the part of Tom, then, because Tom is what Huck most wants to be or achieve: He appears able to escape conventional restraints without losing his place in society.

Just as Twain implicitly contrasted Huck's self-understanding with the reader's reaction to his story in the scene with the slave hunters, so he tries to separate the reader's viewpoint even further from the narrator's at the end—by making that reader sick and tired of all the boyish tricks. Failing to perceive the critical thrust of the disgust that Twain purposely engendered, however, most commentators have simply concluded that his art ran out at the end.[30]

Flouting the law is not a matter of child's play, Twain emphasizes at the conclusion of the novel when Tom gets a bullet in the leg as the conspirators are fleeing from the Phelps farm. And when Tom falls unconscious after his wound has become infected, Twain makes the contrast between courageous manly compassion and boyish games all the more sickeningly apparent. Jim insists that Huck go back into town for a doctor, while Jim stays to tend the sick boy—rather than run for his freedom, as Huck suggested. Jim is willing to risk his freedom out of loyalty and gratitude to his young friend, while—as it turns out—Tom has actually been helping to keep a free man in jail. When Tom regains consciousness, he announces what he has known all along: Miss Watson had already freed Jim in her will!

The novel's conclusion is thus totally ironic. All Huck's adventures have been as irrelevant to the freeing of his friend as Tom's concluding mimicry of the Dumas romances. Freedom is not attained by flight, Twain emphasizes; it is secured, rather, as a matter of conscience enforced by law.

Huck—on the other hand—concludes, "I reckon I got to light out for the Territory ahead of the rest, because Aunt Sally she's going to adopt me and sivilize me and I can't stand it. I been there before" (p. 413). He has not learned anything from his adventures. He is prepared to flee conventional authority again, as he did before.

Why then does Huck—like Ishmael—return to tell his tale? Maybe his adventures have convinced Huck that his distinctive talent lies in the art of telling stories. Indeed, by associating with Tom he may have discovered that writing his own story and becoming an author will make him a certain kind of authority. Then too—by pretending to have been completely innocent—he might not only manage to excuse his own past behavior, but also create sufficient popular sympathy that he will be able to continue doing what he likes without having to flee civil society and be lonely again. Huck is, after all, independently wealthy; and at the end of the story, Jim finally informs him that the feared Pap is dead. Huck could now safely return.[31]

Twain had separated himself from his narrator at the very beginning of the novel by prefacing the story with both a "Notice" and an "Explanatory" by the author. And his presentation of the story gradually works to separate the consciousness of the reader from the consciousness of the narrator. Twain shows his readers not only that Huck's natural sentiments are good, but also that he is young, weak, and vulnerable. Neither compassion nor the most apparently natural form of human association—the family—provides sufficient protection against greed and the desire for dominion. As Huck and Jim experience it, life in the state of nature—outside the law—is dominated by force and fraud. As Huck should have learned at the Wilks's, law is the only effective means of protecting the innocent from the rapacious. But—as Twain's story also shows—law alone will not suffice.

Laws are not always just, and human beings do not always obey them. To be just, the law must be based on recognition of the natural equality of all humans—so dramatically portrayed in the friendship of Huck and Jim. Unfortunately—Twain also shows—there are natural forces that work to undermine both the recognition of that natural equality and the laws based on it. Both the desire for distinction (embodied by Tom) and the desire for ease or an absence of external restraints (characterizing Huck) continually weaken the respect for the rights of others on which republican government depends. The institution of slavery provides the most dramatic example of the problem, because it reminds Americans how convention—mixed with greed and the desire for distinction—can lead some human beings to deny the very humanity of others. As Twain indicates in the Sherburn incident at Bricksville, slavery is but one example of man's inhumanity to man.

Thus, at one level, Twain's novel reaffirms the truths first proclaimed in the Declaration of Independence. First and foremost— that all men are created equal. Jim's concern for the integrity of his family, his willingness to risk life and limb to live as a free man, and his devotion to his young white friends all demonstrate that this black slave is the equal—if not the better—of any white depicted in the narrative. Slavery is clearly based on convention, contrary to nature, and just plain wrong. All humans may have been endowed by their Creator with certain inalienable rights—the Declaration further taught—but to secure those rights, they must establish governments. And in *Adventures of Huckleberry Finn*—Twain shows that neither Jim nor Huck (nor the Wilks heirs, nor anyone else in the novel) can secure either his life or his property from the designs of others except through the agency of law. When these laws fail to secure life and liberty, people like Jim have a right "to alter and abolish them"—that is, to rebel. Twain presents both Huck's and Jim's withdrawals from civil society sympathetically. But he also shows that rebellion does not suffice; only a law based on recognition of the essential equality of all human beings will effectively secure their liberty.[32]

On a second level, however, Twain clearly doubts that people like Huck will ever learn. In *Adventures of Huckleberry Finn* he not only uses Jim's enslavement to remind readers that Americans have not lived up to their professed political principles, but he also indicates the reasons or causes for their failure. Their natural desires to be free of all external constraints and to be recognized as better than others are just too strong.

Like Cooper and Melville, Twain presented in Huck a rather Rousseauian view of the life of a human being in the state of nature. Unlike Cooper and Melville, however, Twain did not think that such a vision would remind his fellow Americans of the true principles of natural right underlying its democratic regime. On the contrary, he suggested by skeptically (if comically) attempting to separate himself and his reader from the narrator that such romantic visions serve primarily to undermine the rule of law and the protection of individual rights—and so, as in the pre-Civil War South, to maximize the role of force and the aristocratic pretensions.

Ridicule as a Means of Teaching Political Moderation

The distinction that Twain stressed between author and narrator reflects the two prongs of his tale. On the one hand, through the plot he affirmed all of Rousseau's basic propositions about human life in the state of nature: Because human beings are concerned first and foremost with their own preservation, their most elemental passion is fear.[33] When they themselves are not in danger, they—like Huck— feel compassion for the suffering of others. But in civil society, that native compassion is overwhelmed—if not totally destroyed—by the amour propre that Tom Sawyer embodies.

Precisely because these propositions are true—Twain concluded— most human beings never recognize their verity. Like Huck, most people continue to define themselves and the value of others in conventional terms. Like Colonel Sherburn or the duke and the dauphin, those who are clever, strong, and daring enough attempt to elevate themselves. As in Bricksville, the weak and timorous shrink back in fear. Rather than assert the equal rights of all and band together to protect those rights with law, they celebrate the degradation of others.

As Twain sees it, the attempt to found a government on the (obviously not) "self-evident" truths of the Declaration was thus doomed to fail—doomed by human nature itself.[34] He observed in his *Autobiography*:

> It is a saddening thought but we cannot change our nature—we are all alike, we human beings; and in our blood and bone, and ineradicably, we carry the seeds out of which monarchies and aristocracies are grown: worship of gauds, titles, distinctions, power.[35]

Twain's understanding of human nature did not lead him to despair of the race, however. As indicated through his characterization of Huck, Twain thought that human beings are essentially innocent. In his *Autobiography,* he also commented along the lines of Ishmael's meditations:

> It is a curious and humorous fact that we excuse all the unpleasant things that the creatures that crawl and fly and swim and go on four legs do, for the recognizably sufficient reason that they are but obeying the law of their nature, which is the law of God, and are therefore innocent; then we turn about and with the fact plain before us that we get all our unpleasant traits by inheritance from those creatures, we blandly assert that we did not inherit the immunities along with them, but that it is our duty to ignore, abolish and break these laws of God. (p. 337)

Like Cooper and Melville, Twain recognized that being essentially innocent does not mean that human beings are harmless or do not injure others. On the contrary, like other animals, they instinctively and necessarily fight to preserve themselves.

Although they fight both for preservation and prestige—he also observed—human beings naturally desire the company of others. They are not driven to associate with each other merely from need or sexual desire. On the contrary—like Huck—they are naturally sociable. And Twain brought out the goodness of this natural desire for companionship in the friendship of Huck and Jim. Like Melville, Twain suggested that the exemplary form of human natural sociability is to be found not in the family with its division of labor and procreative function, but rather in the fellowship of two members of the same sex.

Like Hawthorne, Twain reminded his readers that the family has a partly conventional—indeed, legal—foundation. In the state of nature, he thus depicted a series of broken families. Where there is no legal protection, children can be stolen from their homes, relatives sold "down river," and parents separated or killed. When the family is intact—as at the Phelps—like other conventional associations, it too is constraining. Although the orphan responds warmly to the loving care he receives from the Widow Douglas and Aunt Sally, Huck is therefore always anxious to "light out" once more. Unlike Hawthorne, Twain did not expect domestic bliss to quench the desire for liberty, which human beings think that they once did and still would enjoy—free from all conventional restraints—in the state of nature.

Indeed, by describing human life in the state of nature in terms of the experience of a preadolescent boy, Twain suggested that both the desire to avoid external restraints and the desire to dominate are natural in a way that human sexuality—in the particularized form of attraction that we usually encounter—is not. Here he again followed Rousseau, who had argued that sexual attraction to a specific person requires powers of discrimination that human beings would not have developed in solitude in the state of nature. Once human beings experience the pleasure of dominion over others, moreover, they seek to extend that dominion above everything else.[36]

Whereas Rousseau, Cooper, and Hawthorne all suggested that the desire for distinction is rooted in human sexuality, Twain thought that it is primarily political. He did recognize that the drive for preeminence can be associated with sexual desire in *The Adventures of Tom Sawyer,* when he presents Tom showing off to impress Becky Thatcher. But in *Adventures of Huckleberry Finn,* Twain indicates through his characterizations of the Duke and the Dauphin, Colonel Sherburn, and Tom Sawyer that human beings simply like to be regarded better than others and to order them around.[37]

Because this desire for preeminence is unalterably natural, Twain did not think that people could be talked out of it by a fictional depiction of human life in the state of nature any more than by philosophical argumentation. He decided, therefore, to take a different tack. Rather than preach the evils of vainglory, he could enlist his readers' democratic prejudices by ridiculing the pretensions of others. There are always going to be more "citizens of Bricksville" than there are leaders, whether those leaders are hereditary or elected. As the young Satan observes in *The Mysterious Stranger*:

> All forms of government—including republican and democratic—are rich in funny shams and absurdities, but their supporters do not see it. . . . Will a day come when the race will detect the funniness of these juvenilities and laugh at them—and by laughing at them destroy them? For your race, in its poverty, has unquestionably one really effective weapon—laughter. Power, Money, Persuasion, Supplication, Persecution—these can lift at a colossal humbug, . . . weaken it a little, century by century; but only Laughter can blow it to rags and atoms at a blast. Against the assault of Laughter, nothing can stand.[38]

If fear be more fundamental than compassion and if human beings fear ridicule—as the obverse of distinction—second only to violent death, then Twain might ridicule his readers into better political sense where they could not be directly persuaded.[39] He was definitely aware, however, of the limitations of his art.

"Its circumstances may change," he observed, "but the race's character is permanent."[40] And if human beings themselves cannot be reformed, their political life will always contain a good bit of force and fraud.[41] At most—Twain thought—he might relieve the suffering of the innocent victims, and perhaps even moderate a bit the political excesses of his American readers with a little humor.

Notes

1. Sections of this chapter were previously published in Catherine H. Zuckert, "Law and Nature in *Adventures of Huckleberry Finn*," *Proteus* 1 (Fall, 1984):27–35. They are reprinted here with permission.

2. In the *Green Hills of Africa* (New York: Charles Scribner's Sons, 1935), Hemingway wrote, "All modern American literature comes from one book by Mark Twain called *Huckleberry Finn*. . . . It's the best book we've had. . . .

There was nothing before. There has been nothing as good since" (p. 22). And in an interview at Nagano, Faulkner observed: "In my opinion Mark Twain was the first truly American writer, and all of us since are his heirs, we descended from him." William Faulkner, *Faulkner at Nagano* (Tokyo: Kenkyusha Press, 1957), p. 88.

3. They have tended, therefore, to argue that Twain's art ran out in the end. See Andrew Lang and Newton Arvin, in Arthur L. Scott, ed., *Mark Twain: Selected Criticism* (Dallas; Southern Methodist University Press, 1967), pp. 40, 233; for early examples. Dixon Wecter, "Mark Twain," in Robert Spiller et al., eds., *Literary History of the United States* (New York: Macmillan, 1948), vol. 2, p. 933, and Bernard De Voto, ed., *Mark Twain in Eruption* (New York: Harper and Brothers, 1940), p. 77; Leo Marx, "Mr. Eliot, Mr. Trilling, and *Huckleberry Finn,*" *American Scholar* 22, 4 (Autumn 1953): 423–40.

4. See, for example, Walter Blair, *Mark Twain and Huck Finn* (Berkeley: University of California Press, 1960), pp. 321–70.

5. Both Lionel Trilling, "Huckleberry Finn," in *The Liberal Imagination* (New York: Viking, 1950), pp. 104–17, and George C. Carrington, *The Dramatic Unity of Huckleberry Finn* (Columbus: University of Ohio Press, 1976), pp. 153–59, have pointed out the extraordinary literary unity of *Huck Finn* as a novel.

6. Samuel Clemens, "Literary Offenses of Fenimore Cooper," *North American Review* 161 (July 1895):1–12.

7. Samuel Clemens, *Autobiography* (New York: Harper and Row, 1975), p. 298; emphasis added.

8. Citations are from Samuel Clemens, *Adventures of Huckleberry Finn* (Berkeley: University of California Press, 1985).

9. On the meaning of his pseudonym, see Samuel Clemens, *Life on the Mississippi,* in *The Writings of Mark Twain,* vol. 9 (New York: Harper and Brothers, 1889), vol. 9, pp. 67–68, 367–72. In riverboat terminology, "mark twain" meant two fathoms—deep enough for a riverboat to proceed safely. An old Captain Isaiah Sellars, who made a practice of shaming older pilots who bragged about their superior knowledge of "cubs" by showing that he had knowledge of a much more distant past of which even these pilots were ignorant, first used the term as a pseudonym for some paragraphs on the condition of the river that he published in the New Orleans *Picayune.* After Clemens mocked one of Sellar's paragraphs in his first printed article, the old captain stopped writing. "It was a great pity; for it did nobody worthy service, and it sent a pang deep into a good man's heart. There was no malice in my rubbish; but it laughed at the capt. It laughed at a man to whom such a thing was new and strange and dreadful. I did not know then, though I do now, that there is no suffering comparable with that which a private person feels when he is for the first time pilloried in print." Needing a *"nom de guerre,"* Twain reported, he then "confiscated the ancient mariner's discarded one" and did his "best to make it remain what it was in his hands—a sign . . . that whatever

is found in its company may be gambled on as being the petrified truth." Clemens's pseudonym is therefore a sign of his consciousness both of the power and of the responsibility of the humorist—not to harm the decent but to discredit, as Sellars did, those who would vaunt their false wisdom before the credulous.

10. Kevin Murphy, "Illiterate's Progress: The Descent into Literacy in *Huckleberry Finn*," *Texas Studies in Literature and Language* 26 (Winter 1984):363–87, points out the importance of Huck's becoming literate and how that literacy connects Huck to convention in general and to Tom in particular.

11. Most commentators have made basically the same mistakes with regard both to the structure of the plot and the author-narrator relation in reading Twain's (Clemens's) *A Connecticut Yankee in King Arthur's Court* (Berkeley: University of California Press, 1982). On the function of that novel's frame distinguishing Twain from his narrator, see Catherine Zuckert and Michael Zuckert, " 'In Its Wake We Followed': The Political Wisdom of Mark Twain," *Interpretation* (Summer 1972):59–66.

12. Campbell Tatum, "Dismal and Lonesome: A New Look at *Huckleberry Finn*," *Modern Fiction Studies* 14 (Spring 1968):47–55, goes too far when he suggests that Huck's lonesomeness is pathological. There is a long-standing tradition (stemming from Aristotle) that regards human beings as inherently and naturally social. By showing that Huck strongly desires the society of others, Twain provides a motive—somewhat lacking in Cooper's tales—for his hero's befriending a man of another race in the generally lonesome state of nature. Paul Schacht, "The Lonesomeness of Huckleberry Finn," *American Literature* 53 (May 1981):189–201, also connects Huck's lonesomeness with his "natural" condition.

13. Martha Banta, "Escape and Entry in *Huckleberry Finn*," *Modern Fiction Studies* 14 (Spring 1968):79–80, has also pointed out Huck's attachment to his ease and comfort. This is the essence of the "freedom" that Huck sought.

14. Huck's skepticism about religion would also appear to make him more authentically natural than Natty, since religion is primarily a social phenomenon. William R. Manierre, "Huck Finn, Empiricist Member of Society," *Modern Fiction Studies* 14 (Spring 1968):57–66, emphasizes the way Huck tests the claims of both society and religion in the early chapters.

15. Kenneth Lynn, "Welcome Back from the Raft, Huck honey!" *American Scholar* 46 (Summer 1977):338–47, has also pointed out the way in which life at the widow's represented a desirable alternative for Huck. Everett Carter, "The Modernist Ordeal of Huckleberry Finn," *Studies in American Fiction* 13 (Autumn 1985):169–72, has also argued that earlier critics overstated the revolutionary aspect of Huckleberry Finn by ignoring the way the novel supports the conventions of postslavery middle-class American society.

16. The significance of the broken family in *Huck Finn* has received a good deal of critical attention. Eric Solomon, "Huck Finn Once More," *College*

English 3 (December 1960), has argued that the novel acquires its unity from Huck's search for family. Unfortunately for this argument, Huck consistently resists attempts by the Widow, Pap, and Aunt Sally to "adopt" him. Kenneth S. Lynn, "Huck and Jim," *Yale Review* 48 (Spring 1958):422, has argued—on the other hand—that Huck finds a father in Jim. Unfortunately, because of the slave laws, Jim is more dependent on Huck than vice versa.

17. Jim overheard Miss Watson say that she did not want to sell him but was tempted by the money. He did not wait to find out how she resolved this debate with her conscience. When they argued that Miss Watson's change of heart at the end of the novel is incredible, neither H. N. Smith, *The Virgin Land* (Cambridge, Mass.: Harvard University Press, 1950), nor Leo Marx, "Mr. Eliot," paid attention to the fact that Jim ran before Miss Watson had entirely made up her mind. He tells Huck that "I hear old missus tell de widder she gwyne to seel me down to Orleans, *but she didn' want to,* but she could git eight hund'd dollars for me, en it wuz sich a big stack o' money she couldn' resis! De widder she try to git her to say she couldn't do it, but *I never waited to hear de res!* I lit out might quick." (p. 6; emphasis added). Miss Watson's Christian morals—rigid and strict as we know they are, from Huck— stand against materialism. Jim does not know for a fact that she actually decided to sell him, over her sister's opposition. In any case, she definitely has an attack of conscience later and—strict Christian that she is—she would take such an attack seriously.

18. Thomas Hobbes, *The Leviathan* (Indianapolis: Bobbs-Merrill, 1958), ch. 13.

19. Ibid., ch. 12.

20. The wreck was called the *Walter Scott.* By presenting a highly fictionalized account of life in feudal times as historical fact—Twain wrote in Clemens, *Life,* pp. 308–9, 347–48—Sir Walter Scott had contributed to the outbreak of this steamboat. Twain certainly did not think that fiction is without practical effect. He himself was trying to counteract the effect of romantic "historical" novels by ridiculing Tom Sawyer's tendency to use them as authorities.

21. Harry V. Jaffa, "Tom Sawyer: Hero of Middle America," *Interpretation* (Spring 1972):194–225, has pointed out that Tom was—in many respects—the image of the American hero-politician. At the end of his story, Judge Thatcher describes the boy's future in terms of George Washington.

22. On the contrary, in the very last scene Huck is amazed at Jim's "white" feelings. Huck himself never draws the "obvious" conclusion from his own experience that all human beings are similar by nature—whatever their race.

23. Walter Blair, *Twain and Finn,* pp. 348–49, and William O'Connor, "Why *Huckleberry Finn* Is Not the Great American Novel," *College English* 18 (October 1955):6–10, argued that this conversation was a late and misguided addition because they did not see the centrality of the issue of nature and convention to the plot.

24. Like the tall-tale scene that the editor convinced Twain to excise from

Huck Finn, the Grangerford-Shepherdson feud scene was based on a similar incident reported in Clemens, *Life,* ch. 26. Twain indicated the extent to which the relation between nature and convention was the central theme of *Huck Finn* by adding both the detail that the feud started with the failure of one side to accept a legal settlement, and the marriage at the end. Neither appeared in the *Life* version.

25. In the *Phenomenology of Mind* (New York: Harper and Row, 1967), G. W. F. Hegel argues that human feelings or desires are—in the first instance—immediate. We become conscious of ourselves and our desires only when frustrated. Huck flees all such frustrations.

26. "Thus what for Huck is his worst action—refusing to turn Jim in to Miss Watson—is for the reader his best" (p. 170). James M. Cox, *Mark Twain: The Fate of Humor* (Princeton, N.J.: Princeton University Press, 1966), has pointed out that much of the humor of the novel depends on such inversions of value.

27. As Carson Gibb, "The Best Authorities," *College English* 3 (December 1960), reprinted in Richard Lettis et al., *Huck Finn and His Critics* (New York: Macmillan, 1962), p. 431, has observed: "Custom brutalizes."

28. Twain made the extent to which nature is influenced by circumstance the theme of several of his other works. In Samuel Clemens, *The Prince and the Pauper,* in *The Writings of Mark Twain,* vol. 15 (New York: Harper and Brothers, 1889), he gave the most democratic account of the relation between nature or heredity and circumstance or convention by depicting the prince and the pauper as being virtually interchangeable. In *Pudd'nhead Wilson,* in *The Writings of Mark Twain,* vol. 14 (New York: Harper and Brothers, 1889), however, he showed that circumstances may deform natural potential or prevent it from developing, but circumstances cannot compensate for inherent depravity. The nature—convention relationship is the explicit subject of a posthumously published dialogue entitled *What Is Man?* (New York: Harper and Row, 1917). And in that dialogue, the philosopher concludes by reminding the young man to whom he is speaking: "You remember that you said that I said training was *everything.* I corrected you, and said 'training and *another* thing.' That other thing is *temperament*—that is, the disposition you were born with. *You can't eradicate your disposition nor any rag of it"* (pp. 52–53; emphasis in original).

29. See Alexandre Kojeve, *Introduction à la lecture de Hegel* (Paris: Gallimard, 1947), pp. 9–34, for a pertinent analysis of the master-slave relation.

30. Cox, *Fate of Humor,* represents a notable exception. He, too, argues that the conclusion constitutes something like a "splash of water" in a dreamy reader's face. Post-Civil War readers were so busy identifying themselves in a self-congratulatory way with Huck's attempt to secure Jim's freedom that they did not contemplate the ironic commentary on conventional opinion.

31. Lynn, "Welcome back," suggested that Huck wants to return to take part in one of Tom's plays. I am arguing—on the contrary—that, by writing the novel, Huck "out-Toms" Tom Sawyer.

32. As Leslie A. Fiedler has argued in "Come Back to the Raft Ag'in, Huck Honey!" in *An End to Innocence* (Boston: Beacon, 1955), p. 143, "It is the social fact, our overt behavior toward the Negro, that must be modified to accord with our laws and the, at least official, morality they objectify."

33. It is difficult to draw a hard-and-fast distinction between Hobbes and Rousseau on this point. Although in his *"Discourse on the Origins of Inequality,"* in *The First and Second Discourses* (New York: St. Martin's Press, 1964), Rousseau argued that human beings are peaceable in their solitary natural state, in his essay on *The Origin of Language* (New York: Frederick Ungar Publishing, 1966), he pointed out that—if and when they do encounter others—they tend to react fiercely, and not with compassion, because they are afraid.

34. In Clemens, *Connecticut Yankee,* Twain again showed that ordinary human beings cannot be persuaded of these truths; they are too attached to their own conventions and particular desires. Because he could not persuade the Arthurians to establish a republic peacefully and on the basis of consent, the Yankee eventually had to resort to stealth (or fraud) and force. See Zuckert and Zuckert, "Political Wisdom," pp. 71–87.

35. In De Voto, *Eruption,* p. 66.

36. Rousseau, "Discourse on Inequality," pt. 2, p. 157.

37. So the humorist once commented about an American president: "Mr. Roosevelt is the Tom Sawyer of the political world; always showing off; always hunting for a chance to show off." In De Voto, *Eruption,* p. 49. See Daniel Hoffman, *Form and Fable in American Fiction* (New York: Oxford University Press, 1961), pp. 328–29, and Judith Fetterley, "Disenchantment: Tom Sawyer in Huckleberry Finn," *PMLA* 87 (January 1972):73, for connections between the Duke and the Dauphin, on the one hand, and Tom Sawyer, on the other.

38. Samuel Clemens, *The Mysterious Stranger* (Berkeley: University of California Press, 1970), pp. 165–66.

39. See the passage from Clemens, *Life* quoted in Note 8 above, with regard both to Twain's appreciation of the power of ridicule and to the connection between that recognition and his own pretended name.

40. In De Voto, *Eruption,* p. 66.

41. Twain developed this theme more fully in *Connecticut Yankee* when he showed that, failing to persuade the Arthurians of the superiority of democratic institutions, the Yankee had to resort to "training" and force. At the end, it was not the Yankee's "scientific" educational institutions that prevailed, moreover, but fear of the Inquisition and the Church.

7

Hemingway on Being in Our Time

Ernest Hemingway was one of those readers who were not persuaded by the black humor at the end of *Huckleberry Finn*. "All modern American literature comes from one book by Mark Twain called *Huckleberry Finn*," he observed in the *Green Hills of Africa*. "It's the best book we've had. . . . There was nothing before. There has been nothing as good since." But he counseled, "If you read it you must stop where the Nigger Jim is stolen from the boys. That is the real end. The rest is just cheating" (p. 22).[1]

Hemingway's objections to Twain's conclusion were not simply stylistic; he had doubts about the substance. Those doubts arose from a critique of social contract theory that went even further than Twain's.

By showing not only that Huck withdrew from civil society in search of freedom but also that he had to return to secure it, Twain had dramatically ratified the arguments of the social contract theorists. The humorist had "merely" suggested that such arguments will never persuade people to control their passions, and hence are not truly effective. The arguments supporting social contract theory are indeed contradictory insofar as they suggest that human beings are by nature more emotional than rational, and yet expect them to use reason to check their desires.

Hemingway did not think that the problem was simply rhetorical, however; he thought that it lay in the foundations of social contract theory itself. Like Melville, Hemingway in his Nick Adams stories depicted not only human relations outside the law, but the whole of nature, as constituting a Hobbesian "war of all against all." But in opposition to both the American literary tradition and social contract

161

theory, Hemingway denied that human beings can remove or protect themselves from this deadly combat by promising to obey a government, which would then act to secure their rights. Nor did Hemingway think that humans can find solace and support in private, through (male) companionship or marriage. The reason in all cases is the same. By nature, human beings are sensitive animals; and their natural feelings are essentially transitory. Any oath, commitment, or contract based on such natural feelings will, therefore, eventually find its source or foundation eroded; any institution, partnership, or compact based on perfectly natural desires and passions will inevitably become an empty, external, oppressive shell. There is no natural basis for any enduring form of human community—public or private.

Hemingway's Retelling of Huck Finn

As Philip Young has suggested, Hemingway's Nick Adams stories constitute a kind of retelling of the Huck Finn saga.[2] Like Huck, Nick too grows up on the outskirts of civil society; further like Huck, Nick eventually runs away from home. But, again like Huck, Nick finally returns.

In retelling the story, Hemingway has obviously tried to remedy faults that he perceives in the original, however. The differences are as significant, therefore, as the similarities.

First, Hemingway reverses the direction of the movement or action. Whereas Huck traveled from civil society to the state of nature and back, Nick grows up in the Michigan woods, runs away from home to join the war in Europe, and then returns home to find peace and satisfaction living all by himself in the state of nature. For Hemingway, that which is good in human life is to be found in nature. Characterized by a cycle of birth and death, nature is the beginning and the end.[3]

Second, where Twain depicted Huck and Tom only as "innocent" boys, Hemingway shows Nick maturing to become a husband and father. Like Twain (and Rousseau), Hemingway believes that human beings find pleasure and satisfaction simply in feeling alive—*le sentiment de son existence* or *amour de soi*, as Rousseau called it.[4] But Hemingway indicates even more explicitly than Twain that such pleasures are transitory. Like all his predecessors (both literary and philosophic), Hemingway knows that human beings prefer company— especially the company of members of the opposite sex—to solitude.[5] Like the sheer satisfaction in feeling alive, however, sexual attraction is also based on a transient sensation. It does not provide a firm foundation for lasting social relations. Sexual relations do result in the next generation of children. And most parents—unlike Pap—do love their children. Natural procreation does not enable human beings to overcome the essentially transitory character of life any more than marriage itself does, however. On the contrary, having children forces people to think about the future, and so reminds them of their own inescapable future as individuals—or their own inevitable deaths.

Third, where Huck experienced not only the liberty and equality but also the insecurity of human life in the state of nature on the river, Hemingway therefore shows Nick discovering this fundamental truth about human life in war.[6] (Hobbes had initially characterized the state of nature as a "state of war.") Facing the immediate possibility of his own death for the first time, Nick realizes that human beings all live—because they all die—essentially alone. No one can truly die for another; no political organization can really secure anyone's right to life.

In light of the truth revealed in war, the promises involved in the social contract and the institutions erected on it appear to be fundamentally false. Hemingway thus—fourth—introduces a generational difference into the American story. In earlier versions, the protagonist or narrator himself had withdrawn from civil society to live in the state of nature. In Hemingway's Nick Adams stories, it is the hero's father— a doctor—who flees the Chicago suburbs to raise his son during the summer in the North Michigan woods. The hope that Americans can establish a better life for themselves by beginning anew in nature belongs to the past generation—Hemingway is suggesting—if not to the past century.

Unlike Huck, Nick is not boyishly seeking to escape the uncomfortable constraints of civil society. Like Ishmael, he is looking for a reason to live, and he finds it—finally—at "the big two-hearted river." When Nick returns to nature, he is fundamentally alone. Like Huck and unlike Twain, Hemingway concludes that there is no basis for enduring community in nature.

Postwar Disillusionment

Hemingway's first collection of Nick Adams stories clearly reflects the disillusionment with the results of liberal political experiments that were prevalent following World War I. Like his protagonist, Hemingway himself left the United States to join the Red Cross as an ambulance driver in Europe, and he stayed there after its conclusion. Unlike most of the European artists with whom he associated, however, Hemingway did not let his political disillusionment degenerate into complete cynicism or nihilism. On the contrary, in the concluding story of his first collection, he affirmed that human life is in and by nature good.

Since he admitted that the goodness of immediate or natural sensation is transitory, Hemingway's stance was obviously problematic. To bring out both the merits and the difficulties involved in this affirmation of the goodness of nature in the face of an historical disillusionment with politics, in the concluding section of this chapter I will contrast Hemingway's position with that of the German philosopher Martin Heidegger.[7]

Like Hemingway, Heidegger was writing to a people who were disillusioned with liberal politics. Further like Hemingway, Heidegger argued that the truth about human life is revealed only through a direct confrontation with the possibility of one's own death. In light of that most fundamental of alienating experience—both American novelist and German philosopher agreed—ordinary social and political institutions appear empty and inauthentic. Whereas Hemingway returned to nature to find some satisfaction in life, Heidegger argued that human life is not merely a matter of transient sensations: It is essentially temporal and should be understood as such. Heidegger's insistence that human life be understood in terms of history rather than nature had even worse political implications than Hemingway's retreat into nature, however. The comparison between the American novelist and the German philosopher thus brings out the crisis of natural rights theory in the twentieth century in the opposition between nature and history.

Nature versus History—*In Our Time*

Hemingway wrote the disjunction between individual, personal experience or life (nature) and external, political events or history into the very organization of his first collection of short stories, which he entitled *In Our Time*.[8] There is no unified or unifying narrative. Instead, each story is introduced and separated from the others by an historical vignette.[9]

Despite the fractured and apparently disordered surface, the collection of stories does have a clear organization.[10] In the first half, each story of a boy's growing up in America is prefaced by a scene from World War I.[11] In the second half, each story of a young American's attempt to come to terms with the alienating truth learned in war is introduced by a bullfighting scene. As Hemingway later observed in *Death in the Afternoon,* bullfighting is the art of confronting death par excellencé.[12]

By introducing the story of a young boy's growing up in the hinterlands of the United States with scenes from the war in Europe, Hemingway clearly intends that his readers consider the relation between the two.[13] Americans had fought World War I "to make the world safe for democracy." But—Hemingway suggests—their experiences in that war raised questions about the promise and foundations of American democracy itself. According to the Declaration of Independence, governments are instituted to secure their citizens' rights to life, liberty, and the pursuit of happiness. As the phenomenon of war illustrates so vividly, liberal governments do not and cannot actually achieve what they promise. On the contrary, they lead human beings to their deaths. Hemingway thus prefaces the last story in each half of the collection with a vignette describing not the war or bullfighting, but the operation of the American criminal justice system. Rather than secure life—he implies—the institution of government merely allows certain human beings to act out their hostility toward others with impunity.[14]

In the Declaration, Jefferson had claimed that America's government was to be based on "the law of nature and nature's God." But Hemingway indicates in the title of his first collection that, for people in the twentieth century, God is dead. Like many of the titles that he would select for his later novels, *In Our Time* has not only a literary, but also a religious, source. "Give us peace in our time," the Book of Common Prayer beseeches.[15] In light of its World War I setting, Hemingway's title is clearly ironic. There certainly was cause to seek assistance from on high; and in the seventh preface, Hemingway shows a soldier praying to Jesus while under bombardment at Fossalta. If Jesus would only save him—the soldier promises—he will serve as a witness; he will spread the gospel, "the good news."[16] But when the soldier does survive— Hemingway reports—he goes straight to a whorehouse and says nothing to anybody about Jesus. People in our time do not really believe that there is a God with the power to bring peace.

If God is dead—as Nietzsche announced in the nineteenth century—then establishing peace and order has become especially difficult in our time, because there is no transcendent or enduring foundation for politics or morality.[17] All life is transitory; and Hemingway's book reflects that transitoriness insofar as it depicts disjointed— although intense—incidents, sensations, and experiences.[18]

Nick's Adventures in the State of Nature

In the stories that lead up to his protagonist's being wounded at Fossalta, Hemingway depicts the events or experiences that have caused Nick—like Ishmael—to question the value of life altogether. Like Twain, Hemingway shows life in the state of nature where Nick grows up is not altogether humanly satisfying.

Just as the American troops marching to Champagne in the first vignette are about to be initiated into deadly battle without any real preparation, so in the first story Nick is unintentionally introduced to the mysterious interrelation between life and death.[19] When the doctor takes his son along to the Indian camp where he is expecting to deliver a baby by caesarean section, he wants to show Nick the marvels of modern medicine. In fact, the doctor confronts his son with the ineradicable connection between birth and death.

While the squaws attempt to help the woman in the cabin, the men all move far enough away so that they will no longer hear her screams. When Nick asks if his father can give the woman something to stop her screaming, the doctor explains that he has no anesthetic. "Her screams are not important. I don't hear them because they are not important" (p. 17).[20] Having washed his hands and boiled the instruments, the doctor proceeds to deliver the baby with a jackknife. "That's one for the medical journal," he tells his brother George, who is waiting in attendance. "Oh, you're a great man, all right," George sarcastically responds. The doctor is elated by his success and in a talkative mood until he decides that he "ought to have a look at the proud father," who has been lying—wounded in the leg—in the bunk above his birthing wife. "They're usually the worst sufferers in these little affairs," the doctor observes. "I must say he took it all pretty quietly" (p. 20). Having slit his throat open with a razor, the father could not very well have made much noise.

The screams do matter—to those who might hold themselves responsible for the pain, and even to those who simply care. Medicine cannot cure all, perhaps not even the most important kinds of suffering—

Hemingway suggests—because modern science cannot explain, much less prevent, human death.[21]

The doctor is now sorry that he brought his son along, and tries to reassure him.

> "Do many men kill themselves, Daddy?" Nick asked. "Is dying hard . . .?"
> "No, I think it's pretty easy, Nick. It all depends."

Neither the conversation nor the incident seem to have much impact on Nick, however, for the story concludes: "Nick trailed his hand in the water. It felt warm in the sharp chill of the morning. In the early morning on the lake sitting in the stern of the boat with his father rowing, he felt quite sure that he would never die" (p. 21).

The first and most fundamental lesson that Nick must learn has to do with the inevitability of his own death. He eventually learns this lesson in war; but going to war and learning this lesson do not happen immediately. Nick goes abroad in search of adventure only after he has become dissatisfied and disillusioned with life up in the Michigan woods. Unfortunately, Nick's father provides an all too good model of disillusionment.

The cabin in the upper peninsula of Michigan where Nick receives much of his formative education is on a lake—not far from a lumber mill. Every year, in the process of being towed to the mill, some of the logs come loose from the "boom" and drift to the beach. The lumber companies do mark the logs in case they decide to come back and claim them, but it is not clear that it would actually pay to hire a crew for this purpose. Assuming that it would not and that the logs would simply become waterlogged and rot if nobody used them, the doctor hires Indians to come down from the camp and split them into firewood.

Spoilage constitutes a natural limitation on the right of acquisition or property, as John Locke argued; by nature, a man has a right only to what he can use, because he literally cannot keep or possess goods that are rotting.[22] This natural limitation has been overcome, however—first—by the invention of money (which does not spoil) and—second—by the laws of property.

Taking advantage of the ambiguous relation between natural and conventional right in this situation of the lumber on the lakeshore, a half-breed named Dick Boulton reminds the doctor that—strictly speaking—the log he is working on belongs to the company of White and McNally.

"Don't get huffy, Doc," the Indian taunted. "I don't care who you steal from."

"If you think the logs are stolen," the doctor responded, "take your stuff and get out."

Unable to answer such a challenge to his moral authority, the doctor loses not only the wood, but also the labor that the Indian owes him in exchange for treating his squaw the previous winter. And then the doctor makes himself ridiculous by threatening to use physical force.

"If you call me Doc once again, I'll knock your eye teeth down your throat."

"Oh, no, you won't, Doc." Dick Boulton looked at the doctor. Dick was a big man. He knew how big a man he was. He liked to get into fights. (p. 28)

As in *Adventures of Huckleberry Finn,* we again see Americans with no notion of natural right except force.

Unwilling to concede that might makes right even if he can see no clear alternative, the doctor retreats. Returning to the cabin, he busies himself not with reading the stack of medical journals lying unopened on the floor, but rather with cleaning his gun. He could have used his technical knowledge or equipment "to even up the sides," we are reminded. The doctor's refusal to fight does not stem so much from physical incapacity or fear as from principle. Should a doctor dedicated to relieving pain and preserving life threaten it in order to assert his own economic interest?

Unfortunately, the doctor no longer believes entirely in the validity of his vocation. He does not even demand that his wife recognize its value. Although she is in bed with a perpetual headache, she never looks to him for a cure. She is a Christian Scientist, and the doctor would apparently not have his wife act against her own beliefs any more than the doctor would have the half-breed chop wood that he thinks was stolen.

The doctor does not assert himself because he himself does not know what is right. Thinking that no one else does either, he sees only one way to prevent differences of opinion and interest from generating into conflict and injury: refusing to fight. He thus repeatedly retreats— from the Chicago suburbs where he had a private practice, from the rude Indian, from his wife—to hunt in the woods. He is indeed rather like Ishmael, who went to sea in order to avoid knocking off heads—

his own included. The doctor is trying to escape his despairing sense that no life may be worth living—hence, worth saving—and that his science and vocation are therefore a bitter irony.

Finding his son reading in the woods, the doctor dutifully relates his wife's message: "Your mother wants you to come and see her." But Nick responds, "I want to go with you." At this point, the son gladly joins his father in running off. Whereas a boy can be thoroughly absorbed in the pleasure not only of the hunt itself but also of an escape from constraining authority—if only temporarily—a man cannot. The implicit question is whether the boy will continue to follow his father into the ultimate retreat—suicide—or whether Nick will find some way of affirming the value of life.

When Hemingway next presents Nick in "The End of Something," he is no longer an innocent boy.[23] He has experienced love and discovered that it does not last. He thus faces the unpleasant task of ending an affair with an absolutely unsuspecting girl named Marjorie, with whom—we learn in the following story—he had genuinely and generously discussed marriage. "It isn't fun any more," he tells her. "Not any of it" (p. 40). "Isn't love any fun?" Marjorie asks. "No," Nick answers. Marjorie leaves with great dignity, and Nick is left to seek solace and support from his friend Bill.

But neither male camaraderie nor the assertion of masculine strength and independence suffice to assuage Nick's sense of emptiness and loss.[24] Ironically, he finds relief only when Bill worries that Nick "might get back into it again. Nick had not thought about that. It had seemed so absolute. . . . He felt happy now. There was not anything that was irrevocable" (p. 59).

Just as his experience in the Indian camp involved an unexpected lesson that Nick did not want to learn, so—too—does the affair with Marge. All human passions are transitory; feelings die as absolutely as their authors. But if human attachments and commitments—and perhaps even contracts (recall the half-breed Boulton's breach of faith)—must be based on feelings in order to be genuine, true, and effective, then such commitments are fundamentally unreliable, whatever the present intentions of the parties, because feelings change and passions grow cold. The past is irrevocable; and the future, beyond planning and control.

In fact, Nick does not pick up the affair again. He had been planning to get a job and marry Marge, even though—as Bill reminds him—she comes from a distinctly lower class family. Disillusioned by his parents' empty marriage, Nick does not act on the basis of calculation or convention. He acts out of real feeling; but when that feeling evaporates, he does not know what to do. Having no direction in his life—Hemingway shows us in the subsequent story—Nick decides to bum around.

When Nick leaves home to travel abroad on his own, he quickly discovers that human beings do not hurt others merely from incapacity or indifference. Like the brakeman who knocks Nick off the train, they may enjoy inflicting pain. Perhaps they even inflict it out of affection, as Ad Frances's black companion Bugs does when he blackjacks the ex-fighter to prevent him from going crazy. In either case, there is a certain assertion of control and superiority. Caretaking itself (whether in the name of property rights of the railroad or in the name of friendship) often seems merely to provide a justification for violence.[25]

Camping in the woods to avoid towns, the little white boxer (who looks childlike in repose) with his big black companion cannot but remind readers of Huck and Jim. If these two friends that Nick meets are not currently fugitives from the law, then they are at least ex-convicts. But the life of these modern hobos is hardly pastoral or idyllic; and the things that Nick learns from them about life outside the bounds of civil society are not pretty.

Like Jim in the previous century, the big black man preserves the external marks of the conventional inequality between the races by assiduously addressing both whites as "mister." Nevertheless, Bugs is clearly in control. Whereas Huck was the one who went into town to buy or "borrow" supplies for his friend on the river, Bugs does all the shopping. It is Bugs who invites Nick to join them for supper, and Bugs decides when Nick should go. The black apparently manages the money that Ad's ex-wife sends him; he most certainly manages the ex-fighter himself, with the blackjack.

Once again, an American novelist is reminding his readers that force rules when people put themselves outside the range of legal protection. Unfortunately—Hemingway shows—the law does not protect people's rights to life, liberty, and the pursuit of happiness very well in civil society, either. The law had, for example, allowed another manager to put Ad in so many fights that his brain became as mutilated as his face. However—according to Bugs—what really drove Ad crazy, caused him to be hitting everyone, and therefore got him expelled from society was not his beatings so much as the breakup of his marriage. Looking very much like Ad, his manager/wife had been written up in the newspapers as his sister. When they got married, there was a lot of ugliness about incest in the newspapers. And eventually she left.[26]

If force rules in Nature, conventional opinion rules in society; and neither genuine affection nor willingness to fight is sufficient to counteract its sway. Natural relations—even incest—might be truer and perhaps even kinder than purely legal or economic associations, but they too can be exploitative. Neither Bugs's nor the "sister's" apparently genuine affection for Ad prevented them from living off his misery in one way or another. Civil society does not end the "war of all against all, ceasing only in death." If anything, civil society only makes that war worse.

Death Reveals the False Foundations of Society

Nick's travels away from home eventually take him altogether out of the United States and into the European war where, in the following vignette, we find him wounded. And confronting the immediate possibility of his own death for the first time, Nick self-consciously severs all ties to country and community. "Senta Rinaldi," he says to the man dying beside him. "You and me we've made a separate peace. . . . We're not patriots."

No individual can really die for another, Nick realizes.[27] No organization can actually guarantee anyone's right to life, liberty, and the pursuit of happiness. If he does die—Nick sees—he will no longer benefit from the collective that he has been defending. Nor will he enjoy any posthumous glory and honor. The people at home may never even hear of his "sacrifice." If Nick and all his fellows die, who will there be to tell the tale? As Hemingway subsequently shows in "Soldier's Home," the people whom a soldier has served do not like to be reminded of that fact for very long.

Leaving Nick wounded in Chapter 6 of *In Our Time*, Hemingway does not tell his readers anything more about him until Chapter 11, where the hero announces that he is returning to the states. Until he makes this decision to go home, Nick is still basically just running away. In the interim chapters, Hemingway indirectly presents the dilemma that Nick is facing—by relating the experiences of other characters—because Nick himself is not yet willing or able to face his problem directly.[28]

Americans could not just return from the war and take up life where they left it. As Nick's experience demonstrates, the American regime is based on a series of falsehoods. With the story of the unnamed soldier that follows Nick's wounding, Hemingway reminds his readers that—human passions being transient—human oaths and promises to the contrary are vacuous.[29] And—he suggests in the subsequent vignette depicting the soldier who breaks his promise to Jesus—there does not appear to be any divine power that will force fallible human beings to live up to their word.

Divine love was once taken to be the ground not merely of human community, but of the entire cosmic order. But if war teaches human beings anything—Hemingway seems to be saying—it teaches them that God is dead. Under conditions of modern war, men do not live or die as a result of their individual courage and virtue. Why—for example—should Nick have been wounded by the shelling at Fossalta, and the whoring soldier saved?[30] It is a matter of chance. Evidence of divine justice appears to be just as difficult to find on earth as peace and goodwill among men.[31]

Their experience in war thus sets young American soldiers apart from their compatriots. In "Soldiers Home," Harold Krebs is not able to communicate his feelings to people who have not shared them.[32] And being unable to communicate, he himself loses them.[33] He is left with nothing at all.

Krebs is not even able to preserve the memory of his own manliness and courage in the company of other soldiers. Not everyone had been brave. A man could demonstrate his courage in action for others to see, but merely to talk about bravery would appear to be bragging. Thus

> when he occasionally met another man who had really been a soldier and they talked a few minutes in the dressing room at a dance he fell into the easy pose of the old soldier among other soldiers: that he had been badly, sickeningly frightened all the time. In this way he lost everything.

So "Krebs acquired the nausea in regard to experience that was the result of untruth or exaggeration" (p. 91).[34]

The problem is not that Krebs is completely asocial. On the contrary, he "would like to have a girl." But the girls he watches walking down the street

> lived in such a complicated world of already defined alliances and shifting feuds that Krebs did not feel the energy or the courage to break into it. . . . He did not want to get into the intrigue and the politics. He did not

want to have to do any courting. He did not want to tell any more lies.
(pp. 92–93)

In civil society, it is impossible to maintain and thus to act on the basis of pure, genuine feeling.[35] All conventional social relations are based on lies.

American government represents an even bigger lie and hypocrisy, Hemingway indicates in the next vignette. That government was purportedly established to secure people's rights to life and liberty. In fact, it merely gives to some citizens the license to kill others—in peace, as in war. After a policeman in Kansas City shoots two Hungarian thieves in the back—Hemingway reports—his partner Boyle protests,

> "Hell, Jimmy, . . . you oughtn't to have done it. There's liable to be a hell of a lot of trouble."
>
> "They're crooks, ain't they? . . . They're wops, ain't they? Who the hell is going to make any trouble?" Drevitts responded.
>
> "That's all right maybe this time . . . but how did you know they were wops when you bumped them off?"
>
> "I can tell wops a mile off."

Even the immigrants who specifically came to the United States to escape Old World oppression and to begin anew as Americans have not proved able to overcome divisive ethnic prejudices and old nationalistic ties. Irishmen shot Hungarians (mistaken for Italians) with official—even legal—sanction in the United States just as well as in the war in Europe.

To believe that human beings can overcome the war of all against all by constructing a new political order requires that people—like the revolutionist of the next story—ignore their own experience as well as American history. But to believe that government is the source of the problem and that men would live in peace as brothers if only the state were abolished is equally naive.[36]

The communist alternative is no better than liberal democracy. At the center of the book, Hemingway thus takes himself and his protagonist out of the "cold war" debate that has continued to define twentieth-century politics.[37] Government cannot secure any individual's life or liberty any more than it can bind that individual to others. Nor will government wither away. It may be more apt—as Hemingway relates in the next story—to put the opposition in jail.

"The Revolutionist" is the story of a young Hungarian communist.

(After the communists overthrew the Hungarian monarchy—Hemingway reminds his readers—Colonel Horthy displaced them and established a fascist regime.) "Horthy's men had done some bad things to him"—so the revolutionist seeks asylum, first in Italy and then in Switzerland. He has no money, but—out of sympathy for his sufferings—his comrades take him in and feed him before they pass him on to their fellows at the next railroad station.

The youth "was delighted with Italy. It was a beautiful country, he said. The people were all kind." In a land of plenty—the young communist believes—people would live together in peace and harmony. Hearing that the movement is not going well in Italy, he thus assures his comrade: "It will go better. . . . You have everything here. It is the one country that everyone is sure of. It will be the starting point of everything."

The young communist does not understand the source and character of his own political movement any more than the young Americans understand theirs. He "had been in many towns, walked much, and seen many pictures," the narrator reports. "Giotto, Masaccio, and Piero della Francesca he bought reproductions of and carried them wrapped in a copy of *Avanti*. Mantegna he did not like" (p. 105). As his dislike of Mantegna indicates, the youth refuses to countenance the role of martyrs and suffering as they are used to foster mutual sympathies in producing revolutions. Mantegna's painting of St. Sebastian is a reminder that human beings seek salvation out of suffering—not contentment—and that they often persecute agitators whom they hold to be responsible for disturbing their peace. Perceiving the youth's unwillingness to see his own situation and the world around him, the narrator does "not say anything." He merely states that "the last I heard of [the young communist] the Swiss had him in jail near Sion" (p. 106).

The brotherhood of all mankind thus represents the dream of a naive youth who refuses to take account of his own experience, Hemingway is suggesting. Life in the twentieth century gives people no more reason to believe that they can achieve peace and goodwill on earth by instituting a new world order than it does to maintain faith in divine justice.[38]

Disillusioned with both religion and politics, people in our time must come to terms with their mortality as no generation before them. They must live and die without hope either of saving themselves or of creating a better life for posterity. What they need above all is to find some satisfaction in *this* life, and Nick finds it—finally—at "the big two-hearted river." Death would not be so terrible if life in itself were not good, Hemingway recognizes. Because the pleasure merely in feeling alive is transient, however, nature does not provide a basis for a lasting or just community.

Unable to believe in either God or country, the postwar generation seems to have no alternative but to form small private societies of *cognosci,* who know that there is nothing to live for but the present moment. In the five stories leading up to Nick's return to the Michigan woods, Hemingway thus portrays the lives of a series of American émigrés.[39]

All the émigrés depicted here are intellectuals, who live more according to ideas they have gotten from books than according to real feelings or experience. For example, in the third story the narrator observes that a "young gentleman" is amazed when his guide orders Marsala, because "that's what Max Beerbohm drinks" (p. 127). The young gentlemen know the tastes and even the affectations of the literati, but they never notice the habits of the local populace.

These American émigrés are much less daring and unconventional and much more pretentious and uncomprehending than they themselves realize. Having arranged for an Italian ex-soldier to take him and his companion trout-fishing out of season, the young gentleman was relieved when the expedition failed. "He was no longer breaking the law" (p. 133).

The intellectuals do not understand the source of their failure to form lasting communities, nor the price. They do not see that they are running away—at bottom—from the prospect of death.[40]

Although political and nationalistic ties constitute illusions—Hemingway suggests—human sexuality seems to indicate that society does have a natural foundation. All of the young American gentlemen whom he describes living in Europe have women, or "wives." These couples have difficulty conceiving and raising children, however.[41] Alienated not merely from their own particular nation but also from the natural generative cycle, their lives are empty and full of frustration.[42]

Procreation is the natural outcome of human sexuality. In the next story—noticing that their waitress is pregnant and without a wedding band—Nick explains to his friend George that men in the Swiss hinterland do not marry women until they have proved themselves able to bear children. The American émigrés are living in defiance of the natural cycle. But Hemingway indicates also that literally producing a new life—that is, having a baby and assuming responsibility for its upbringing—does not represent an adequate or satisfying response to an individual's confrontation with death.

Like Krebs the ex-soldier, the young American émigrés are tempted to postpone—if not altogether to avoid—assuming their conventional adult responsibilities: settling down and having a family. "Didn't you wish we could just bum together?" George asks in "Cross-Country Ski." "[We could] take our skis and . . . repair kit and extra sweaters and pyjamas in our ruck-sacks and not give a damn about school or anything" (p. 144). "Yes," Nick responds, "and go through the Schwartzwald . . . where [I] went fishing last summer" (p. 145). Like Twain, Hemingway believes that there is a fundamental tendency in human beings to "light out."

In contrast to Twain, however, Hemingway indicates that it is not the desire to avoid responsibility and its associated constraints that fundamentally moves these young men. George does go back to school. Nick and his wife Helen return to the States—even though they do not want to—because she is pregnant. And when George observes sympathetically, "It's hell, isn't it," Nick responds, "No, not exactly." He might not be happy to be going home, but he is glad that Helen is having a baby.

Procreation constitutes the natural way of overcoming the prospective loss of individual life, through the perpetuation of the species. Men as well as women want to have children, Hemingway observes. They hope to live on—in a way—through their sons. The problem in our time is that men like Nick are not sure that they want to live on.

Once people have children, they must think about the future. But—Hemingway indicates—it is impossible to look toward the future without coming to terms with the past. In order to greet the birth of his son completely cheerfully, Nick must come to terms with his feelings about his own father; and he is not yet able to do this. "My Old Man" addresses Nick's problem indirectly by depicting the disillusionment of an émigré's young son at his father's death.[43]

The Goodness of Life Makes Death Even Harder

The fundamental problem or weakness that Nick's father has bequeathed to him is the doctor's inability to affirm that life is worth living. At the end of the book, we see Nick—in contrast to his father—conclude that life is good.[44] According to Hemingway's own later testimony, "Big Two-hearted River" is a "story about coming back from the war [although] there was no mention of the war in it."[45] The boy who "felt quite sure that he would never die" now knows that he indubitably will. He returns—almost—to the locus of his childhood, with a new sensibility.[46]

Finding the town of Seney and the surrounding countryside burned to the ground, Nick is reminded that nature can be as destructive as war. He knows that it cannot all be burned, however; he has already seen the river and the trout swimming in it. Life goes on. He experiences the continuity in himself. "He felt all the old feeling. . . . He was happy" (p. 179). Picking up a pack that he realizes is too heavy, Nick nevertheless feels a certain relief because he has "left everything behind, the need for thinking, the need to write, other needs" (p. 179). So when he later makes camp—exhausted from the hard walk with the heavy pack—he is still happy.

> He had not been unhappy all day. This was different though. . . . It had been a hard trip. . . . He had made his camp. He was settled. Nothing could touch him. It was a good place to camp. . . . He was in his home where he had made it. (p. 187)[47]

Nick is so much at home that he can allow himself to think, to recall a friend who went off after striking it rich, and to laugh when the coffee made according to that friend's recipe turns out to be bitter.

Nick's satisfaction will not last, however. Hemingway reminds his readers of the fundamental human problem in the vignette that divides the two halves of "Big Two-hearted River." "They hanged Sam Cardinella at six o'clock in the morning," the newspaper report reads. Is this the reality that Nick must wake up to?

"Be a man," a priest urges as they carry the prisoner onto the gallows. But "when they came toward him with the cap to go over his head Sam Cardinella lost control of his sphincter muscles. The guards who had been holding him . . . were both disgusted." Disgust does not keep the guards from hanging Cardinella, however, any more than compassion prevented the revolutionaries from shooting the minister too sick to stand up against the wall of the hospital in the vignette that introduced Chapter 5. In both cases, the executioners simply prop up their victim with a chair. Cardinella's gross—if rather natural—reaction to the prospect of his own imminent death raises a serious question, however: Is the truth revealed in this death scene that "man" is no more than a dung-producing reflex? Hemingway is never quite sure.[48]

In the second half of "Big Two-hearted River," Hemingway indicates the limits of Nick's recovery from his wartime experience, when he goes fishing the next day. Nick is emphatically alone. After he loses his first big trout, he feels shaky and wants to sit down. "The thrill had been too much. . . . He did not want to rush his sensations any" (p. 204). After he catches two other large trout, he calls it a day. He does not want to try too much. In particular, he does not feel ready to enter the swamp, "to hook big trout in places impossible to land them. . . . In the swamp fishing was a tragic adventure."

In the swamp Nick would again have to confront his own limits directly. He would not be able to catch trout in the deep dark waters, and would then be reminded of the ultimate futility of all striving. When he kills a trout at the swamp's edge, he is reminded of his own death. Contemplating all that the swamp means, Nick wishes that "he had brought something to read" (p. 211). He wants to use his mind and imagination to escape the prospect of inevitable physical decay.

Art Does Not Constitute an Adequate Answer

Hemingway explored the possibility that human beings might come to terms with their inevitable demise—indirectly—through art. Because he is a writer, Nick can express and so preserve the "cool and clear" sense of his own existence that Krebs lost.[49] In the draft of an alternative conclusion, Hemingway thus presented Nick as the author of all the stories. In "On Writing," Nick finally rushes back to camp to write down what is in his head.[50]

In nature, Nick has found a kind of truth. And Hemingway recognized that in truth there is a kind of individual—if not societal—morality. "So far"—he wrote in *Death in the Afternoon*—"about morals I know only that what is moral is what you feel good after and what is immoral is what you feel bad after" (p. 4). One can lie about one's memory and about one's intentions; but one cannot deceive oneself about immediate feelings.

Above all, Hemingway strove to recapture those feelings in his own prose.[51] Because he found truth and hence a kind of morality in immediate sensation, he did not—like many of his Paris associates—embrace art for art's sake. For Hemingway, art was not the means by which human beings bring order out of a natural chaos and so give their lives a significance otherwise lacking. For Hemingway, writing remained a means of expression. Rather than stress the means of expression, Hemingway sought to communicate experience as directly and purely as possible. The artistry of his prose is therefore radically understated. Because he was trying to communicate what really happened—without any interpretative embroidery or exaggeration—his writing is intentionally rather flat and journalistic. He began his writing career as a reporter, and his fiction is always emphatically realistic. Nevertheless, he clearly distinguished the fiction to which he aspired from journalistic factuality.

> In writing for a newspaper you told what happened, and with one trick and another, you communicated the emotion aided by the element of timeliness which gives a certain emotion to any account of something that has happened on that day; but the real thing, the sequence of motion and fact which made the emotion and which would be as valid in a year or in ten years or, with luck and if you stated it purely enough, always, was beyond me and I was working very hard to get it.[52]

Journalism has an impact basically because of its timeliness, whereas Hemingway was seeking to capture the enduring core of the seemingly transitory, historical incidents or events in human life.

Nevertheless, he concluded that art is no better and no more enduring a response to the fact of individual death than politics or procreation. The self-reflective conclusion called "On Writing" was detracting from the immediacy of the experience depicted in "Big Two-hearted River," and so he deleted it. In the finished version of the story, Nick does not look back on the fellowship of his youth from the later vantage point of marriage. Hemingway does not make explicit Nick's stance toward his past or toward civil society. Nor does he indicate Nick's final stance toward death. For Hemingway, the problem is fundamentally insoluble.

Human beings kill in rebellion against their mortality, Hemingway later explained in *Death in the Afternoon*.[53] And in its final form, "Big Two-hearted River" ends with the killing of the trout at the outer edge of the swamp. His solitary fishing trip has made Nick happy—temporarily—but it has not solved all his problems. It has simply postponed them. "There were plenty of days coming when he could fish the swamp" (p. 212).

There Is No Lasting Solution

Nick's problems are not merely personal, as Hemingway reminds his readers in the last vignette by pointing to the connection between events in Europe and the now somewhat ambiguous meaning of the return to nature in America. In "L'Envoi," a reporter interviews the deposed Greek king in the palace gardens where the revolutionary committee has been—in effect—holding him prisoner. Pruning his roses, the king appears to be the image of an English country gentleman.[54] Not wanting to seem a bad sport or a sore loser, the king even praises his captor: "Plastiras is a very good man, . . . but frightfully difficult. I think he did right, though, shooting those chaps" (p. 213). "Those chaps" are the six ministers whose execution was depicted in the preface to Chapter 5. In prosecuting an otherwise unnecessary war against Turkey, these ministers no doubt thought that they were loyally serving their king—furthering his interests by extending his empire. Loyalty is not rewarded in this world, though, Hemingway indicates. Political order is not founded on tradition or consent so much as on force, even in constitutional democracies. "If Kerensky had shot a few men," the king reflects, "things might have been altogether different."

"Of course," the king then comments, "the great thing in this sort of an affair is not to be shot oneself." If the first lesson of politics is the need to use force, the second is the need to attend to one's own interests. The king may seem indifferent to his loss of power and status, but he is by no means oblivious to his personal safety. (Hence— we suspect—the praise of his captors, which is being delivered to a journalist who might be expected to report it.) For a man facing his own impending death—Hemingway consistently shows— politics, position, regime, and wealth become secondary considerations.

"It was very jolly," the reporter concludes. "We talked for a long time. Like all Greeks he wanted to go to America" (p. 213). In the wake of imperialistic wars and revolutionary reaction, it is— ironically enough—the king who wishes the opportunity to begin anew in the New World, free from class prejudices.

America was the source of the revolutionary hope that human beings could secure liberty, equality, and fraternity by founding a new political order based on the right of nature. Unfortunately—Hemingway thinks—modern history has shown that this hope was as ill founded as the faith in king and church that preceded it. Human beings do not treat each other as equals—much less, brothers. Like all animals, they live in competition with one another, and hence in an essentially hostile relation.

In contrast to civil society—which attempts to justify the present sacrifices and burdens individuals make in war with promises of future glory or peace and prosperity for generations to come—nature reveals the fundamentally transitory character of all existence in a perpetual cycle of prey and predator, birth and death. Nature is not a "garden" any more than American government is a protector of life and liberty. On the contrary—as Nick discovered at the big two-hearted river— nature constitutes a war of all against all, in which grasshoppers, fish, and men alike struggle to live and then live only at each other's expense.

Nature does not, therefore, provide an adequate foundation for human life or society. Although a return to nature can remind one that life is good, it also gives proof that nothing endures beyond the cycle of birth and death. Nature is indeed two-hearted.

Hemingway and Heidegger

Death therefore remained an insuperable problem for Hemingway. It was death itself that was the problem, however, not fear. Like Melville, Hemingway showed that nature as a whole does consist of a "war of all against all." But he did not conclude like Twain (and Hobbes) that human beings act primarily from fear of violent death. If Nick had simply feared death, he would not have voluntarily gone to war. He did not particularly seek honor; and he did not make his "separate peace" because he was afraid. He left the United States for the same reason that Ishmael shipped aboard the *Pequod*: He wanted to discover a reason to live. And—Hemingway showed—Nick was able to appreciate what is good in life itself in the state of nature only after he had directly confronted the possibility of his own death.

In emphasizing the confrontation with the immediate possibility of death as the definitive experience in the life of an individual, Hemingway anticipated the influential analysis of human existence that the postwar German philosopher Martin Heidegger offered in *Being and Time* only a few years later.[55] To fear death, Heidegger argued, is to treat it as an external phenomenon—something that might even be avoided.[56] Like Hemingway, he considered death to be actually the most personal, inalienable, "own-most" possibility that an individual human being ever faces.[57] Only direct confrontation with the ever-present possibility of death would show an individual the fundamental uncertainty and radical insecurity of human existence.

As Melville had observed in "The Line" (Chapter 60 of *Moby Dick*), few human beings can continually live in the face of such radical insecurity. So, Heidegger argued, they "fall" or turn away from contemplating the possibility of death into the comforting— although fundamentally illusory—routines and opinions of everyday life. By dramatizing the courage that it takes even the lowliest sailor to live actually in the face of death, Melville thought that he was reminding his readers of the true grounds of democratic fellowship. Unfortunately—Hemingway and Heidegger agreed—confronting the ever-present possibility of one's own death does not, as Ishmael suggested, lead human beings to appreciate the essentially interdependent character of their existence or arouse a sense of compassion. Contemplating the possibility of their own demise leads them rather to perceive the essential emptiness of all social and political opinions and institutions.[58]

If the truth of human life is found only in the prospect of death "authentically" contemplated as one's own, neither that truth nor that life can really be shared. Neither liberal democracy nor its communist alternative has a valid foundation, Hemingway and Heidegger both concluded. To promise to secure an individual's right to life is to deny the fundamental truth of human existence, by suggesting that his life can be preserved by institutional or other cooperative means. Likewise, to promise that all human beings can live as brothers is to deny the individuating experience of death.[59]

Beyond disillusionment with both major modern forms of egalitarian politics, however, the postwar American novelist and the postwar German philosopher came to strikingly different conclusions from a common insight. To come to terms with the ever-present possibility and inescapable necessity of one's own death—Heidegger argued—is to perceive the essentially temporal character of human existence. Human beings do not live in a series of isolated moments called "the present." They live instead by projecting their past experiences into the future. And they understand that past (and hence themselves) "traditionally," in terms of concepts that they have acquired— largely imbedded in the language itself—from the people among whom they were born.[60] Fundamentally, therefore, temporal existence is historical existence. But the fact that human beings live historically does not mean that their lives are entirely determined or unfree. On the contrary, the individual who sees that death is an ever-present possibility thereby also sees that he or she has actually always lived—if only implicitly—by choice. Human beings can make their lives—not only individual, but also communal—more authentic, by making that choice explicit. The choice is not an abstract determination among indefinite possibilities. Rather, it is a choice between continuing to live as one has lived in the past, in the particular circumstances in which one finds oneself—or ceasing to do so. To live historically is to live as part of a particular people, not as an isolated individual or as a member of the human race per se.[61] Heidegger thus embraced the fascist reaction against both liberal individualism and communist universalism, because he thought that it was truer to the historical nature of human existence.[62]

For Hemingway, on the other hand, the fascist reaction against both liberalism and communism simply constituted yet another example of a political movement—originating in natural desires, but then serving primarily to justify official violence when those natural desires had dissipated. As the politics of "the people" (*Volk*) defined basically through ethnic ties, fascism could claim to have the same natural foundations as the family. In contrast to both Melville and Twain, Hemingway suggested that the desire to mate and procreate is as strong as—if not stronger than—the fear of violent death and the desire for human fellowship. But he also indicated that politics based on family ties have no more lasting or genuine natural foundations than those based on the fear of violent death or the pleasures of male camaraderie. Family relations do not guarantee future affection any more than childhood friendship. On the contrary, as Hemingway reminded his readers through the historical vignettes, extended family relations in the form of ethnic ties merely provide an excuse—in America as well as in Europe—for the violent oppression of others.

Hemingway's insistence on the simple goodness of pure, natural sensation thus saved him not only from complete nihilism, but also from the fascist reaction to that nihilism.[63] But it created a gap between nature and history that he himself found impossible to bridge.

Because they feel that life is good—he saw—human beings try to preserve it. Failing that, they engage in violent killing—they hunt and they war—in rebellion against their inescapable fate. Like the satisfaction of simple sensation or the more intense thrill of sexual pleasure, however, the exultation in conquest is short lived. In the death of another living creature, every human being cannot help but see prefigured his or her own demise.

Like Heidegger, Hemingway thought that the confrontation with death as one's own-most possibility revealed not only that the continuation of human life fundamentally constitutes a choice, but also that human existence is essentially historical. Therein lay the difficulty with which the novelist incessantly struggled without coming to a satisfactory solution: Why should a human being self-consciously choose to persist in the face of ultimate defeat? On what grounds can a son hope to live more satisfactorily than his father? To recognize the historical character of human existence is to recognize its essentially transitory character. If all human institutions developed basically to preserve human life, then—in time and with experience— the impossibility of achieving that goal will necessarily become clear. Having perceived the essential emptiness of family, church, and polity, the people in our time must confront the question of the value of life itself in an unprecedented way.

On the other hand—Hemingway recognized—confrontation with the possibility of one's own death would be neither so fearful nor so revealing if human beings did not fundamentally feel that life itself is good. Heidegger had reduced the present to the venue through which human beings project the past into the future. Hemingway contrasted the satisfaction that one can find in simple sensations at the present moment with both the anxiety produced by an uncertain future and the disillusionment necessarily associated with the past.[64]

For Hemingway, there were two insoluble problems. First, he was unable to affirm what he himself saw as the distinctively human characteristic: the foresight into one's own death that makes human existence essentially historical. Because human beings are not the only sensitive animals, Hemingway identified what is good about life itself with nature as a whole. In thus opposing nature and history, he lost a sense or conception of *human* nature. Consequently, he was also unable to find any way human beings could relieve their alienation and suffering by joining together. Although he saw both that human beings are naturally attracted to one another and that they do not live happily in isolation, he did not think that they could form an enduring union that would not become an empty, inauthentic, and hence ultimately oppressive sham.

By showing how a celebration of the generative natural cycle could be combined with a sense of history, William Faulkner—then—was not simply attempting to provide a better, more complete picture of human nature. He was seeking to reveal the true grounds of human community and to show that political progress is possible.[65]

Notes

1. Ernest Hemingway, *Green Hills of Africa* (New York: Charles Scribner's Sons, 1935).

2. Philip Young, *Hemingway: A Reconsideration* (University Park: Pennsylvania State University Press, 1966). Following Young, Joseph M. Flora also claims that Nick is Hemingway's most important character. *Hemingway's Nick Adams* (Baton Rouge: Louisiana State University Press, 1982), pp. 1–4.

3. In some respects, Nick does not represent a latter-day version of Huck so much as he constitutes a twentieth-century reinterpretation of Natty Bumppo. The strongest echo of Natty in Nick Adams may be found in the fragment of an unfinished novel, "The Last Good Country," where Hemingway shows Nick take a rifle and flee from the law after catching trout out of season. Ernest Hemingway, *The Nick Adams Stories* (New York: Charles Scribner's Sons, 1972), pp. 70–82. Cooper's novels had explicitly been dedicated to teaching his countrymen that there were natural principles of right that could form the basis of a just polity—the very claim that Hemingway puts into question. Like Natty and unlike Huck, Nick acquires much of his formative education from the Indians. That education does not concern the skills of self-preservation or stoical endurance, however, so much as the complex interrelation of love, birth, and death. In a later story, Hemingway shows that Nick first learned both the pleasures of sex and the pangs of infidelity from an Indian. "Ten Indians," in Ernest Hemingway, *Men without Women* (New York: Charles Scribner's Sons, 1927), pp. 97–102.

4. See Huck's famous description of the joys of living on a raft: "When we got her out to the middle, we let her . . . float wherever the current wanted her to . . ., dangled our legs in the water and talked about all kinds of things. . . . We was always naked, day and night, whenever the mosquitoes would let us. . . . It's lovely to live on a raft." Samuel Clemens, *Adventures of Huckleberry Finn* (Berkeley: University of California Press, 1985), p. 180.

5. Nick's withdrawals are thus always rather explicitly temporary. For example, coming down from the mountains into the town in "An Alpine Idyll," he reflects: "I was a little tired of skiing. We had stayed too long. I was glad there were other things beside skiing, and I was glad to be down, away from the unnatural high mountain spring into this May morning in the valley." Hemingway, *Without Women*, p. 110.

6. Philip Young also observed, Hemingway: *Reconsideration,* p. 40, that Nick's relation to civilization is different from Huck's, just as Nick's relation to his father is much different from Huck's relation to Pap—in large part because Nick's father is utterly unlike Pap.

7. Hence the amalgam of *Being and Time* with *In Our Time* in the heading for this chapter.

8. I have concentrated on Hemingway's first collection of Nick Adams stories because I think this collection reveals most clearly both the promise and the problems that Hemingway saw in the return to nature. Examined carefully—I believe—this early collection contains all the themes and thoughts that animate his entire corpus. Hemingway himself suggested that the whole could be seen in the part, if that part were viewed carefully enough. See *Death*

in the Afternoon (New York: Charles Scribner's Sons, 1932), p. 278: "Let those who want to save the world if you can get to see it clear and as a whole. Then any part you make will represent the whole if it's made truly."

9. By separating each story from its sequel and so destroying a facile sense of narrative continuity, the vignettes were intended to give the collection of stories something of the actual character of human experience, in which certain incidents stand out and are remembered as significant turning points even though the meaning or the reasons why they stick in the memory continues to elude the particular individual. Wesley A. Kort, "Human Time in Hemingway's Fiction," *Modern Fiction Studies* (1980):582, has also pointed out that, whereas the action in the vignettes tends to be public and external, the stories themselves are more private and give an internal view.

10. See Robert M. Slabey, "The Structure of *In Our Time*," Clinton S. Burhams, Jr., "The Complex Unity of *In Our Time*," and Jackson J. Benson, "Patterns of Connection and Their Development on Hemingway's *In Our Time*," in Michael S. Reynolds, *Critical Essays on Ernest Hemingway's "In Our Time"* (Boston: G. K. Hall, 1983), pp. 76–119, for somewhat different accounts of the structure and order. David Seed, " 'The Picture of the Whole': *In Our Time*," in A. Robert Lee, ed., *Ernest Hemingway: New Critical Essays* (London: Vision, 1983), has pointed out many of the thematic links among vignettes and stories. See also Charles G. Hoffman and A. C. Hoffmann, " 'The Truest Sentence': Words as Equivalents of Time and Place in *In Our Time*," in Donald R. Noble, *Hemingway: A Reevaluation* (Troy, N.Y., Whitston Publishing, 1983), pp. 99–114.

11. E. R. Hagemann, " 'Only let the story end as soon as possible': Time and History in Ernest Hemingway's *In Our Time*," *Modern Fiction Studies* 26 (Summer 1980): 255–61, has shown that the vignettes cover the period from 1914–23.

12. "Now the essence of the greatest emotional appeal of bullfighting is the feeling of immortality that the bullfighter feels in the middle of a great faena and that he gives to the spectators. He is performing a work of art and he is playing with death, bringing it closer, closer, closer to himself, a death that you know is in the horns because you have the canvas-covered bodies of the horses on the sand to prove it." Hemingway, *Death*, p. 213.

13. Stephen Cooper concluded in *The Politics of Ernest Hemingway* (Ann Arbor: University of Michigan Research Press, 1987), p. 23, that Hemingway omitted all political commentary in *In Our Time*, because he ignored the interrelations between stories and vignettes.

14. "Where you see gratuitous cruelty most often is in police brutality," Hemingway observed in *Death*, pp. 187–88, "in the police of all countries I have ever been in, including, especially, my own. . . . After one comes, through contact with its administrators, no longer to cherish greatly the law as a remedy in abuses, then the bottle becomes a sovereign means of direct action. If you cannot throw it at least you can always drink out of it."

15. Quoted in Slabey, "Structure of *In Our Time*," p. 77.

16. Hemingway originally planned to stress the transient, disordered character of both life and "the news" in our time not only through his title and his flat journalistic style, but also graphically by framing each page with a collage of newspaper articles. Carlos Baker, *Ernest Hemingway: A Life Story* (New York: Scribner's, 1969), pp. 115–16.

17. Hemingway read Nietzsche's *Thus Spoke Zarathustra*. See Michael S. Reynolds, *Hemingway's Reading 1910–1940* (Princeton, N.J.: Princeton University Press, 1981), p. 163.

18. Hemingway was a personal friend of Picasso and a lifelong admirer of Braques, so it is not altogether surprising that he produced a rather "cubist" work—almost, but not quite, a novel—in which ordinary relations of sequence, time, and narration are fractured and reorganized on an apparently flat surface created by his studiedly simple, "objective," reportorial prose style. Kenneth G. Johnston, "Hemingway and Cézanne: Doing the Country," *American Literature* 56 (March 1984): 28–34, has traced the influence of postimpressionist painters on the novelist. Hemingway explicitly mentioned Cézanne's influence in "On Writing"—the conclusion that he drafted, but then excised, from *In Our Time*.

19. There is, in fact, a definite connection between each introductory scene and subsequent story. In a letter to Edmund Wilson, Hemingway explained that the introductory scenes "give the picture of the whole before examining it in detail. Like looking with your eyes at something, say a passing coastline, and then looking at it with 15X binoculars. Or rather, maybe looking and then going and living in it— and then coming out and looking at it again." Edmund Wilson, *The Shores of Light* (New York: Farrar, Straus, and Young, 1952), p. 123.

20. Citations are from Ernest Hemingway, *In Our Time* (New York: Charles Scribner's Sons, 1925).

21. Hemingway made the same point about the inability of modern medicine to account for the ineradicable connection between birth and death in "The Quai at Smyrna," which he later added as an introduction to the entire collection. On a quai full of refugees—a British officer reports—women continued to have babies. The problem was that "you couldn't get the women to give up their dead babies. . . . Had to take them away finally. Then there was an old lady, most extraordinary case. I told it to a doctor and he said I was lying." Brought before him on a litter, the woman drew up into a birthing position as she died. "I told a medical chap about it and he told me it was impossible" (p. 10).

22. John Locke, *The Second Treatise of Government* (New York: Liberal Arts, 1952), ch. 5.

23. The story is introduced by a vignette describing the surprise on a German soldier's face when the Americans "pot" him as he reaches the top of a wall and is preparing to jump down into an unidentified garden. In the

story itself, Marge is also surprised when she goes to meet her lover by the lake—in the apparent peace of a natural garden. There is no security or "Garden of Eden" free from the threat of death and the resulting inconstancy—however apparently pacific and even idyllic the circumstances. Likewise—Hemingway suggests—there is no real innocence or loss thereof. As Melville suggested in "The Line" (Chapter 60 of *Moby Dick*), all human beings face the prospect of immediate death—whether they recognize it or not.

24. Hemingway indicates how thoughtless and cruel such camaraderie can become in the introductory vignette. Having set up a wrought-iron house gate as a road barrier, the narrator then celebrates the ease with which his team shoots down the German officers who try to climb over—forgetting the purpose of the war as well as any sense of humanity. The narrator reports, "We were frightfully put out when we heard the flank had gone, and we had to fall back."

25. By describing in the introductory vignette the execution of six Greek ministers shot against the wall of a hospital, Hemingway reminds his readers that institutions specifically established to preserve human life do not and cannot counteract the destructive effects of competition and conflict. Politics is an arena—even a cause—of such conflict, more than it is a solution.

26. Bugs is rather ambiguous, in fact, about Ad's relation to his wife. After insisting that "they wasn't brother and sister no more than a rabbit," Bugs twice reiterates that she "looked enough like him to be twins" (pp. 77–78). Hemingway suggests that there is a natural tendency toward incestual relations between brother and sister in the story "Soldier's Home" (see below in the text) as well as "The Last Good Country." In the latter, he shows Nick run off to the woods with his sister "Littleness."

27. Despite both his love for Maria and his sympathy for the Spanish republicans, Roberto in Hemingway's *For Whom the Bell Tolls* (New York: Charles Scribner's Sons, 1940), p. 463, comes to exactly the same conclusion. Unable to ride away from an attack with his girl and the gypsies because he is wounded, Roberto insists that she go on without him: "What I do now I do alone. I could not do it well with thee. . . . That people cannot do together. Each one must do it alone." As Hemingway demonstrates in the stories that follow Nick's wounding, love cannot overcome the fact of death.

28. All the protagonists of the next five stories have something in common with Nick, even though no one of them is identical with him. Wirt Williams failed to see the point of the difference between Nick and the other protagonists—they represent alternative possible outcomes—when he found it hard "to accept Krebs as Nick in 'Soldier's Home,' and George as Nick in 'Cat in the Rain,' [although] the logic of the chronicle insists upon it." *The Tragic Art of Ernest Hemingway* (Baton Rouge: Louisiana State University Press, 1981), p. 36.

29. Since the unnamed soldier in the story following Nick's wounding has an affair with a nurse named Luz in the hospital—as Frederick Henry does with Catherine Barclay in Hemingway's subsequent novel, *Farewell to Arms*

(New York: Charles Scribner's Sons, 1929)— it is tempting to identify the soldier with Nick, and both with Henry. (Henry also has a friend named Rinaldi.) Like Catherine, Luz stays on night duty; and like Henry, the soldier on crutches does many of her rounds. Again like Catherine and Henry, "they wanted to get married, but there was not enough time for the banns, and neither of them had birth certificates. They felt as though they were married, but they wanted everyone to know about it, and to make it so they could not lose it" (p. 84). They do lose it after the armistice, however, when the soldier goes home to find a job and Luz takes up with a major. The major never marries Luz as he promised, and "[a] short time after, [the soldier] contracted gonorrhea from a sales girl in a Loop department store" (p. 85). Love does not enable human beings to conquer death, because—like all things human—love, too, is transitory. (Catherine does not leave Henry for another man, but she dies in childbirth.)

30. Just as in Chapter 5 of *In Our Time,* the six ministers are shot against the wall of a hospital, so the wounded soldier is pulled next to the wall of a church. Neither institution provides any real protection from death, Hemingway suggests. Readers learn that Nick was wounded at Fossalta only in a later story, "A Way You'll Never Be," in Ernest Hemingway, *Winner Take Nothing* (New York: Charles Scribner's Sons, 1927), pp. 63–85. The fact that Richard Cantwell also returns to Fossalta as the place where he was wounded at the beginning of Hemingway's *Across the River and into the Trees* (New York: Charles Scribner's Sons, 1950), pp. 17–18, indicates the extent to which Hemingway has his protagonists share the same fundamental, formative, shattering experience.

31. In the next story, when Harold Krebs's mother urges him to settle down and get a job because "God has some work for everyone to do. . . . There can be no idle hands in His kingdom," the ex-soldier thus responds, "I'm not in His kingdom" (p. 98).

32. Having been at Belleau Wood, Soissons, the Champagne, St. Michel, and in the Argonne, Krebs does not want to talk about the war when he first arrives home. Later when he feels the need to talk, no one wants to hear about it. His town has heard too many atrocity stories to be thrilled by actualities. Krebs finds that to be listened to at all he must lie; and after doing this twice, he too has a reaction against the war and against talking about it.

33. "All of the times that had been able to make him feel cool and clear inside himself when he thought of them; the times so long back when he had done the thing, the only thing for a man to do, easily and naturally, when he might have done something else, now lost their cool, valuable quality and then were lost themselves" (p. 90).

34. Nausea at the emptiness of modern life is a theme of Nietzsche's work, as it became also a theme in the work of Jean-Paul Sartre. Unlike Hemingway, neither Nietzsche nor Sartre associated that nausea particularly with untruth, however. Hemingway made the association, because he thought that meaning is to be found in pure—that is, true—feeling. That truth is what Krebs lost.

35. In the sequel to the story Hemingway reminds his readers that there were women somewhat ready at hand. "He was still a hero to his two young sisters." Harold's favorite sister even tells all her friends that he is her beau.

"Couldn't your brother really be your beau just because he's your brother?"
"I don't know."
"Sure you know. Couldn't you be my beau, Hare, if I was old enough and if you wanted to?"
"Sure. You're my girl now." (p. 97)

As in the story of Ad, Hemingway again hints that incest may be the most natural—certainly it is the least conventional—form of association. Brother need not be introduced to sister; they are already tied by affection and common experience.

36. Whereas Plato in the *Republic* (New York: Basic Books, 1968), passages 414b–15c, suggested that a just government would have to be founded on a "noble lie," Hemingway concludes that all governments are based on lies and that none can therefore be just.

37. Hemingway had originally published the vignettes separately in a volume entitled *in our time*. (Using no capitalization in the title was the publisher's idea—not Hemingway's. The absence of capitals in the title of the original collection provides a convenient way of distinguishing the earlier collection of vignettes from the later collection of vignettes and stories.) By leaving "L'Envoi" as an unnumbered postscript and making two of the original 18 vignettes from *in our time* into "stories," Hemingway created a book of 15 chapters in which one of the original vignettes—"The Revolutionist"—became central.

38. As a journalist, Hemingway reported both the revolutionary conditions in Italy following the disastrous Allied defeat at Caporetto and the likelihood of nationalistic fascist response. Although Northern Italian workers supported revolution—he observed— they were not willing to undertake the harsh measures necessary actually to bring it about. He also predicted the probability of a fascist reaction. See Robert O. Stephens, *Hemingway's Nonfiction* (Chapel Hill: University of North Carolina Press, 1968), pp. 180–92.

39. Hemingway's first novel, *The Sun Also Rises* (New York: Charles Scribner's Sons, 1926), was also intended to be a response to—rather than an affirmation of—Gertrude Stein's comment, "You are all a lost generation." Although Hemingway took the title of the novel from the section of Ecclesiastes that he quotes after quoting Stein on the frontispiece, most critics seem to have ignored the significance of the recurring natural cycle: "One generation passeth away, *and another cometh; but the earth abideth forever*. The sun also rises, and the sun goeth down . . .; unto the place from whence the rivers come, thither they return again" (emphasis added). Unlike the Biblical author, Hemingway regards the source to which all return as natural, rather than divine. In both *In Our Time* and his subsequent novel, he presents life or the generative cycle as a kind of response to European nihilism.

40. In the third of the émigrés stories, Hemingway shows that the young

gentleman and his wife have been arguing, probably over the prospect of an abortion. (See the more explicit argument in "Hill like Elephants," in Hemingway, *Without Women,* pp. 39–44.) Their guide does not understand what is bothering them. Excited by the prospect of beginning a new life as a guide, he attributes all the misunderstanding to differences in language: "Part of the time he talked in d'Ampezzo dialect and sometimes in Tyroler German dialect. He could not make out which the young gentleman and his wife understood best so he was being bilingual. But as the young gentleman said, Ja, Peduzzi decided to talk altogether in Tyroler. The young gentleman and the wife understood nothing" (p. 130). Misunderstanding is not merely the result of a failure to communicate, Hemingway indicates. It is rooted in a more fundamental form of alienation. The much older guide had hoped to become part of a new little free and egalitarian society. Having called the young man *"caro"* several times with no objection, Peduzzi is looking forward to repeating the expedition the next day. But the young gentleman warns him, "I may not be going . . . very probably not" (p. 135). Hemingway later reveals that he omitted "the real end of it which was that the old man hanged himself. This was omitted on my new theory that you could omit anything if you knew that you omitted and the omitted part would strengthen the story and make people feel something more than they understood." *The Moveable Feast* (New York: Charles Scribner's Sons, 1964), p. 75. (The statement refers to what has often been dubbed Hemingway's "iceberg" theory of writing after his earlier statement in *Death,* p. 192: "If a writer of prose knows enough of what he is writing about he may omit things that he knows and the reader, if the writer is writing truly enough, will have a feeling of those things as strongly as though the writer had stated them. The dignity of movement of an iceberg is due to only one-eighth of it being above water. [On the other hand, a] writer who omits things because he does not know them only makes hollow places in his writing." Hemingway may have taken this notion from the postimpressionist painter of whom he was so fond. Cézanne also intentionally left out a great deal. Richard W. Murphy, *The World of Cézanne 1839–1900* (New York: Time-Life, 1968), p. 77. The order of the stories in *In Our Time* points to the suppressed meaning, however. Like Peduzzi, all the émigré couples are disappointed in their own desire to find a new life, because they fail to face the source of their dissatisfaction with the old.

41. The first such émigrés depicted by Hemingway are "Mr. and Mrs. Elliot [who] tried very hard to have a baby," but—at 40— she proves too old. Fifteen years her junior, Hubert Elliot had not really intended to marry Cornelia. "He had been in love with various girls before he kissed Mrs. Elliot and always told them sooner or later that he had led a clean life. . . . He wanted to keep himself pure so that he could bring to his wife the same purity of mind and body that he expected of her. . . . Nearly all the girls lost interest in him" (p. 110). Cornelia first praised his purity (she was Southern by birth), and then his lovemaking. They were married, and he took her to Europe—just

as he later takes some friends who admire his poetry to the château in Touraine that he has rented for the summer. Touraine turns out to be hot, so Elliot's friends follow another rich (unmarried) poet to the seashore. The Elliots get tired of trying so hard to have a baby in the big hot bedroom. Ceding his bed finally to the older female companion whom his wife convinced him to bring to Europe, Elliot writes poetry late into the night in his own room. He has already sent the check to the publisher to bring out his volume. Hemingway leads the reader to doubt that Elliot's poems will have any more passion or perception than his married life. Neither art nor education constitutes a substitute for experience, and Hubert has very little. He remains a man of pure ideas.

42. In the following story, Hemingway shows another young American couple—living in Italy—in which the wife wants to settle down and have a child. Looking out the window of their hotel, she spots a kitty trying to avoid the rain by hiding under a table, and insists on going out to get it. Finding the cat gone, she returns to the room and expresses her sense of dissatisfaction to her husband George: "Don't you think it would be a good idea if I let my hair grow out? . . . I get so tired of looking like a boy" (pp. 120–21). When he responds that he thinks she looks "pretty darn nice," she continues: "I want to pull my hair back tight and smooth and make a big knot at the back that I can feel . . . I want to have a kitty to sit on my lap and purr when I stroke her. . . . And I want to eat at a table with my own silver and I want candles." Impatient with such domestic desires, George tells her to "shut up and get something to read." Like Nick as a boy at the cabin in the Michigan woods, George uses books as a means of escape.

43. Like the boy Nick who used to put down his book to go squirrel hunting, Joe in "My Old Man" loves his father. He does not know that his father helped fix races—trying to amass enough money to return home to the States with his son. Joe does remember his "old man" telling him about when "he was a boy in Kentucky and going coon hunting, and the old days in the States before everything went on the bum there. And he'd say 'Joe, when we've got a decent stake, you're going back to the States and go to school.' 'What've I got to go back there to go to school for when everything's on the bum there?' I'd ask him. 'That's different,' he'd say." (p. 168) When his father is killed in an accident, Joe is thus shocked to hear a bystander comment as they take the body away: "The crook . . . had it coming to him." Although the old friend comforting the boy urges him not to "listen to what those bums said. . . . Your old man was a swell guy," Joe concludes, "I don't know. Seems like when they get started they don't leave a guy nothing" (p. 173).

44. I therefore disagree fundamentally with Kenji Nakajima's presentation of *"Big Two-hearted River" as the Extreme of Hemingway's Nihilism* (Tokyo: Eichosha, 1979). Nakajima provides a useful summary of many different critical interpretations of the story.

45. Hemingway, *Moveable Feast*, p. 75. Sheridan Baker, *Ernest Heming-*

way: An Introduction and Interpretation (New York: Rinehart, 1976), pp. 31–38, has interpreted the whole story— especially the short tense sentences and Nick's stated desire not to think—as a reaction to his wounding in the war.

46. The fact that Nick does not return to his family's cabin—but goes, rather, to fish on another river in the same general neighborhood—is but one indication that he has not entirely settled the problem represented by his past, and particularly by his father.

47. Nick's satisfaction with finding a "good place" and making it his home should be contrasted with the waiter's meditations on the plight of the old man in "A Clean Well-lighted Place" in Hemingway, *Winner*. Having tried to commit suicide the week before, the old man stays in the "clean, well-lighted cafe" until forced to go home. "What did he fear?" The waiter muses. "It was not fear or dread. It was a nothing that he knew too well. It was all a nothing and man was nothing too. . . . Some lived in it and never felt it but he knew it all was nada y pues nada y nada y pues nada. Our nada who art in nada. . . . Now, without thinking further, he would go home to his room. He would lie in the bed and finally . . . go to sleep. After all, he said to himself, it is probably only insomnia" (pp. 23–24). After he was wounded, Nick also suffered insomnia, but he conquered it—as he does his nihilistic disillusionment following the war—by going "back to trout-fishing, because I found that I could remember all the streams and there was always something new about them, while the girls, after I had thought about them a few times, blurred." "Now I Lay Me," in Hemingway, *Without Women*, p. 137. Nick finds himself at home and at peace only when he is alone in nature.

48. When Lieutenant Cantwell revisits Fossalta in Hemingway, *Across the River*, he stoops to relieve himself at the very place where he (and also Nick) was wounded. As part of the natural cycle, human beings first make dung, and then themselves finally decay.

49. Because Nick has been wounded, he is aware of his own vulnerability. As a result, he has an even keener sense of how good it is simply to feel alive. In *Death*, Hemingway argued that a matador has not really been tested until he goes back into the ring and faces death *after* being wounded.

50. Hemingway, *Nick Adams Stories*, pp. 240–41.

51. "I found the greatest difficulty, aside from knowing truly what you really felt, rather than what you were supposed to feel, and had been taught to feel, was to put down what really happened in action; what the actual things were which produced the emotion that you experienced." Hemingway, *Death*, p. 2.

52. Ibid.

53. Hemingway, *Death*, pp. 232–33: "One of [the] greatest pleasures [of killing] is the feeling of rebellion against death which comes from its administering."

54. Charles Fenton, *The Apprenticeship of Ernest Hemingway* (New York: Farrar, Straus, 1954), quoted by Slabey, "Structure of *In Our Time*." Jeffrey

Meyers, "Hemingway's Second War: The Greco-Turkish Conflict, 1920–22," *Modern Fiction Studies* 30 (Spring 1984): 25–36, gives the actual historical background for both this scene and the execution of the six ministers.

55. *Being and Time* was originally published in 1927, two years after *In Our Time*. Martin Heidegger, *Being and Time* (New York: Harper and Row, 1962).

56. Ibid., div. 1, ch. 5, sect. 30.

57. Ibid., div. 2, ch. 1, sects. 46–53. "Own-most" represents a translation of *eigentlich*—often less precisely rendered as "authentic."

58. See ibid., div. 1, ch. 5, sect. 38.

59. See Martin Heidegger, *Introduction to Metaphysics,* (New Haven, Conn.: Yale University Press, 1959), p. 37: "From a metaphysical point of view, Russia and America are the same; the same dreary technological frenzy, the same unrestricted organization of the average man."

60. Heidegger, *Being,* div. 2, chs. 4 and 5.

61. Most English- and French-speaking commentators have missed the historical definition of "possibility" and the connection between the individual's fate and his or her nation's destiny. Mark Blitz, *Heidegger's "Being and Time" and the Possibility of Political Philosophy* (Ithaca, N.Y.: Cornell University Press, 1982), and Michael Allen Gillespie, *Hegel, Heidegger, and the Ground of History* (Chicago: University of Chicago Press, 1984), represent exceptions. See also Otto Poeggler, *Der Denkweg Martin Heideggers* (Pfullingen, FRG: Neske, 1963), and Alexander Schwan, *Politische Philosophie im Denken Heideggers* (Cologne and Opladen, FRG: Westdeutscher Verlag, 1965).

62. Heidegger's statement about the absence of any difference between America (the United States) and Russia (the Soviet Union) in his *Introduction to Metaphysics* continues thus:

> At a time when the farthermost corner of the globe has been conquered by technology and opened to economic exploitation; when any incident whatever, regardless of where or when it occurs, can be communicated to the rest of the world . . . simultaneously; . . . time as history has vanished from the lives of all peoples. . . . We are caught in a pincers. Situated in the center, our nation incurs the severest pressure . . ., but our people will only be able to wrest a destiny from it if *within itself* it . . . takes a creative view of its tradition. All this implies that this nation, as a historical nation, must move itself and thereby the history of the West beyond the center. (pp. 31–32, emphasis added)

Although Heidegger was an active official of the Nazi party for only a short time—and the famous "turn" in his thought resulted in a much more passive stance toward the world—he never apologized for or disavowed his Nazi allegiance, even though the Nazis finally sent him to the Eastern Front. On the contrary, when his *Introduction to Metaphysics* was translated and reissued in the 1960s, Heidegger kept a statement about the "essential truth of National Socialism" in the text. He very explicitly continued to maintain that both liberal and Marxist-Leninist political systems need to be superseded. Because his philosophy influenced writers on the left like Jean-Paul Sartre even more—

perhaps—than it did thinkers on the right, the relation between Heidegger's philosophy and his politics continues to be a hotly debated topic. See Victor Farias, *Heidegger et le Nazisme* (Paris: Editions Verdier, 1988), for the latest round.

63. See Martin Heidegger, *Nietzsche: Nihilism* (New York: Harper and Row, 1982), for Heidegger's argument—first—that Nietzsche represents not the overcoming but the completion of nihilism, and— second—that people have to live through the nihilism necessarily associated with technology in order to see the light on the other side.

64. From Heidegger's point of view, Hemingway's attachment to a conception of nature in general and to pure sensation in particular kept the novelist within the traditional metaphysical understanding of "being" (originally equated with "nature" by the Greeks) understood as "presence." Heidegger would not, therefore, have been surprised that the American novelist proved unable to integrate his attachment to nature with his insight into the necessarily historical character of human existence—an insight that results from an authentic confrontation with the possibility of one's own death.

65. Hemingway dramatized the failure of human effort to have any lasting effect, in another story of a return to the state of nature: *The Old Man and the Sea* (New York: Charles Scribner's Sons, 1952). The old man Santiago risks everything to capture the marlin of his dreams, only to see it eaten up by sharks on his way back into the harbor. When he returns, the old man must therefore again depend on the boy whom he has taught how to fish for food— just as he did at the beginning of the story, before his great trial. Nothing changes.

8

Faulkner on Nature and History

William Faulkner tried to bridge the gap between nature and history that had made Hemingway despair of political progress, by showing that human nature itself is essentially historical. In *Go Down, Moses,* he reminded readers that human beings derive their sense of individual identity only by piecing together their experiences and memories over time. Likewise, in *Intruder in the Dust,* he showed that a sense of community is not rooted merely in a general feeling of shared experience. It rests—more fundamentally—on a sense of shared goals or aspirations that are held out as a promise or commitment into the future.

The view of the relation between nature and history that Faulkner presented in *Go Down, Moses* and *Intruder in the Dust* is very much like that of the French philosopher Henri Bergson.[1] Like Bergson, Faulkner insisted that nature is vital and dynamic, rather than static and dead.[2] Also like Bergson, he suggested not only that human beings are distinguished by their historical sense, but that this historical sense is also the ground of both freedom and progress.[3] Unlike the French philosopher, however, Faulkner made explicit the political implications of a creative view of nature and an historical understanding of humanity.

Human beings are all born with an equal right to life, liberty, and the pursuit of happiness, Faulkner affirmed. Having a right to liberty does not mean that all people are actually free, however. Like the authors of the Declaration of Independence, Faulkner recognized that these rights must be secured. History has generally been the story of human rapacity and oppression. But in contrast to Twain and Heming-

197

way, Faulkner insisted that there has also been progress.[4] The founding of the United States itself provided an example of such progress; the declaration of natural right as the only legitimate basis of government represented a step forward. Like Twain and Hemingway, Faulkner saw that Americans have not lived up to the principles of their own Declaration of Independence in the past. Past failure is not so much a reason to jettison the principles—he suggested—as to continue striving to realize them. The "self-evident" propositions of Declaration do not merely describe the freedom and equality that human beings had enjoyed in a prepolitical original condition; they announce an aspiration or goal to be achieved in the future.

Go Down, Moses

Both in *Go Down, Moses* and in its sequel—*Intruder in the Dust*—Faulkner inquired, in effect, what we should make of Americans' past failure to live up to their own political principles. As a result of his education in the state of nature in "The Bear," Isaac McCaslin gives the traditional American answer: They should disavow the past and begin anew.

When speaking in his own name, however, Faulkner expressed skepticism about the whole notion of a return to nature. Asked by an interviewer whether he—like Rousseau—thought that "we should return to nature to recover our whole and proper humanity," the novelist responded,

> I don't hold to the idea of a return. . . . Once the advancement stops then it dies. It's got to go forward and we have got to take along with us all the rubbish of our mistakes and errors. We must cure them; we mustn't go back to . . . an idyllic condition, in which the dream [made us think] we were happy, . . . free of trouble and sins . . . , because if time is a [forward] and continuous thing which is a part of motion, then we have to run into that [trouble and sin] again sooner or later and go through it again.[5]

Like George Santayana, Faulkner thought that when people are ignorant of history, they are doomed to relive it.

As in Twain's *Adventures of Huckleberry Finn,* so also in *Go Down, Moses,* there is a significant difference between the views of the protagonist and those of the author. From his Indian mentor, Ike thinks he has learned that he can free himself of the evil heritage of slavery by giving up all property claims and thereby returning to a more natural form of existence. Retelling Ike's story, Faulkner shows that it is impossible for human beings to return to the state of nature or to a purely natural level of consciousness because human nature itself is historical.

In reading *Go Down, Moses,* it is therefore important to consider the account that Ike gives of the reasons he has decided to repudiate his patrimony as told in "The Bear" within the context that Faulkner originally set for it.[6] Although *Go Down, Moses* might appear to be merely a collection of stories about race relations in the United States,[7] each story was designed—in fact—to shed further light on Ike's interpretation of his own, his family's, and his nation's history.[8]

"Was"

Like Hemingway, Faulkner wrote the problem of understanding human historical experience into the very structure of his work. By fracturing the story into many separate units narrated by different characters at different times and places, Faulkner replicated the way human beings actually learn about the past. They put together accounts of events—events that they themselves have not and could not have witnessed—from other people representing a variety of perspectives, whose accounts taken in isolation from one another are unreliable because they are colored by the narrators' own interests, passions, and inabilities. People never really learn their own history in a smooth, chronologically organized narrative flow.

Like Isaac McCaslin, people are affected by things that happened before they were born or were fully conscious. Since they themselves cannot witness such formative events as their own birth, people must rely on the testimony of others. But—as Faulkner comically demonstrates by describing conditions in Ike's family through the eyes of his nine-year-old cousin, Cass—there is no such thing as an objective account. Just an external description of what happened—in the absence of any understanding of the passions and thought that produced the actions—is virtually unintelligible. In "Was," Faulkner does tell his readers something about Isaac's background. But the telling is clearly ironic.

Without any experience of sexual passion himself, Cass does not understand the force that drives Tomey's Terrel repeatedly to run away from the McCaslin plantation to hang around the cabin of a female slave named Tennie, who is owned by their next-door neighbor (Isaac's uncle-to-be), Hubert Beauchamps.[9] Nor does the boy perceive why his Uncle Buddy is so anxious to retrieve "Turl" before Hubert can catch him and bring him back—along with Hubert's sister Sophonsiba (Isaac's future mother)—for an extended visit.

Living with his uncles, the boy has also never seen the violent oppression undergirding the institution of slavery. He never asks, therefore, why his uncles do not keep Turl at home by chaining or whipping him. He certainly does not recognize—as readers of the entire family history will discover—that, as the product of his great-grandfather's incest with a black daughter, Turl is more purely a McCaslin than McCaslin "Cass" Edmonds himself. In the eyes of the boy, the hunt for the slave and the subsequent card game in which Hubert bets his sister and her dowry against the price of a slave is all just fun and games.

By implicitly contrasting the perspective of his narrator with that of his twentieth-century readers, however, Faulkner reminds the latter of how unjust and unnatural race-based slavery was. Isaac has reason to repudiate his past.

In the first place—Faulkner shows—slavery made it impossible to recognize the obvious family relation among human beings as a species. Turl cannot marry Tenny, for example, because Hubert Beauchamps will not "have that damn white half-McCaslin on his place even as a free gift" (p. 6).[10] Miscegenation is proof of a common nature; but to admit that common nature—Beauchamps intuits—is to recognize the injustice and forceful oppression at the base of the South's economy.

Race-based slavery did not merely divide and disrupt black families, moreover. It distorted white society, as well. Although Cass does not recognize it, his twin uncles Buddy and Buck are fundamentally opposed to the South's "peculiar institution." In pre–Civil War Mississippi, however, they cannot legally free their blacks. In practice, they come as close as they can, though. When his great-grandfather Carothers died—Cass reports—his uncles moved the "niggers" out of the slave quarters and into the big house that Carothers had not had time to finish. Securing the front door of the manor each night with a single nail, the twins let the blacks roam free—in effect—by leaving the windows and back door open.

Their opposition to slavery also has a great deal to do with their bachelor status. Women were closely associated with the social ambitions and pretensions underlying the slave system. Sophonsiba insists on calling her brothers' estate "Warwick"—for example—and on having a boy trumpet for meals from the top of two posts that she calls "gates." But the connection between marriage and slavery went much deeper than a fake facade.[11] With a family, a man acquires dependants and so must produce more than he himself consumes—if only to trade with others for things that he cannot produce. Thus, with a family, the man himself also becomes dependent on others.

To free themselves from the taint of slavery, Buck and Buddy had to minimize their economic needs. By doing all the domestic work himself, Buddy relieves the two brothers of any need for household help— slave or wifely. Living off the land themselves, they run the plantation primarily to support their black dependants.[12]

Slavery is unnatural because it denies the family relation of the human species. But the twins' opposition to slavery leads them—just as unnaturally—to deny the erotic drive and the consciousness of living in time, both of which are at the root of the human family as a social institution.

By remaining bachelors and living all by themselves in a cabin in the woods, the twins may appear to have preserved a boyish, Huck Finn–like existence—free from social convention and the associated restraints. Buck puts on his one tie when he goes to visit the neighboring plantation. In their wild household, dogs chase foxes indoors as well as out.

But the fact that their life is unconventional does not make it either free or natural. On the contrary, the twins appear to represent a case of arrested development. Sixty years old, they are still called "Buck" and "Buddy." They do not appear to have accepted adult responsibilities. These men are not contemptibly attempting merely to preserve the freedom of their youth or to avoid adult responsibilities, however. They are trying to respect the humanity of others, and thereby act morally. As a result, they find themselves in an inescapable bind. Their opposition to slavery—ironically enough—makes any change in existing conditions impossible. Things thus return to the *status quo ante* at the end of the story. Until the South loses the Civil War and slavery is abolished, Buddy will not permit Buck to marry Sophonsiba, and Hubert will not allow a half-white McCaslin on his land.

By rejecting their family's past and denying themselves all future progeny, Buck and Buddy find themselves living—in effect—outside of time. Outside of time, there is not only no progress; there is also no passion, because such intensity of feeling can be built up and sustained only over time—through memory. A man who forgets what he wants from moment to moment can hardly yearn for his beloved or grieve at her loss. Like his Biblical namesake, Isaac is born into his father's old age; but from "Was," we never learn how.

In "Was," Faulkner thus foreshadows the difficulties that Ike will encounter when he—like his father—repudiates the plantation that he inherited, in an attempt to free himself and his progeny from the injustice of slavery. Even more emphatically than his father, Ike also eventually finds himself living without a real family and outside of time. He is not, therefore, really part of any community. And as a result, he is not able to act effectively to overcome the errors and injustice of the past.

There is no purely private solution to past oppression and injustice. Effective action must be public. As Faulkner reminds his readers in the next story, however, legal enactments do not suffice. The Thirteenth Amendment may have formally freed the slaves, but it did not make whites recognize the natural liberty and equality of blacks.

"The Fire and the Hearth"

Human beings may be equal by nature, because of their family or species relation. But that common origin does not necessarily make them free. What then is the source and nature of their natural liberty?

In the confrontation between Cass's grandson Carothers "Roth" Edmonds and Carothers McCaslin's black great-grandson Lucas Beauchamps, Faulkner shows that human freedom does not consist in the absence of external restraints. The major barrier that individuals encounter in realizing their desires is, in fact, the free will of others. Roth will not recognize Lucas's equality, as the black desires; and Lucas will not admit his white relation's superiority, as Roth wants. The antagonistic relations between the races in the American South testifies—ironically—to the limited extent of freedom in the members of both.

Although human beings are not able either to choose their external circumstances (for example, the place and family into which they are born) or to control the thoughts and desires of others, they can and do shape their own lives. Like the philosopher Bergson, Faulkner observed that each individual has the power to create a personal identity as a result of the internal time consciousness that enables the individual to bring all his or her life experiences to mind at once and so to produce a unity out of the discrete events. Present frustrations provoke one to think about the past causes of those frustrations, as well as to contemplate ways of relieving them in the future. No one perceives his or her life simply as a series of essentially unrelated, accidental events. The unity of an individual's experience is not produced by any external cause, however. One creates the connections among one's various experiences through a process whereby past is continually interpreted and reinterpreted in terms of present and future.[13]

Individuals tend to make visible the distinctive principle of unity on the basis of which they create an identity out of their various experiences, through some fateful decision. Like Isaac, both Lucas and Roth make choices that determine the course and character of their entire lives. These choices are not dictated by any general, external factors—not biological, economic, historical, nor political. In the case of all three men, the fateful decision is a reflection of the character's own distinctive, internally produced understanding of their common heritage. By implicitly contrasting Isaac's interpretation of the family's history with the reactions that two other McCaslins have to their common ancestry, Faulkner shows that Isaac's understanding is by no means the only one possible. Because human freedom lies primarily in our ability to create our own identities as individuals through a reconstruction and reinterpretation of the past—Faulkner suggests—freedom is internal and intellectual more than it is external and political.

Because the source and character of human freedom is not externally visible, in the second story Faulkner uses an objective narrator to let readers see inside the minds of the major characters. He structures "The Fire and the Hearth" around two parallel scenes in which Lucas and Roth think over the entire course of their respective lives as each approaches the door of the other.

All interpretations of the past are not equally valid nor equally liberating. Despite their opposed understandings of their common heritage, Lucas and Roth both live in a constant state of frustration and rage. Neither feels free, because he defines his value as a human being too much in terms of the recognition of others—that is, in external rather than intrinsic terms.

The common biological origin that has been a source of shame for white McCaslins proves—somewhat ironically—to be a source of pride for the black. The fact that Carothers was his great-grandfather leads Lucas to believe that he is the equal of any white McCaslin (and better than most other people). By challenging Zack Edmonds—Roth's father—to a duel, Lucas proves to his own satisfaction that he is a "man." (Lucas thus has the same understanding of what makes a man a "man" as Colonel Sherburn in *Huck Finn.*) Whites generally refused to grant his equality, however; and Lucas is angry.[14]

Now as he approaches the door of the plantation manager, Lucas realizes that his anger dates back to the day of Roth's birth. On that day—having risked his life while fetching a doctor to assist the white woman in birth—Lucas discovered on his arrival home not only that Roth's mother had already died in childbirth, but also that his own wife—Molly—had moved into the big house to nurse the white baby along with her own. After she had stayed there for six months, Lucas felt the need to show that another man cannot simply seize, possess, and then dismiss his wife at will—not without a fight. So he went to Zack Edmonds's bedroom to challenge him.

> You knowed I wasn't afraid, because you knowed I was a McCaslin too.
> . . . You never even thought that, because I am a nigger too, I wouldn't dare. No. You thought that because I am a nigger I wouldn't even mind.
> (p. 53)

To make Zack recognize that he has feelings and a sense of honor as deep as any white man's, Lucas proposes to kill Zack, even though he expects to be lynched as a result.

Lucas proves to himself and to Zack that he is a "man," but he cannot force the rest of white society to recognize his equality. And without such public recognition, Lucas fails to secure it even within his own family. He "never forgot the amazed and incredulous rage with which he thought, *Why she ain't even knowed unto right now that I ever even suspects*" (p. 49, emphasis in original). And he concludes, *"Women. I wont never know. I dont want to. I ruther never to know than to find out later I have been fooled"* (p. 59). Twenty years later, Molly still urges him to follow "Mr. Roth's" directions about planting—orders that Lucas has regularly ignored. And those same 20 years later, Zack's son Roth treats Lucas as a "nigger"; and Lucas starts up his still in a secret insistence on his rightful independence from white rule.[15]

Like Lucas, Roth too is continually frustrated and enraged. His anger can also be traced to a conscious decision about the meaning of their common heritage. He made it the "day the old curse of his fathers, the old haughty ancestral pride based not on any value but on an accident of geography, stemmed not from courage and honor but from wrong and shame, descended to him. He did not recognize it then. He and his foster-brother Henry were seven years old" (p. 111).

On that day—asserting his superiority simply because he was able to—Roth forbade Henry from sleeping in the bed with him, and found himself "lying in a rigid fury of the grief he could not explain, the shame he would not admit" (p. 112). When Roth does become able to admit that shame and grief, it is too late. Lucas and Molly and their son Henry now serve him; he is no longer a member of the family.

Having exiled himself from the only family he has ever known, Roth then becomes angry when Lucas refuses to acknowledge the superiority of whites by acting like "a nigger." As he approaches Lucas's house, he finds that he is "raging—an abrupt boiling over of an accumulation of floutings and outrages covering not only his span but his father's lifetime too, back into the time of his grandfather McCaslin Edmonds" (p. 104).[16] Casting his mind back over the 20 years that he has managed the estate, "they seemed to him one long and unbroken course of outrageous trouble and conflict, not with the land or weather (or even lately, with the federal government) but with the old negro who in his case did not even bother to remember not to call him mister" (p. 116).

In contrast to his father, Roth has found it impossible to regard Lucas as an equal.[17] To recognize the black's humanity would not only be to deny his superiority as a white man, but also to admit his own injustice—and consequent inferiority.[18] To Roth, the evidence of their common origin and nature has thus become a source of "amazement and something very like horror."[19] Unwilling to admit that they are equals, Roth fears that, if Lucas be not his inferior, then he must be his superior.

Lucas merely insists on parity. "I'm the man here," he responds when Roth comes to plead with Lucas to give up the search for buried gold that had so distressed Molly. "I'm the one to say in my house, like you and your paw and his paw were the ones to say in his" (p. 120). To avoid letting the white man order his private affairs, Lucas initially agrees to a divorce.

Lucas takes back his agreement and promises to give up his search for the buried gold, however, just as Roth is about to take Molly before the judge. There is one thing more important than gaining recognition as an equal. That is maintaining "the fire on the hearth"—the symbol of the ongoing commitment of husband to wife, "for better or for worse, for richer or poorer." After all, it was primarily to have this commitment respected that Lucas had fought Zack in the first place.[20]

In opposition to the doctrine of the American Declaration of Independence, Faulkner seems to say that enduring communities cannot be founded merely on an assertion of rights. As in the case of Lucas and Roth, the assertion of rights merely produces an antagonistic standoff. Like the marriage between Lucas and Molly, enduring communities are founded on contracts, but the essence of the contract lies in a commitment to maintain the community in the future despite mutual disagreement and misunderstanding in the past.

"Pantaloon in Black"

Individual alienation and social divisions are both products—ironically—of human free will; but—Faulkner suggests—human beings can also use their free will to overcome both alienation and antagonism, by compacting to form a community. Or can they? Individual liberty is grounded in the human being's consciousness of living in time, but that consciousness itself can be traced to an awareness of his or her own future death—which distinguishes human from beast. Because it ultimately separates each individual from all others—Hemingway had argued—a real confrontation with the prospect of one's own death shows that a community based on true feeling is impossible. In light of the transitoriness of all things, all promises of lasting affection or concern become empty lies. In "Pantaloon in Black," Faulkner disputes this claim of Hemingway. It is failure of communication—Faulkner suggests—not mortality itself, that separates one human being from another.

Rider and Mannie had "built a fire on the hearth on their wedding night as the tale told how Uncle Lucas Beauchamp, Edmonds' oldest tenant, had done on his forty-five years ago and which had burned ever since" (p. 138)—the narrator explains. But six months later, Mannie died. Like Hemingway, Faulkner seems to suggest not only that human existence is essentially transitory and uncertain, but also that personal mortality constitutes an insuperable obstacle to the founding of an enduring union. Also like Hemingway, Faulkner seems to suggest that there is no reason or justice in human suffering. When Rider's uncle urges him to "put yo faith and trust in Him," the black man responds like one of Hemingway's postwar émigrés: "What faith and trust? . . . Whut Mannie ever done ter Him? Whut He wanter come messin wid me and—" (p. 145).

Rider is not distraught at the prospect of his own death, however. His inconsolable grief arises from the loss of his wife—and with her, all his hopes of future happiness. He desperately wants loving companionship. He is unable to find solace in the compassion of others, because he is unable to express his grief in terms that they can comprehend. External observers do not know what to make of the black's strange behavior. In the absence of the conventional signs of mourning, they cannot imagine what moves him to act as he does.[21]

Retold in Part 2 of "Pantaloon in Black" from a white deputy's external and conventional perspective, Rider's story no longer expresses the tragic, unfulfillable yearning to be reunited with his beloved that Faulkner dramatized in Part 1.[22] To the observer with no understanding of his inner anguish, the black's actions appear ridiculous— like those recounted with an equal lack of understanding in "Was." As the title of this story indicates, from the white deputy's point of view, Rider has become a "pantaloon in black."

> Them damn niggers. . . . They look like a man and they walk on their hind legs like a man, and they can talk and you can understand them and you think they are understanding you. . . . But when it comes to the normal human feelings and sentiments of human beings, they might just as well be a damn herd of wild buffaloes. (p. 154)[23]

In reflecting thus on Rider's strange behavior, the deputy has nevertheless made a decisive observation. Human beings are not defined by their external appearance or form. Their nature is to be found in their internal life.

The major source of the racial divisions that have plagued the American polity—Faulkner suggests in his third story—is too external a view of what it is to be a human being. So long as people fail to perceive that others are moved by the same hopes and fears that they themselves are moved by, they will continue to misunderstand and distrust one another. By making visible the inner passions that produce human behavior, the novelist not only shows his readers how to understand their history, but also brings out the true grounds of community in com-passion.

"The Old People"

Human beings do not understand what they share by nature because it is difficult, in fact, to discover what their nature is. To find out what human beings are like by nature, philosophers and poets have tried to discover their origins. As Rousseau reminded his readers in the "Discourse on the Origins of Inequality,"[24] however, these prehistoric orgins are neither directly observable nor recorded. It appears almost impossible to know for certain what "the old people" living in a "state of nature" were like.

Nonetheless, in relating the story of Isaac McCaslin's attempt to return to nature, Faulkner suggests that human beings can come to understand their own nature through a certain kind of introspection. Because their internal time consciousness enables them to bring past, present, and future together, they can discover the source of the continuities in human existence as well as of the divisions and differences in themselves. Isaac himself never comes to appreciate the fundamentally historical character of his own experience, however. Because he thinks of history as the record of human injustice and error, he continually seeks to escape his own sense of living in time by immersing himself in "timeless" nature.

Isaac learns about nature under the tutelage of an old Indian named Sam Fathers. Like many teachers, Sam influences his student as much through the example he sets as by his precepts. By withdrawing from civil society to live in the woods like his forebears—Isaac observes— Sam has freed himself from the heritage of slavery and recaptured his natural liberty. Isaac concludes that, by following Sam's example and relinquishing all claims to property, he too can free himself of the unjust heritage of the past by returning to a more natural form of existence.

Cass tells Ike that Sam has been able to regain his natural freedom because of his Indian blood.

> He was a wild man. When he was born, all his blood on both sides, except the little white part, knew things that had been tamed out of our blood so long ago that we have not only forgotten them, we have to live together in herds to protect ourselves from our own sources. (p. 167)

In retelling Sam's history, however, Faulkner shows that the Indian does not recapture his natural liberty and equality merely as a result of birth or race.

In fact, Sam was not born free—but a slave. His father Ikkemotubbe was a full-blooded Chickasaw chief. However, blood relationship did not prevent the chief from selling his son along with the boy's mulatto mother to Carothers McCaslin two years after Sam was conceived. Ikkemotubbe may have been corrupted by his contact with white society. In any case, his blood certainly had not preserved him from the evil effects of civilization.

If human beings be free and equal by nature, neither their freedom nor their equality is a product simply of biological inheritance. Nor—the story of Ikkemotubbe indicates—are they naturally held together in families or other forms of community by mere biological relation. As Faulkner suggested in "The Fire and the Hearth," both individual liberty and enduring community originate in the human being's consciousness of living in time. And that consciousness is transmitted to succeeding generations—he shows in "The Old People"—through history of a certain kind.

Both Cass and Ike attribute Sam's return to the ways of his forebears to his blood because it is by no means clear how else he could have acquired knowledge of his ancestry. Sam never knew his father; he was raised entirely by and among blacks. No one could understand how Sam's heritage had been transmitted to him. Isaac thought that Sam might have first heard the stories he tells about the old people—his ancestors—from another Chickasaw named Jobaker.

Whatever the source, the boy himself can testify to the stories' extraordinary effect. For, as Sam talked,

> those old times would cease to be old times and would become a part of the boy's present, not only as if they had happened yesterday but as if they were still happening. . . . And more: as if some of them had not happened yet but would occur tomorrow, until at last it would seem to the boy that he himself had not come into existence yet. (p. 171)

Past experience could be revived by its becoming part of a living person's present consciousness. That revival occurs through the telling of tales that lead listeners to empathize with the desires and frustrations of their ancestors. Without such empathy—Faulkner showed in the preceding stories—it is impossible to understand history or to recognize human nature as such.

By bringing together past, present, and future, the inner time consciousness that makes human passion and personal identity possible also enables each individual to perceive the continuity in human history. And in that continuity—in the consciousness of living in time that distinguishes human beings from other forms of existence—each finds his or her nature, as well. In "The Old People," Faulkner thus suggests that human nature is more spiritual than it is physical. Indeed, at the end of the story, he indicates that nature as a whole is pervaded by a vital spirit. It is a mistake to conceive of nature merely in terms of the mechanical movement of dead matter. No one and no thing wants to die and be forgotten.[25]

"The Bear"

Past experience or life is preserved by becoming part of the consciousness of a present human being; but in the process of incorporation, the past is also changed. In "The Bear," Faulkner shows that Isaac never simply recaptures Sam's almost animal level of consciousness. Where Sam is essentially a "wild man," Isaac is emphatically a man of conscience.

Like Sam and Isaac, all human beings share a certain natural heritage. As living creatures, they all ultimately have the same biological origin; they all participate—one way or another—in the history of the race as a whole; and they all possess the temporally structured consciousness that enables each to create his or her own identity. But precisely because human beings are individuals, by nature, the differences are as important as the similarities.

Although all human beings strive to produce some kind of unity out of the conflicting elements of their experience and heritage, those elements are different in each case because people live at different times and places and among various nations and races. According to Isaac's cousin Cass, Sam's consciousness is the arena of a battle between his black blood (or experience of submissive servitude) and his Indian blood (or fierce desire to be independent).[26] In "The Bear," Faulkner shows that Isaac's conscience or consciousness—also—is the locus of a battle, between different parts of his spiritual heritage. And because his battle is essentially a spiritual one, Isaac's story reveals more clearly than Sam's what human nature really is. If human life is essentially historical, any individual's nature cannot be known simply from biological origins. It is necessary to see something of what that individual can become over time.

Unlike Sam, Isaac—as a white American—has Christian "gifts." And Christianity presents a seemingly contradictory teaching about nature. As God's creation, nature as a whole is good. Human beings are a part of that creation, but—following Augustine—Christian theologians insist that humans are permeated with "original sin." That sin is essentially connected, moreover, to their knowledge of good and evil—or morality—and to their freedom of will.[27]

Because Isaac acts out of a sense of inherited guilt, his consciousness is always more explicitly historical than Sam's. Isaac always looks out of a defective past toward the future, in the hope of achieving something better. In returning to nature, he is not—like Sam—attempting to free himself from the errors of his immediate ancestors by reassuming older, more traditional patterns of behavior.[28] In returning to nature, Isaac is not just seeking a return to the past; he is seeking something better—even though he himself is never entirely sure what that "better" is. This yearning, this hope in the absence of any concrete knowledge of its object, is the force—Faulkner shows—that has animated all human history, if not nature as a whole. Although Isaac himself embodies it, he never entirely understands it. It is—in a word—love.

By returning to the state of nature on an annual hunting expedition into the woods, Isaac has learned that nothing can ever be simply saved or retained.[29] In the continual strife and striving of the hunt, no creature merely attempts to preserve itself. If living things do not continue to grow by destroying and consuming others—or are not themselves appropriated and incorporated—they will die and disintegrate into nothing.[30]

Like Hemingway, Faulkner suggests here that a human being cannot learn the truth about life or creation without directly confronting the fact of death. Before he was ten years old and allowed to accompany the men to the Big Bottom—Isaac reports—it had seemed to him that "they were going not to hunt bear and deer but to keep yearly rendezvous with the bear which they did not even intend to kill" (p. 194). In effect, he had conceived of nature, simply in terms of ritualistic repetition. His was a purely theoretical, external view. Only after he has actually seen "the print of the enormous warped two-toed foot" does Isaac realize "for the first time . . . that the bear . . . was a mortal animal and that they had departed for the camp each November with no actual intention of slaying it, not because it could not be slain but because so far they had no actual hope of being able to" (pp. 200–201).

By nature—Isaac sees—all living creatures must die. The embodying of the spirit of the wilderness is itself mortal.[31] The men had not been able to hunt it successfully because they did not have a dog large and strong enough to bay the huge animal. Loving the bear as the embodiment of the spirit of the wilderness, Isaac thrice reminds us that "he should have hated and feared Lion," because Lion is the dog who finally bays and kills Old Ben.

> Yet he did not. It seemed to him that there was a fatality in it. . . . It was like the last act on a set stage. It was the beginning of the end of something, he didn't know what except that he would not grieve. He would be humble and proud that he had been found worthy to be a part of it too or even just to see it too. (p. 226)[32]

Death is a necessary part of life, he has learned. Isaac does not, therefore, try to save the bear any more than he later tries to save the wilderness from the lumber company.

Merely witnessing the hunt, however, Isaac keeps himself from really participating in it. Once he even had an opportunity to kill the bear, when he ran under its raised paws to save a foolish little fyce. But he did not. And since he never really participates in the hunt, he does not entirely comprehend it or the spirit in which it is conducted.

His cousin Cass tried to help him understand his reticence—Isaac recalls—by reading to him from Keats's "Ode on a Grecian Urn."

> *She cannot fade, though thou hast not thy bliss, . . . Forever wilt thou love, and she be fair!*

Isaac did not get the point.

> *"He [wa]s talking about a girl,"* he said.
> *"He had to talk about something,"* McCaslin said. . . . *"He was talking about truth. Truth is one. . . . Courage and honor and pride, and pity and love of justice and of liberty. They all touch the heart, and what the heart holds to becomes truth, as far as we know truth."* (p. 297; emphasis in original)

Isaac did not want to kill the bear, Cass suggested—because he wanted the hunt to continue. Life is a perpetual chase, which would cease if its object or goal were ever realized. It is the striving—rather than the goal itself—that really matters.[33]

Although Isaac loves the chase, for him it retains the character of a ritualistic repetition because he does not understand the force that drives it. That force is love, Faulkner shows. The bear is killed not only as a result of Lion's size and the strength of his instinctive urge to hunt and kill, but also through the man Boon's love of the dog— however unnatural that love may appear.[34]

Boon always took Lion to his bed, until one day when—after Lion bayed Old Ben—Boon fired five shots from 25 feet and missed. Boon did not really care—apparently—whether his love were requited or not, but he was clearly capable of feeling shame before his beloved. Leaving the dog with Sam, Boon explains, "I aint fit to sleep with him" (p. 226). But in the end, his love enables Boon to do what he has never been able to achieve simply as a hunter. When Lion locks his jaws on Old Ben's throat and the bear begins ripping the dog's entrails out, Boon jumps on Ben's back and plunges his knife into the old bear's heart.

Not having experienced love himself, Isaac is no more able than the nine-year-old narrator of "Was" to identify its myriad forms and consequences. To witness is not to feel. His education in the state of nature is—Faulkner thus suggests—fundamentally defective. Isaac does not understand love and sex at 16 years of age, when he learns the full shame of his heritage—which has included not only slavery, but also incest—nor at 21, when he repudiates that heritage.

Reading the ledgers that record his family's history, Isaac discovered that—like Ikkemotubbe—his great-grandfather Carothers had travelled to New Orleans to purchase a mulatto slave whom he apparently did not really need. Whereas Ikkemotubbe eventually sold the slave and the child that he had by her, Carothers kept both mother and daughter as slave and eventually had a child—a boy—with the daughter. Ashamed of the incest, the mother committed suicide. Carothers eventually left to Tomey's Terrel a $1,000 bequest in his will—with no further explanation—"to be paid only at the child's coming of age, . . . not out of his own substance but penalising his sons with it. . . . *So I reckon that was cheaper than saying My son to a nigger* [Isaac] thought. . . . *But there must have been love. . . . Some sort of love"* (pp. 269–270; emphasis in original).

But what sort of love was it? Carothers seems to have been almost entirely indifferent to the fate of his progeny—and yet, not quite.

The similarities between the stories of the origins of Sam's and Isaac's families suggest that there has been a general, natural force at work. Like all animals—Faulkner reminds us—human beings are born as a result of sexual intercourse. The initial attraction does not hold the partners together, nor make them care for their progeny. Animals do not enslave their mates or their young, however. Nor do they forbid incest. On the contrary, intergenerational mating is fairly common among beasts. The two acts that Isaac most abhors in his family's history—slavery, and the abrogation of the incest taboo—both involve distinctively human institutions. Faulkner does not make explicit the connections between the two, however. He expects the reader to figure them out.

If we were to follow Isaac's initial suggestion and—like Aristotle and Marx—regard slavery as the basic manifestation of economic exchange, property, and the division of labor, we would see that forced labor and the incest taboo have formed the twin supports or foundations of the basic human family structure.[35] Like Carothers, men have taken wives not merely to satisfy their immediate sexual desires but also to give them children who will carry their name and the memory of their deeds into the future. To satisfy this desire to be remembered, men have supported women—as it were—in exchange for a guarantee of paternity through the domestication or limitation of female sexuality. To house and feed their women and children, men found that they needed both land and people to work it. As Aristotle argued, slavery is grounded in forethought—that is, the distinctive human ability to look to the future. Faulkner concludes that the most "natural" of all human associations, the family—being rooted in a sense of living in time—is itself fundamentally historical. In human life, nature and history cannot be separated.

Whereas the basic family structure embodies a clear sense of the necessary succession of generations, incest denies it through intermixture. By fathering a child on his own child, Carothers did almost become a "fatherless progenitor." Like Oedipus, he sought—in effect—to overcome both the physical and temporal limits of his own existence, by becoming himself the source of all.[36] His incest thus embodied the infinite, timeless quality of nature that Isaac feels in the woods. (p. 195). But Carother's "crime" also reveals an absence of the distinguishing characteristic of human existence: the sense of living in time.

Isaac himself does not understand all of this. He takes his grandfather's incestuous relation with his own daughter to exemplify the evils of slavery, because it represents a denial of the importance of respecting humanity, as such—the common relation—in its most extreme form. *"His own daughter. No No Not even him"* (p. 270).

Human beings do not respect family relations by nature—Faulkner insists—if by "nature" is meant simply biological origin. They form families and have children to perpetuate their name, because they recognize that they cannot—as Carothers perhaps only unconsciously desired—perpetuate their personal existences by becoming their own fatherless progenitors.[37] In direct opposition to Hemingway, Faulkner thus suggests that human society is rooted in our foresight into our own personal deaths.

As both Carothers and Ikkemotubbe demonstrate, human beings are not originally—or, in this sense, naturally—compassionate. As Isaac should have learned from the bear, nature as a whole is indifferent to the fate of individuals.[38] Human beings learn to recognize and respect the feelings of others only over time. By nurturing their children, they come to care first for tribe and then for nation. (They will—Faulkner predicted—finally even come to be concerned about the fate of the human race as a whole.[39])

As Isaac sees it, the inhumanity that Carothers and Ikkemotubbe displayed toward their brethren was due to the desire for property. In depicting his protagonist's return to the state of nature, Faulkner shows Isaac to be wrong about this. He has been too impressed with the external meaning of Sam's example. In nature—as Ike himself experienced at the Big Bottom—appropriation is a part of life. After all, the bear himself had staked out a territory. Property claims are not contrary to nature—not in the way Isaac thinks of them.[40]

Explaining why he refuses to accept the plantation that he has inherited, Isaac argues: God gave the world to mankind in common. Neither the Indians who sold it nor the white men who bought it had a right to seize and alienate the land. People like his grandfather acquired land and enslaved other people to work it because the former were greedy and wanted money. If human beings would control their acquisitive desires and would take only what they need to survive, injustice and oppression would cease. The whole notion of possessing "property" is based on a fundamental illusion. People cannot hold anything in perpetuity. They themselves are mortal, and things in nature are constantly changing.

If property is so very contrary to God's will—Cass responds to Ike's argument—then why has He allowed so many men to claim it? What does Isaac have to say, moreover, about the sons of Ham? There are stories in the Bible that seem to justify not only racial segregation, but even incest. Is there a fundamental difference or tension between Scriptural history and nature?

Neither Faulkner nor his protagonist accepts such a disjunction. Announcing a principle of interpretation that ought to be applied to his own story, Isaac suggests that the people who wrote down God's word sometimes got it wrong.

> Because they were human men. They were trying to write down the heart's truth out of the heart's driving complexity, for all the complex and troubled hearts which would beat after them. . . . It had to be expounded in the everyday terms which they were familiar with and could comprehend, . . . because if they who were that near to Him as to have been elected . . . to transcribe and relay His words, could comprehend truth only through the complexity of passion and lust and hate and fear which drives the heart, what distance back to truth must they traverse whom truth could only reach by word-of-mouth? (pp. 260–61)

In fact—Isaac asserts—human history constitutes a divine lesson in human suffering. The American South provides a prime example. Like the Biblical Jews whose liberation is celebrated in the Negro spiritual from which Faulkner took his title,[41] Southerners had been a stiff-necked people who needed drastic disciplinary measures. They had to endure not only the Civil War but also reconstruction and its aftermath to learn that "a nation of people could be founded in humility and pity and sufferance and pride of one to another" (p. 258).[42]

If Isaac is correct, property claims have—ironically and indirectly—been the cause of human improvement. Over time, the suffering occasioned by human rapacity has taught people to be more compassionate and—in that compassion—revealed the true grounds of human community. If human beings have indeed become better as a result of their historical experience, it is important both to remember the lesson and to continue the process. By trying to forget the past through a return to nature, Isaac does not draw the logical conclusion from his own analysis of American history. Faulkner expects that some of his readers will.

In retelling the story of Isaac's repudiation of his inheritance, Faulkner proposes a rather radical reinterpretation of the significance of the American Founding. It is possible—he suggests—to substitute an emphatically moral account for the commonplace and essentially economic understanding of the principles of the American regime.

The traditionally accepted rationale for the principles contained in the U.S. Declaration of Independence is taken from the philosophy of John Locke. Like Isaac, Locke argued that the earth originally belonged to humanity in common. Everyone had a right to appropriate what he or she needed to stay alive. Food that could not be eaten would spoil, so there was also a natural limitation on acquisition. (Who would work only to watch the fruits of that labor rot?) With the invention of money, however, this limitation vanished. The "rational and industrious" acquired most of the land; and the escalating conflict between those who owned land and those who needed food to eat threatened the lives, liberties, and possessions of all. To secure their rights, all joined together to establish government. Although wealth continued to be unequally distributed—Locke concluded—everyone was better off as a result of the enhanced level of production that followed from the securing of rights.[43]

As the expression of a deeper and vital natural urge—Faulkner suggests—the appropriation of property is itself neither the source of the problem nor the solution. The betterment of human beings involves more than their standard of living. American history shows, moreover, that the institution of government does not suffice to guarantee the rights of all people living under its jurisdiction.

In "The Bear," Faulkner thus proposed an alternative account of the history encapsulated in the famous "self-evident" truths. In the state of nature, human beings were free and equal insofar as no one had a right to rule anyone else. Paternity alone did not generate authority.[44] The institution of the family itself did not arise simply as a result of animal instinct; it depended on the human consciousness of living in time, and that consciousness was initially quite minimal. In the absence of any effective form of external restraint, individuals who were greedy and power hungry like Ikkemotubbe and Carothers not only sought but succeeded in obliging others to be the slaves of their desires, by means of forceful domination. The establishment of government was necessary to restrain such individuals. As the institution of legalized slavery in the United States illustrates, however, merely instituting government does not suffice. In fact, it enables men like Carothers to satisfy their desires even more effectively. Such people must be oppressed themselves (like the Puritans in England, and the Southerners after the Civil War) to learn that the only way they can secure their own lives and liberties is to respect the rights of others. Although they have made progress, Americans still have a way to go.

By coming to see that others share the same hopes and fears, human beings develop a sense of fellow feeling (or moral conscience) only over time. This progressive development of "humanity" arises out of the conjunction of the two sources or kinds of morality and religion— as explicated by Bergson[45]—which Faulkner dramatizes in the exchange between Isaac and Cass. Ike embodies the somewhat inchoate religious yearning that leads men and women of conscience to leave their past behind in search of a better life. Cass, on the other hand, represents the more worldly force of both natural and historical continuity. He conscientiously does what is necessary to keep individual, family, nation, and—ultimately—species alive. (Unlike Isaac, Cass has a son.) Thus, like Isaac and Cass, these two impulses exist in tension with one another. Nevertheless—Faulkner shows—neither form of morality is sufficient in and of itself.

You cannot repudiate your heritage—Cass argues—because you yourself are a product of that heritage, and that heritage is not all bad. Buck and Buddy tried to free the slaves—only to find that they had to take care of them, instead. Having found Turl's daughter starving in the "freedom" of her Northern husband's farm in Arkansas, how can

Isaac really believe that merely ceding the land to the blacks will constitute any more effective restitution than legal manumission? Would it not be better to carry on the work begun by his father: to affirm the good, rather than repudiate the bad? By giving up his place and position in society, Isaac will make himself unable to offer concrete help (as he himself recognizes when Lucas comes to claim his part of the legacy). Isaac's principled stance against slavery may be perfectly moral; but if so, morality appears to be perfectly ineffective.

Good intentions alone do not enable people to do good. But good works without good intentions are equally problematic. Isaac may not be able to overcome the ongoing effects of slavery; but by managing the plantation so efficiently, Cass is perpetuating the economic system that keeps blacks in thrall.[46]

To become effective, Isaac's desire to free human beings from past oppression must be shared and acted upon by others. Because people like Isaac do not entirely understand the spirit in which they act, however, any particular set of institutions that they join together to found is apt to be based partly on error—and to prove, in operation, to be somewhat unjust. Neither continuity nor progress can be realized, therefore, simply by persisting in past practice. By nature— Faulkner insists—nothing can be preserved. To found a nation on nature is—he suggests—to found it on an explicit recognition of human potential for improvement. That improvement is neither a matter of nor achieved through changes in external circumstances—economic or political. It originates in the human consciousness of living in time, and can therefore only be realized through changes in that consciousness.

"Delta Autumn"

In the last view Faulkner gives us of his protagonist, Isaac never does recognize the time-based, future-oriented character of the natural desire that he himself embodies: Because he wants—above all—to lose his sense of inherited guilt, Isaac thinks that the goodness both of sexual ecstacy and of his return to nature lies in the loss of all consciousness of self and time through immersion in a greater unity.

Isaac had initially experienced sex as the greatest temptation. When his wife tried to seduce him into reclaiming the plantation, he resisted even in surrender—saying,

> No, I tell you. I wont. I cant. Never . . . and he thought, *She was born lost. We were all born lost* then he stopped thinking and even saying Yes,

it was like nothing he had ever dreamed, let alone heard in mere man-talking. (pp. 314–15; emphasis in original)

Sexual ecstasy constitutes the greatest temptation of all for Isaac because the loss of self-consciousness is so complete.

The loss of self-consciousness in sexual union is only temporary, however. Travelling to the Big Bottom for the last time, he reflects on the difference between the transiency of human life compared to the eternity of the natural cycle.

summer, and fall, and snow, and wet and saprife spring in their ordered immortal sequence, the deathless and immemorial phases of the mother who had shaped him if any had toward the man he almost was, mother and father both to the old man born of a Negro slave and a Chickasaw chief who had been his spirit's father if any had. (p. 326)

He "would marry someday"—he recognized—"and they too would own for their brief while that brief unsubstanced glory which inherently of itself cannot last and hence why glory: . . . but still,"—he concludes—"the woods would be his mistress and his wife."

Associating sex with original sin, Isaac does not see the close connection between sexuality and the vital force that he—like Cass—sees pervading all creation. In trying to become reunited with nature, he does not even regard himself as the product of the sexual union between two discrete individuals. He understands himself more as a part of nature as a whole than as a distinctively *human* being.

Having withstood temptation on grounds of the essential goodness of nature, at the end of his life Isaac no longer believes in original sin. Indeed, he finally concludes that the moment of sexual unity is divine. As the origin of all existence, or Creativity—Isaac tells his companions on his last hunting trip—God realizes Himself completely only through sexual intercourse. "I think that every man and woman, . . . at that instant the two of them together [are] God" (p. 348).

No longer believing in original sin, Isaac is thus taken aback when he discovers that—like his grandfather—Isaac's nephew Roth Edmonds has merely left money for a son he had by a black woman (who is herself a McCaslin). The "sins of the fathers" do appear to descend through the generations. Human nature is not—as Isaac had come to believe—simply good.

And in Isaac's encounter with the woman, Faulkner dramatizes the inadequacy of Isaac's response to historical injustice. "Forget all this, forget it ever happened,'' he characteristically advises her. ''Go back North. Marry: a man in your own race. That's the only salvation for you—for a while yet, maybe a long while yet. We will have to wait'' (p. 363). Even Isaac still believes in the possibility of progress. *''Maybe in a thousand or two thousand years in America,* he thought. *But not now!''* (p. 361; emphasis in original). Progress depends, however, on the hope and passion that Isaac has always attributed especially to women.[47] ''Old man''—the woman responds—''have you lived so long and forgotten so much that you dont remember anything you ever knew or felt or even heard about love? (p. 363)

Contrary to Isaac's impression, history does not simply repeat itself. In contrast to his great-grandfather, Roth did not know that the black woman was related to him. He had acknowledged partial responsibility for his deeds, moreover, by leaving money himself—not shifting the burden to his descendants. There is, therefore, some ground for hope.

Progress does occur, but only incrementally and indirectly. The black woman had hoped for too much. She wanted to reform her lover. ''I would have made a man of him,'' she tells Isaac. ''You spoiled him. You, and Uncle Lucas and Aunt Mollie. But mostly you . . . when you gave to his grandfather that land which didn't belong to him . . . by will or even law'' (p. 360). As Faulkner showed in ''The Fire and the Hearth,'' Roth made himself the man he was by his own choice. His guilt was not simply or primarily a result of Isaac's decision not to accept responsibility for managing the plantation that he inherited. No one can free another or make that person better. Because every human being is inherently free, each has to decide for himself.

Isaac himself had acted with a hope of improvement in the future, Faulkner reminds his readers. He, too, was moved by love. As an old man thinking over his life, Ike recalls that he repudiated the land because of all the wrong and the shame, even while knowing he could not cure the wrong or eradicate the shame—''for his son at least'' (p. 351). Like his wife and the black woman, Isaac himself also had hoped for too much. Because he would not reclaim the plantation, his wife refused to have sexual relations with him after her one attempt at seduction. So in ''saving and freeing his son,'' he lost him. Like his father and uncle before him, Isaac had effectively denied himself any future progeny as a result of his attempt to repudiate the past entirely.

Because human beings live in time—Faulkner concludes—it is virtually impossible for them simply to forget. In any case, forgetting would merely return them to their barbaric beginnings. The only hope is to act into the future in such a way as to change the meaning of the entire course of events. Isaac himself continually looks over the course of his life and draws different conclusions from it.[48] Because the meaning of human history is not externally or finally determinable, people are free to change the character and significance of their own lives—as individuals and as nations.

"Go Down, Moses"

In the last and title story, Faulkner thus emphasizes the difference between himself and his protagonist by dramatizing the importance of remembering, rather than forgetting. All hopes of improving relations between the races in the United States depends on preserving the story of past injustice and all its consequent misunderstanding, so that people in the future can improve on the mistakes.

At the beginning of "Go Down, Moses," Lucas's wife Molly comes to the town lawyer, Gavin Stevens, to ask him to find her grandson Butch. "It was Roth Edmonds sold him," she says. "Sold him in Egypt. I dont know whar he is. I just knows Pharoah got him. And you the Law" (p. 371).

Molly had not succeeded in teaching her grandson "to be gentle with his inferiors, honorable with his equals, generous to the weak and considerate of the aged, courteous, truthful and grave to all" (p. 117) any more than she had Roth. Ordered off the plantation for stealing from the commissary, Butch Beauchamps had broken out of jail and fled north after he swung an iron pipe at the officer who caught him red-handed, stealing from a store in town. Stevens finally does locate him only because Samuel Worsham "Butch" Beauchamps reveals his true name to a census officer just before they execute him in Chicago for shooting a cop in the back.

In consideration of the old woman's feelings, Stevens works not only to raise money for a proper funeral—casket, hearse, flowers—but also to keep the story—the reasons why Butch died—out of the local papers. The lawyer is thus amazed when the editor relays Molly's final request. "Is you gonter put hit in de paper? I wants hit all in de paper. All of hit" (p. 383). Now that her grandson is dead, Stevens thinks, "she doesn't care how he died. She just wanted him . . . to come home right. She wanted that casket and those flowers and the hearse and she wanted to ride through town behind it in a car" (p. 383).

But Stevens is obviously wrong. Molly blames Roth for her grandson's death, and she is not satisfied by the conventional ritual. She wants the whole story remembered—in all its complexity. As a natural heir of old Carothers, Butch might have thought that he had a better right to the goods in the commissary than the "female-made" Edmonds. For the blacks, the law represents the force whereby the whites have kept them in subservience.[49]

Law represents an empty, superficial notion of human justice— Faulkner seems to say—because it cannot account for the "complexity of passion and lust and hate and fear" that produces crime as well as community effort. If Americans are to realize either their freedom as individuals or their unity as a people, they will have to found their nation in something more—something truer than a legal contract. They will have to join together more consciously in the striving to become something better that is human nature. As a novelist, Faulkner thus attempts to show his readers what their nature really is.

Intruder in the Dust

Faulkner did not intend to undermine either the justice or the utility of law in the United States. To be just and effective—he insists in the sequel to *Go Down, Moses*—law must rest on a deeper sense of community—of shared grief as well as glory—in which citizens recognize others as human beings like themselves.

In *Intruder in the Dust,* Lucas Beauchamps is saved from execution for a murder that he did not commit, by a youth named Charles "Chick" Mallison whom Lucas once rescued from drowning. The education that Chick subsequently receives from the black McCaslin is better—Faulkner thinks—than the education that Ike received in the state of nature."[50]

The first thing Lucas teaches Chick is that human relations are not merely matters of exchange. When Chick awkwardly tries to pay Lucas for the dinner that Molly has given him, the black man tells Chick's friends to pick up the money the boy dropped. And when Chick sends Lucas a Christmas present the next year, Lucas responds by sending Chick a jar of molasses. The price of a human life (or even relieving one's conscience—that is, one's sense of obligation) is not so cheap. Even more important, by refusing to act like a "nigger," Lucas forces the boy to question conventional Southern beliefs about the "natural" inferiority of blacks to whites.

Lucas does eventually ask Chick to do something for him—not in exchange for his own service or as a reward, but as a human being to a human being. Found holding a smoking gun in his hand over the body of a white man named Vinson Gowrie who was shot in the back, Lucas is arrested and put in jail. Knowing the prejudices of Southern white men and the law that they enforce, the black man refuses to tell his lawyer—Gavin Stevens—about the evidence that would exonerate him. Instead, Lucas asks Chick to go dig up the corpse.

It is a dangerous mission. Everyone in town thinks that Vinson Gowrie's red-neck family and friends are coming out that night to lynch his "nigger" murderer, and that they will certainly not take kindly to someone tampering with the grave. Gavin Stevens proves accurate Lucas's suspicions about the support and trust he is likely to receive from white men, moreover, when he forbids his nephew Chick from going out.

Nevertheless—Faulkner also shows—Southern whites are not so bad as Lucas thinks. Nor is the law so weak. Several white men risk their own lives in order to guarantee a fair trial for this "nigger" whom they believe to be guilty. Sitting behind the open doors of the jailhouse with a rifle across his knees, Will Legate admits,

> "I don't expect to stop them. If enough folks get their minds made up and keep them made up, aint anything likely to stop them from what they think they want to do. . . . But then, I got you and that pistol to help me."
>
> "Me?" the jailer cried. "Me get in the way of them Gowries and Ingrums for seventy-five dollars a month? Just for one nigger? And if you aint a fool, you wont neither."
>
> "Oh I got to," Legate said in his easy pleasant voice. "I got to resist. Mr. Hampton's paying me five dollars for it." . . .
>
> Suddenly the jailer . . . : "Don't mind me. I'm going to do the best I can; I taken an oath of office too. . . . But dont think nobody's going to make me admit I like it. I got a wife and two children; what good am I going to be to them if I get myself killed protecting a goddamn stinking nigger? . . . And how am I going to live with myself if I let a passel of nogood sonabitches take a prisoner away from me?" (pp. 53–54)[51]

Neither the individual's sense of duty nor the effectiveness of law is accurately described in terms of a contract, grounded in a calculation of self-interest. Both are matters of conscience.

Had the Gowries and the Ingrums come from the Beat Four neighborhood that night to take Lucas from the jailhouse and lynch him, neither the principled lawmen nor Chick's midnight trip to the graveyard would have saved the black. But—contrary to the expectations of the townspeople, both black and white—the lynch mob does not materialize. As Chick discovers on seeing the father at the grave site, the Gowries have stayed home to mourn their loss of a son. Like the white deputy in "Pantaloon in Black"—Faulkner shows—the people of Jefferson have denigrated their own humanity by failing to see not only the black victims but also their poor white oppressors as suffering, grieving human beings like themselves.

Once Chick, his black friend Aleck Sander, and the old and impoverished aristocrat Miss Habersham have dug up the grave, discovered that Vinson Gowrie's body is not in it, and reported that fact to Stevens, then the law represented by Sheriff Hampton works quickly and efficiently to get to the bottom of the matter—which turns out to have been fratricide. Stevens not only admits that his conventional preconceptions prevented him from discovering the truth and acting justly, but he also praises his nephew's courage and independence in challenging the established order. "Just dont stop," the lawyer reiterates (p. 210).

Chick is distressed, however, by the failure of the expectant mob to make any gesture of apology to Lucas. He is ashamed of his native people "who ran, fled not even to deny Lucas but just to keep from having to . . . say they were sorry . . . so they wouldn't have to say out loud that they were wrong" (p. 196).

Chick's uncle reassures him, however:

> Lucas will ultimately get his [apology and much more]; they will insist on it, they will have to . . . and not just Lucas . . . since what sets a man writhing sleepless in bed at night is not having injured his fellow so much as having been wrong. (p. 199)

According to Stevens, the mob did not flee from its conscience, but on account of its conscience. Although human beings almost universally deplore murder, they do not look on it with quite the horror with which they regard fratricide.

Humanity's conscience is rooted in the feeling of family, and Chick is reminded that he is part of the Southern family—its conscience, as it were. He would

> spring to defend them from anyone anywhere so that he might excoriate them himself without mercy since they were his own and he wanted no more save to stand with them . . . : one shame if shame must be, one expiation since expiation must surely be but above all . . . one: one people one heart one land. (pp. 209–10)

Feeling this unity so strongly, the youth accedes to his uncle's opposition to Northern attempts to make Southerners treat blacks as equals.

As he himself is the product of a complex heritage, so Chick realizes that his people and race are united (or divided) to the extent in which they share a common experience and understanding. Looking down at the Mississippi—the tie linking his region to the nation as a whole—the youth reflects on the causes of the division that was growing in the mid–twentieth century. Northerners and Southerners were becoming alienated from one another because Northerners had not shared the excruciating experience of war and defeat. The war that was fought to preserve the Union had—in fact—divided it even further. Lacking all understanding of Southerners' shame and suffering, Northerners misconstrued the intentions and actions of their fellow citizens—just as the white deputy had misunderstood Rider.[52]

And as Faulkner had suggested in the "The Old People," kinship is a matter of shared experience and understanding much more than it is a matter of blood or law. "Whereupon *once more his uncle spoke at complete one with him* and again without surprise he saw his thinking not be interrupted but merely swap one saddle for another" (p. 153; emphasis added).

As Isaac's education in "The Bear" culminated in his debate with a father substitute—his cousin Cass—so Chick rises to self-consciousness by deliberating with his uncle. But whereas Isaac and his cousin ended up being alienated from one another, Chick and his uncle come to full agreement.

In defying "the North . . . , not even a geographical place but an emotional idea" (as Chick puts it), Southerners—according to Stevens—

are not really resisting . . . progress and enlightenment. We are defending not actually our politics or beliefs or even our way of life, but simply our homogeneity from a federal government to which in simple desperation the rest of this country has had to surrender voluntarily more and more of its personal and private liberty in order to continue to afford the United States. (p. 153)

In resisting the North, Southerners are acting to preserve the true American heritage of self-government.

Americans form one people—Stevens argues—because they share the same notions of what is right. And because Americans believe that all men are created equal, blacks will eventually be fully integrated into white society.

Someday Lucas Beauchamp . . . will vote anywhen and anywhere a white man can and send his children to the same school anywhere the white man's children go and travel anywhere the white man travels as the white man does it. But it wont be next Tuesday. (p. 155)

Not the South, but the North, has failed to learn the lesson of American history. Rather than appealing to the conscience of their fellow citizens, Northerners continue to try to enforce equality with law. Attached to their own liberty, Southerners will not be dictated to or forced to obey the will of others. Rather than helping blacks by trying to force integration—Stevens continues—the North is thereby setting blacks back by forcing the Southern whites who have always helped them "willynilly into alliance with them with whom we have no kinship whatever in defence of a principle which we ourselves begrieve and abhor."[53] Southern whites are then

in the position of the German after 1933 who had no other alternative between being either a Nazi or a Jew or the present Russian (European too for that matter) who hasn't even that but must be either a Communist or dead. (p. 216)

The gravest danger to the preservation of human liberty in the twentieth century—Faulkner suggests—is that Americans will repudiate their own heritage on the grounds that it is unjust. Like Isaac, the nation would then cut itself off from the future—and thus all hope of realizing its highest aspirations—by repudiating the past.

Not just Southerners, but Americans generally, have failed to live up to their principles. That is what makes it so important for individuals like Isaac and Chick to stand up and say, "That is enough. This is wrong." But—Faulkner also reminds his readers—such acts of individual moral courage are effective only because they reawaken the conscience of the broader community. Were there no shared notions of right and wrong—just and unjust—individual acts of resistance would represent nothing more than futile protests, quickly silenced and easily forgotten.

Faulkner's Political Teaching

After he won the Nobel Prize for Literature in 1950, Faulkner became a cultural ambassador, sponsored by the U.S. State Department. In this capacity, he made many specifically political remarks; and in these remarks, the novelist made even more explicit the political implications of the view of human life that he had been presenting in his fiction.

"All men are born with the equal right to attain freedom, not to be given freedom, but the equal right to earn freedom and keep it as they are responsible and are strong and are truthful," Faulkner told an audience in the Philippines.[54] Taking the words of the Declaration of Independence literally, he emphasized that human beings are all born with a *right* to liberty—not liberty itself.

But—he concluded—individual freedom cannot therefore be secured by political action. "It is only man that can settle his problems; it can't be done by ideologies, by government, by politics, but by man himself. He has got to do it, and he has got to do it by believing in man."[55]

Like life, liberty can be destroyed by government, however. Preserving limited government—the rule of law, rather than arbitrary force—is necessary to secure human beings' right to attain freedom, even if it cannot secure freedom itself. Faulkner was therefore a pronounced anticommunist.

> I would say that the urgent question—truth—is freedom; that people—man—shall be free. And it seems to me that in the world today are not two ideologies facing one another that keep everybody else in fear and trembling. I would say that it is one ideology against a simple natural desire of people to be free, . . . and I don't believe that man can be free under a monolithic form of government. I think that he has got to have the liberty to make mistakes, to blunder, and to find his way, but primarily he must be free to say what he wants. . . . He must have complete freedom within a government which allows him the right to be a check on that government, that when he does not like that government, he can . . . try to change it.[56]

In order to maintain free government, however, people must believe that it is right. Political life requires a moral foundation. As Faulkner showed in his novels, human beings do not form lasting communities solely on the basis of sexual desire or economic interest. Without a common standard of right and mutual respect, there is no enduring basis of unity. Echoing Abraham Lincoln's "House Divided" speech, Faulkner thus predicted that blacks would eventually achieve all the rights enjoyed by whites in the United States, because the nation could not remain half slave and half free.

Because Faulkner emphasized the importance of historical continuity in maintaining a sense of community, M. E. Bradford has suggested that the novelist had a fundamentally Burkean perspective.[57] Like Edmund Burke, Faulkner insisted that change could only occur gradually. Like Burke, Faulkner also criticized the idea of beginning anew through a return to nature. Unlike Burke, however, Faulkner denied the possibility—much less the legitimacy—of conservatism per se, because "all life is in a constant flux. The only alternative to motion is stasis—death."[58] Where Burke was primarily concerned with maintaining the institutions that human beings had developed over time, moreover, Faulkner saw the ground of all human hope and value in the individual consciousness or conscience.

Although—in his opposition to totalitarian systems—Faulkner reaffirmed fundamental American commitments to the essential freedom and equality of all human beings and to limited government, his novels thus constitute a fundamental critique of the traditional philosophic basis of the state-of-nature theory underlying the Declaration of Independence. His novels ought to be of particular interest to political theorists precisely because he sought to ground American political principles in the sort of contemporary historical philosophy usually thought to undermine liberal beliefs.

Human beings are all "created equal," Faulkner insisted. But, as he showed in the story of Isaac McCaslin, undifferentiated nature does not provide an adequate foundation for either community or individual conscience. In the stream of becoming, all forms of existence are essentially equal because all are essentially transitory. By nature, individuation or individuality is simply ephemeral. The source of human value cannot be found in what humans share in common with the beasts, but must be located in their distinctive characteristic: their historical consciousness. The sense that human beings have of living out of the past and into the future is at the root not only of each individual's understanding of his or her own identity, but also of the most basic of all human communities: the family.

The Declaration speaks of the acts of "the people," but how—Faulkner implicitly asked—do individuals come together to form one nation or one people? Neither contract nor exchange represents an adequate accounting for the origins of an ongoing tie—much less, obligation. Contracts merely specify the terms on which obligations can be satisfied and terminated.

Individuals are able to extend themselves beyond the physical and temporal limits of their bodily existence—Faulkner observed—by means of their historical consciousness. Their sense of shared experience—a common heritage or history—as well as a common aspiration or goal unite them with others. The foundation of all communities is to be observed most simply in the family. That is why Faulkner could use a single family—the McCaslins—as a paradigm or model of the fate not merely of America, but even of all mankind. Where there is no desire to carry over something of the past into the future, there will be—as in the case of Buddy and Isaac—no family. Where the common origin is denied—as between Roth and Lucas—there will be no people. That origin is not simply biological (although people do tend—like Cass and Lucas—to understand it as such); it consists also in a common aspiration to have commonly held hopes realized in the future.

Individuals are never completely or permanently united with one another—not only because they live in separate bodies, but also because each consciousness is fundamentally unique. Alienation is a necessary consequence of individuation. There is a certain amount of mutual incomprehension and consequent division in every association—between husband and wife (for example, Lucas and Molly) and between parent and child (for example, Isaac and his father figure: his older cousin Cass) in the family; among blacks; between and among respectable and poor whites (as in the town of Jefferson); between North and South in the nation; between the United States and Europe in the West; and among the various nations and races in the world as a whole.

Some misunderstanding is inevitable—but the novelist can help. The difficulty with which Faulkner began is that the integrity, identity, and essential liberty of each individual lie in his or her consciousness, and that consciousness is not directly or externally observable. Through storytelling, however, the novelist can bring that inner life into the open and thus show his readers the true basis of both individuality and community.

By recalling their past achievements, the writer reminds his people of their higher aspirations.[59] Therefore, Faulkner saw himself—above all—as a public teacher. Such public teaching is particularly important in the United States—he thought—because Americans tend to forget their fundamental commitments to human liberty and equality by incessantly striving for material success.

> Today, we are too busy with physical well-being, but I do believe that all people want to be braver, kinder, more generous than they are. And that when they are brought to remember that they are not quite as generous as they might be, not as brave, that they have done not quite enough . . .

that they change. And that is the writer's position, his job: to remind people that people must be braver than they were, that they must be more generous, that they must have compassion. . . . And I think my people in the United States respond to that.[60]

Like Cooper, Faulkner emphasized the importance of maintaining a moral—rather than an economic—interpretation of the principles animating the American republic. And further like Cooper, Faulkner saw his task as an American author to be—first and foremost—that of maintaining this political morality.

Notes

1. Faulkner made explicit both his agreement with and his debt to Bergson. See "Interview with Louic Bouvard," in James E. Meriweather and Michael Millgate, eds., *Lion in the Garden* (Lincoln: University of Nebraska Press, 1963), p. 70. "When I asked if he were thinking of the God of Bergson, [Faulkner] said, 'Yes, a deity very close to Bergson's.' " Faulkner also stated that he "agree[d] pretty much with Bergson's theory of the fluidity of time." In 1949, he recommended Henri Bergson, *Creative Evolution* (New York: Random House, 1944), to his young protégé, Joan Williams, on the grounds that "it helped me." Joseph Blotner, *Faulkner: A Biography* (New York: Random House, 1974), p. 1302. Donald M. Kartiganer, *The Fragile Thread: The Meaning and Form in Faulkner's Novels* (Amherst: University of Massachusetts Press, 1979), has observed, "The philosopher Bergson is a clear presence in Faulkner's fiction, whether there by design or a common understanding" (p. 166). John Conder, *Naturalism in American Fiction* (Lexington: University of Kentucky Press, 1984), pp. 160–95, has given a Bergsonian reading of *The Sound and the Fury* (New York: Random House, 1956). See also Paul Douglass, *Bergson, Eliot, and American Literature* (Lexington: University of Kentucky, 1986).

2. Bergson, *Creative Evolution*.

3. See Henri Bergson, *Time and Free Will* (New York: Harper, 1980). In responding to Hemingway, Faulkner thus—in effect—also disagreed with Heidegger. In *Being and Time* (New York: Harper and Row, 1962) as well as in his lectures on *The Basic Problems of Phenomenology* (Bloomington: Indiana University Press, 1982), Heidegger had insisted that human life should be understood in historical—as opposed to natural—terms. Like Bergson, Faulkner suggested that the historical should be understood as a modification of nature, which is itself changing and evolutionary. In *Being and Time,* Heidegger had criticized Bergson's conception of time as an internal flux. Time has a structure, Heidegger insisted; it consists of a unity of past, present,

and future. The problem with the traditional conception of time is not, therefore—as Bergson had argued—that it substitutes an external, physical conception measurable in terms of motion through space for internal consciousness. The problem with the traditional conception is that—in conceiving of "being" (intelligible existence) as "presence"—the temporal or historical basis, context, and hence meaning of "presence" had been lost.

4. Serving as a cultural ambassador for the United States after World War II, Faulkner reiterated his belief in progress many times. For example, in Japan he commented, "And so, we get rid of the tyrants . . . , we get rid of a great deal of the misery which we created for ourselves [, as for example,] of little children who don't have to work in sweat factories any more. There's a certain amount of protection against a merchant selling one poison food, the condition of women is better, and the condition of the people who were slave people is better. That's some advancement. The artist has more freedom, at time he had to please some lord or baron for his daily bread, . . . he doesn't any longer. The philosopher can say what he wants." Meriweather and Millgate, *Lion,* pp. 109–10.

5. Quoted in ibid., p. 131. The specific examples of evils that Faulkner thought we could not avoid by returning to nature were wars and the atomic bomb.

6. When "The Bear" was published as a separate short story in *The Portable Faulkner* (New York: Viking Press, 1946), the novelist thus objected, "That story was part of a novel. . . . If [the publisher] had told me he was going to print it separately, I would have said, Take [section four] out, this doesn't belong in this as a short story, it's a part of the novel but not part of the story." Quoted in Michael Millgate, *The Achievement of William Faulkner* (New York: Random House, 1963), p. 202.

7. Faulkner initially described the volume in such terms to his publishers.

8. Critics and editors have been skeptical about Faulkner's claim that *Go Down, Moses* is a novel. Not only were most of the "chapters" first published separately as short stories, but there also is no single, unifying narrative. Faulkner clearly rewrote the component parts of the collection, however, to make it an artistic whole. Unlike all the other stories in the collection, "The Bear" was written especially for *Go Down, Moses*. Faulkner used a story called "Lion" that he had published in *Harper's* as the basis for section two of "The Bear," but most of the story was new. He also rewrote many of the other stories—changing them in important respects to integrate them. For example, he added the dramatic contrast between Lucas's and Roth's reflections on their past to "A Point of Law," "Gold Is Not Always," and "An Absolution" in composing "The Fire and the Hearth." Likewise, he expanded the meaning of an unpublished version of "Delta Autumn" by making Roth the father of the black woman's child. See John Pilkington, *The Heart of Yoknapatawpha* (Jackson: University of Mississippi Press, 1981), pp. 244–49.

9. Faulkner later explained that "the germ of the story was one of the

three oldest ideas that man can write about, which is love, sex. And to me it was comic. . . . Also it had a certain sociological importance in—to show my country as it really was in those days. The elegance of the colonial plantation didn't exist in my country. My country was still frontier." Frederick L. Gwynn and Joseph L. Blotner, eds., *Faulkner at the University* (Charlottesville: University of Virginia Press, 1959), p. 131; hereinafter *FU*.

10. Page citations are from William Faulkner, *Go Down, Moses* (New York: Random House, 1942).

11. See Aristotle, *Politics* (Chicago: University of Chicago Press, 1984), passages 1252a25–54b, on the roots of family organization in a combination of the male–female and master–slave relations.

12. Even so, human erotic desire threatens to undermine their economy. "They couldn't keep [Turl] at home by buying Tennie from Mr. Hubert"— Cass explains—"because Uncle Buck said he and Uncle Buddy had so many niggers already that they could hardly walk around on their own land for them" (p. 5).

13. Speaking to Bouvard, Faulkner stated, "I agree pretty much with Bergson's theory of the fluidity of time. There is only the present moment, in which I include both the past and the future." Meriweather and Millgate, *Lion*, p. 70. According to Bergson in *Time and Free Will*, the fluidity of the internal time consciousness is the source of an individual's freedom to create and recreate his or her own identity. "The free act takes place in time which is flowing and not time which has already flown [that is, the free act takes place in the individual's becoming conscious of the essential unity in the midst of the ongoing flow—and hence of the cumulative change that the duration of his or her own consciousness itself produces]. All the difficulties of the problem [concerning the relation between time or history and free will] arise from the desire to endow duration with the same attributes as extensity, to interpret a succession by simultaneity, and to express the idea of freedom in a language into which it is obviously untranslatable" (p. 221).

14. Lucas is angry when Faulkner first introduces him—because he has to stay up all night, dismantling and burying his still all by himself. He cannot get his wife and daughter to help, because he is burying his own still so he can call in the authorities to put his son-in-law-to-be George out of the business. George's careless stupidity would bring the sheriff down on every still in the neighborhood; and Lucas wants to keep his own in operation—as he has for the last 20 years—because now Roth has forbidden any "nigger" to do so. From the very beginning of the story, Faulkner thus shows that Lucas's desire to be recognized as an equal is threatening the integrity of his own family.

15. Myra Jehlen, *Class and Character in Faulkner's South* (New York: Columbia University Press, 1976), pp. 120–22, was thus simply wrong when she claimed that Faulkner does not dramatize Lucas's search for equality. Compare Margaret Walker, "Faulkner and Race," in Evans Harrington and Ann J. Abadie, eds., *The Maker and the Myth* (Jackson: University of Missis-

sippi Press, 1978), pp. 105–21, who has observed that Lucas is a black reader's favorite character; and Erskine Peters, *William Faulkner: The Yoknapatawpha World and Black Being* (Darby, Pa.: Norwood Editions, 1983), p. 159.

16. Warren Beck ignored the beginning of this statement of Roth's thoughts in *Faulkner* (Madison: University of Wisconsin Press, 1976), pp. 351, 547, when he suggested that Roth acts primarily out of gratitude to Molly. She raised him, and he is presumably going to talk to Lucas on her behalf; but he "was . . . if he told himself the truth, not [angry out of] concern for her at all."

17. Roth remembers asking his father about Lucas's refusal to call him "Mr. Zack." His father never seemed to mind. "You think that because Lucas is older than I am, old enough even to remember Uncle Buck and Uncle Buddy a little, and is a descendant of the people who lived on this place where we Edmonds are usurpers . . . is not reason enough for him not to want to say mister to me? . . . We grew up together, we ate and slept together and hunted and fished together, like you and Henry. We did until we were grown men" (p. 114). Concerned first and foremost about maintaining his own position, Roth responds "We're not usurpers. . . . That's not enough."

18. Like Buck and Buddy—Faulkner shows in "Delta Autumn"—Roth is unable to marry and have children because he feels guilty about the oppression of blacks. Manliness and sexual mastery are connected in his mind. As he thinks over the past, Roth comes to understand that something "had happened between Lucas and his father . . . because they were . . . men, not stemming from any difference of race nor because one blood strain ran in them both" (p. 115). And then in his late teens, he realizes it had been a woman. "My father and a nigger man over a nigger woman. . . . He didn't even think Molly's name. That didn't matter. *And by God Lucas beat him . . . else Lucas wouldn't be here*" (pp. 115–16; emphasis in original).

19. To Roth, their common origin and progenitor has thus become a source of "amazement and something very like horror. . . . He [Lucas] is more like old Carothers than all the rest of us put together, including old Carothers. He is both heir and prototype simultaneously of all the geography and climate and biology which sired old Carothers and all the rest of us and our kind . . . even nameless now except himself who fathered himself, intact and complete, contemptuous, as old Carothers must have been, of all blood black white yellow or red, including his own" (p. 118).

20. The "point" of "A Point of Law," from which Faulkner developed the first section of "The Fire and the Hearth," was that, by giving a wife immunity from testifying against her husband, the law itself recognizes the sacred character of the marriage relation—that it involved a confidence not to be breached even for the sake of obtaining legal justice.

21. In reaction to his wife's death, the black man first attempts a superhuman test of his physical strength by picking up a log ten times his weight. Then he tries to drown his sorrow with uncured whiskey. "Hit look lack ah just cant quit thinking," he laughs "with tears as big as glass marbles running across his face" (p. 159). After he slits the throat of a white foreman who has been

cheating his black logging gang at craps for years, Rider finds the oblivion that he sought—in death. Although the whites put him in jail—partly for his own protection—Rider escapes and is lynched by the foreman's relatives.

22. Because it does not concern the life of a member of the McCaslin family—Stanley Tick has argued—"Pantaloon in Black" is the only story that does not fit into the whole. "The Unity of *Go Down, Moses,*" reprinted in Linda Welsheimer Wagner, ed., *William Faulkner: Four Decades of Criticism* (Lansing: Michigan State University Press, 1973), pp. 327–34. "Pantaloon" does not dramatize an incident from Ike's or his family's life—I am suggesting—because it is designed to bring out the role of the novelist in portraying that life.

23. In light of the deputy's disparaging remarks about the nonhumanity of "niggers," it is important to note that the sheriff attempted to explain to Rider's aunt "what would happen to her too if them Birdsong kin catch us before we get him locked up." He thought that "her being in the car might be a good thing if the Birdsongs did happen to run into us." It might stave off violence. If the Birdsongs did try to take Rider, the sheriff would have to resist "because after all interference with the law cant be condoned even if the Birdsong connection did carry the beat for Mayhew last summer" (p. 157). As Faulkner shows even more dramatically in *Intruder in the Dust,* there were whites who risked their own lives to guarantee a black's right to a fair trial—less from concern for the black person, than from their own principles and conscience.

24. Jean Jacques Rousseau, "Discourse on the Origins of Inequality," in *The First and Second Discourses* (New York: St. Martin's Press, 1964).

25. When Ike tells Cass about the ghostly buck that Sam showed him the day he killed his first deer and was initiated into manhood, his cousin muses, "Think of all that has happened here, on this earth. All the blood hot and strong for living, pleasuring, that has soaked back into it. For grieving and suffering too [for] even suffering and grieving is better than nothing. . . . But you cant be alive forever, and you always wear out life long before you have exhausted the possibilities of living. And all that must be somewhere; all that could not have been invented and created just to be thrown away. . . . And the earth dont want to just keep things, hoard them; it wants to use them again. Look at the seed, the acorns, at what happens even to carrion when you try to bury it; it refuses too, seethes and struggles, too until it reaches light and air again" (p. 186).

26. Sam's "only visible trace of negro blood was a slight dullness of the hair and the fingernails, and something else which you did notice about the eyes, . . . in their expression, and the boy's cousin McCaslin told him what that was: not the heritage of Ham, not the mark of servitude but of bondage; the knowledge that for a while that part of his blood had been the blood of slaves. 'Like an old lion or bear in a cage,' McCaslin said. 'He was born in the cage and has been in it all his life; he knows nothing else. Then he smells something.

It might be anything. . . . But there for a second was the hot sand or the cane-brake that he never even saw himself . . . and probably does know he couldn't hold his own with it. . . . Then . . . all he could smell was the cage. That's what makes his eyes look like that.' 'Then let him go!' the boy cried. . . . 'His cage aint McCaslins,' he said'' (p. 167).

27. The tension between nature and history in the Western tradition has often been associated—even more broadly—with the tension between the Greek philosophical heritage, based as it was on the concept of an eternal nature, and the Scriptural notion of a God who reveals himself only in time, through history.

28. Faulkner emphasizes the difference between Sam's and Isaac's consciousness of their roots or the past at the end of "The Bear." During his last trip to the Big Bottom, Isaac comes upon a huge old rattlesnake, which he salutes as Sam had saluted the ghostly buck that embodied the spirit of the hunt: "Oleh, Grandfather." The difference in the symbolic progenitors is revealing: The buck represents the spirit of the hunt, but the serpent is the sign of the fallen angel. (Before a class at the University of Virginia, Faulkner stated that "the snake is the old grandfather, the old fallen angel." *FU,* p. 2).

29. As Faulkner later explained, his intention in "The Bear" was not to have his readers choose between man and wilderness. What he sought was rather to help readers understand "that change . . . must happen. . . . That no matter how fine anything seems, it can't endure, because once it stops, abandons motion, it is dead." *FU,* p. 277.

30. At first there was nothing" (p. 163).

31. Like Melville's white whale, critics have taken the bear to symbolize almost everything: God, nature, life, death, good, evil, and so on. Speaking at the summer seminars in American literature held at Nagano, Japan, in August 1955, Faulkner himself explained, "To me, the wilderness was man's past. . . . The bear was a symbol of the old forces, not evil forces, but the old forces which in man's youth were not evil, but that they were in man's blood, his inheritance, his impulses from that old or ruthless malevolence, which was nature." For Faulkner, history and nature are both always part of humanity's inheritance.

32. The casting of the hunt in the form of a tragedy should remind the reader of Ishmael's reflections on Ahab's quest in *Moby Dick.* (Faulkner reread Melville's novel every four years.)

33. It is not an accident, therefore, that—like the white whale—the bear has been taken to symbolize almost everything.

34. "It was as if Lion were a woman"—Ike observes—"or perhaps Boon was the woman. That was more like it—the big, grave, sleepy-seeming dog which as Sam Fathers said, cared about no man and no thing; and the violent, insensitive, hardfaced man with his touch of remote Indian Blood and the mind almost of a child" (p. 220).

35. Aristotle, *Politics,* passages 1252a25–54b; Karl Marx, "The German

Ideology,'' in Robert C. Tucker, ed., *The Marx-Engels Reader,* 2nd ed. (New York: W. W. Norton, 1978), pp. 149–63.

36. *Oedipus Tyrannus* exhibited basically the same drive and was there-fore—according to Seth Benardette—essentially a tyrant. He countenanced no limitations on his desires. "Sophocles' *Oedipus Tyrannus,*" in Thomas Wood-ard, ed., *Sophocles* (Englewood Cliffs, N.J.: Prentice-Hall, 1966), pp. 105–21.

37. In Plato's *Symposium* (Cambridge, Mass.: Harvard University Press, 1925), passages 206e–212a, Diotima suggests that human beings express their desire for immortality in three ways: by having children, by seeking fame, and by engaging in philosophy.

38. Sam observes of the bear: "He dont care no more for bears than he does for dogs or men neither" (p. 198). The contrast here between the in-difference of nature and the compassion that human beings show is—to this extent—like that Melville presents in *Moby Dick.*

39. See the discussion of Faulkner's political thought in the last section of this chapter.

40. The story of Isaac's education in nature thus ends not only with his witnessing the destruction of the woods by the saws of the lumber company, but also—rather ironically—with his confronting yet another claim to property. Emerging from the woods into a clearing, Isaac comes upon Boon. The slayer of the bear who embodied the spirit of the wilderness is pounding the pieces of his dismembered gun in front of a tree swarming with squirrels and shouting: "Get out of here! Dont touch them! They're mine!" The appropriation of property is not simply the negation or antithesis of natural community, Faulkner suggests; it is an expression of the vital force that constantly seeks to transform everything. Since no one can ever keep anything from changing—much less, in perpetuity—property understood as possession is an illusion. (The end of "The Bear" is clearly ironic—if not downright comic—because there is clearly no way that Boon can effectively maintain his claim to the squirrels.) Understood as appropriation and—so—change in one's physical circumstances, however, property is fundamentally an expression of humani-ty's essentially historical existence—of one's desire to distinguish oneself and so to give oneself an identity apart from the timeless lack of differentiation in nature.

41. The spiritual goes: "When Israel was in Egypt's land, Let my people go! Oppressed so hard they could not stand/ Let my people go! Go Down Moses/ 'Way down to Egypt's land/ Tell old Pharoah/ 'Let my people go!' " Harry T. Burleigh, ed., *Negro Spirituals* (New York: American Museum Science, 1922).

42. Isaac is careful, however, not to exonerate the North. On the contrary, he suggests that the abolitionists were hypocrits. "[When God looked] upon this land this South for which He had done so much with woods for game and streams for fish and deep rich soil for seed . . . and saw no hope anywhere and

looked beyond it where hope should have been, where to East North and West lay illimitable that whole hopeful continent dedicated as a refuge and sanctuary of liberty and freedom from what you called the old world's worthless evening. . . . [He] saw the rich descendants of slavers . . . passing resolutions about horror and outrage . . . to whom the outrage and the injustice were as much abstractions as Tariff or Silver or Immortality and *who employed the very shackles of its servitude* . . . as they did . . . the whirling wheels which manufactured *for a profit* the pristine replacements of the shackles and shoddy garments as they wore out and spun the cotton and made the gins which ginned it and the cars and ships which hauled it . . . *for that profit"* (p. 284; emphasis added). If Americans had traded natural liberty and bounty for oppression and profit, then the Northern manufacturers of textiles were even more guilty than the Southern slaveholders who supplied their raw materials.

43. John Locke, *The Second Treatise of Government* (New York: Liberal Arts, 1952), chs. 5 and 9.

44. Locke agreed that "parental" power was not the source of political power. *Second Treatise,* ch. 6.

45. Henri Bergson, *The Two Sources of Morality and Religion* (Garden City, N.Y.: Doubleday, 1935).

46. Some readers have taken McCaslin Edmonds as Faulkner's spokesman. But Faulkner indicates his differences with Cass quite clearly in an interview with Russell Howe: " 'My position is this,' said Mr. Faulkner. 'My people owned slaves and the very obligation we have to take care of these people is morally bad. It is a position which is completely untenable.' " Meriweather and Millgate, *Lion,* p. 258.

47. "Women hope for so much. They never live too long to still believe that anything within the scope of their passionate wanting is likewise within the range of their passionate hope" (p. 352).

48. Most significantly, at 21 years of age Isaac thought that "Sam Fathers set me free" (p. 300). But after his wife tried to seduce him, he concluded that "no man is ever free and probably could not bear it if he were" (p. 281).

49. The "furious laughter" that Butch emits through his teeth with blood and curses the night he is apprehended by the Jefferson policeman ought to remind readers of both Isaac's wife (who ended her attempt at seduction with laughter that he first mistook for crying) and Rider (who laughed with tears running down his face).

50. Hearing that Ike was a certain reporter's favorite character, Faulkner asked her: "And do you think it's a good thing for a man to reject an inheritance?

Q: Yes, in McCaslin's case. He wanted to reject a tainted inheritance. You don't think it's a good thing for him to have done so?

Faulkner: Well, I think a man ought to do more than just repudiate. He should have been more affirmative instead of shunning people.

Q: Do you think that any of your characters succeed in being more affirmative?

Faulkner: Yes, I do. There was Gavin Stevens. He was a good man but he didn't succeed in living up to his ideal. But his nephew, the boy, I think he may grow up to be a better man than his uncle. I think he may succeed as a human being." (Meriweather and Millgate, *Lion,* p. 215.)

51. Page citations are from William Faulkner, *Intruder in the Dust* (New York: Random House, 1948).

52. "With the whole vast scope of their own rich teeming never-ravaged land of glittering undefiled cities and unburned towns and unwasted farms so long-secured and opulent you would think there was no room left for curiosity. [Yet Chick perceived,] there looked down upon him and his countless row on row of faces which resembled his face and spoke the same language he spoke and at times even answered to the same names he bore yet between whom and him and his there was no longer any real kinship and soon there would not even be any contact since the very mutual words they used would no longer have the same significance and soon after that even this would be gone because they would be too far asunder even to hear one another: only the massed uncountable faces looking down at him and his in fading amazement and outrage and frustration and most curious of all, gullibility: a volitionless, almost helpless capacity and eagerness to believe anything about the South not even provided it be derogatory but merely bizarre enough and strange enough" (pp. 152–53).

53. Critics have insisted—correctly—on the difference between the character Gavin Stevens and the author William Faulkner. The novel is basically a story about a boy's initiation into manhood; and Chick's actions constitute a powerful critique of his Uncle Gavin's opinions. E. G. Andrew Lytle, *The Hero with Private Parts* (Baton Rouge: Louisiana State University Press, 1966), p. 131; Patrick Samway, "*Intruder in the Dust:* A Re-evaluation," in Glenn O. Carey, ed., *Faulkner: The Unappeased Imagination* (Troy, N.Y.: Whitston Publishing, 1980), pp. 83–109. Faulkner himself, nevertheless, said quite similar things about the civil rights movement in his own name. He agreed with Stevens to the extent that Chick does. See Charles P. Peavy, *Go Slow Now: Faulkner and the Race Question* (Eugene: University of Oregon Press, 1971), and "Interview with Russel Howe," in Meriweather and Millgate, *Lion,* pp. 157–66.

54. Meriweather and Millgate, *Lion,* p. 199.

55. Ibid., p. 200.

56. Ibid.

57. M. E. Bradford, *Generations of the Faithful Heart* (La Salle, Ill.: Sherwood, 1983).

58. Joseph L. Fant and Robert Ashley, eds., *Faulkner at West Point* (New York: Random House, 1964), p. 91.

59. "The writer must believe always in people, in freedom; he must believe that man must be free in order to create the art; and art is in my opinion one of the most important factors in human life because it has been art, literature, folklore, music, painting, which have been the record of man's rise from his beginnings. It is the writer's duty to show that man has an immortal soul. The

writer, the artist, the musician is the one factor which can show him the shape of his hope and aspirations of the future by reminding him of what he has accomplished in the past." Meriweather and Millgate, *Lion,* p. 212.

60. Ibid., p. 106.

9

Natural Right: An American Fiction?

American novelists' attempts to disclose the grounds of a politics based on natural right have become especially interesting in the twentieth century, because the development of contemporary scientific and historical theory has made the whole notion of right "by nature" (and hence the philosophical foundations of the U.S. constitutional system) highly questionable. By describing the world in terms of matter in motion, modern physical science suggests that there are no natural standards of right or justice. By showing that human beings evolved out of other species and that the things human beings value most highly have varied from era to era and from people to people, modern social science has indicated that there is nothing inherently human. And contemplating human history, many more people than just Isaac McCaslin have concluded that it illustrates human rapacity and injustice more than it records progress toward universal liberty and equality. Many Americans have now come to share the doubts of the disillusioned nineteenth-century reformers whom Hawthorne and Melville depicted. On both scientific and historical grounds, they have begun to wonder whether "America" represents the politics of natural equality and liberty or of economic exploitation and the power of technological force.

The justice of the American regime depends on its adherence to the principles of the Declaration of Independence. And, as the novelists following Cooper repeatedly showed, Americans have not lived up to their own stated ideals. There is, however, an even more fundamental problem: the status or foundation of these principles themselves. The "truths" of the Declaration are not really "self-evident."

241

According to the Declaration, governments are instituted to secure people's inalienable rights to life, liberty, and the pursuit of happiness. But—all our novelists saw—it does not make sense to secure the right to self-preservation unless life is worth preserving. The rationale for government thus depends on a previous demonstration of the value of human existence. It is difficult to determine exactly the natural rights of human beings or in what they inhere, however, because the things that make human life worth living are not externally visible. In attempting to show their readers what is truly good about human life—by nature—these novelists thus self-consciously undertook a task of fundamental political importance.

Our novelists usually presented their political teaching indirectly— even covertly—because they recognized popular resistance to explicit preaching. The indirect presentation was not merely a matter of rhetorical technique, however. If the goodness of human life is not externally visible, American political institutions ultimately must be founded in an appreciation of the beauty of the inner life of an ordinary person. As Cooper and his successors realized, that beauty cannot be described historically or analyzed theoretically. It can only be revealed through the work of the literary artist.

Because such revelations are explicitly fictional, their political and philosophical import has generally been ignored. Should contemporary readers become more aware of the ontological and epistemological limitations not merely of "science" but of discursive reason more generally, however, they might—as Martin Heidegger has argued— come to see the way in which poetic "fiction" not only can but also does shape communal human existence.[1]

These American novelists saw that modern science was challenging traditional American principles of natural right; and they responded— essentially—that modern science does not possess a true or adequate understanding of human nature. As a result, science is not able to account for its own source or roots, nor for its broader social and political effects. Cooper pointed out just such a lack of self-understanding in his savage satire of Dr. Bat. Hawthorne echoed Cooper's critique in his short story "The Birthmark" by suggesting that the intellectual pride epitomized by medical science, which refuses to accept the inherent limitations of human nature associated with mortality, has deadly practical effects. Melville also identified science with intellectual pride in his depiction of Ahab; and—like Cooper—he indicated that such pride ultimately undermines science itself, because a true scientist is forced to recognize and admit the limits of his own knowledge. Twain delivered a blistering attack on enlightenment politics in *A Connecticut Yankee in King Arthur's Court* by showing that the Yankee's attempt to modernize what we would call an "underdeveloped nation" (sixth-century England) culminated in a technological holocaust. And Hemingway insisted on the inadequacy of medical science in understanding the most fundamental issues of human life—the issues, literally, of life and death—from the very first story of *In Our Time*.

Because they agreed that a scientific view of human life is inadequate, these novelists did not concern themselves with science nearly so much as they did with the relation between nature and history. Literary fictions depict human experience, and the question confronting our novelists was—partly—whether that experience is more accurately portrayed in terms of a common nature or the story of a shared past. Here—we have seen—these were authors divided. Cooper, Melville, and Hemingway all sought to remind their readers of the essential goodness of human life by nature. Hawthorne, Twain, and Faulkner all responded that such idealized accounts of life in the state of nature constitute dangerous illusions with deleterious political results.

In one way or another, both groups of novelists subscribed to the basic tenets of social contract theory. Like Hobbes and Rousseau before them, they all suggested that human beings are essentially innocent.[2] Although much has been made of their "blackness,"[3] authors like Hawthorne and Melville showed that human beings harm others less from malice than through well-intentioned attempts to reform and save them. Their passions are greater than their knowledge, but—with the exception of the "naturally perverse" (that is, unnatural) like Claggart—human beings are not evil by nature.

Natural innocence does not preclude violent attacks on others. On the contrary, as all our novelists showed, passionate human beings with limited rationality will necessarily come into competition and conflict. Human beings might have been peaceable living in solitude in the state of nature, as Rousseau had argued. But all the novelists agreed with Hobbes (and also Rousseau) that, once humans encounter each other, they become engaged in a war of all against all. To secure peace, it was therefore necessary to establish a new form of polity.

However, our novelists disagreed about how successful that polity had been or could be, in light of American history. They disagreed about the significance of American historical experience with regard to the truth or adequacy of the American doctrine of natural right—in part, because they had different notions about what history is.

Like Aristotle, Cooper understood history as the recitation of factual detail—in opposition to the more philosophical poetic depiction of types.[4] And, Cooper concluded, the fundamental question that American history raises—whether might makes right—cannot be answered through such factual details.

Hawthorne—on the other hand—regarded history as the record of the results of human beings acting out their deepest passions. By observing the effect of unrestrained passion in the past—he hoped—people can learn the need for self-restraint.

Like Hemingway, Melville saw history primarily as the record of human suffering. In *Billy Budd* he finally took an ironic stance toward that history, because he realized that so much of the suffering has not been necessary. There are natural foundations for morality—or general human notions of right—as well as for political order and leadership; but pride in their intelligence makes human beings like Ahab and Vere perversely turn against their own natural sentiments.

If human nature remains the same—Twain concluded—human beings will continue making the same errors.[5] His contemporaries' faith in progress was thus fundamentally unfounded.

For Hemingway—even more than Twain—history constituted a record of the failures of political reform, and was therefore a source of profound disillusionment. For Faulkner—on the other hand—history represented not the antithesis, but the essence, of human nature.

More fundamentally—however—the novelists divided on the question of the relation between nature and history, because neither an appeal to nature in abstraction from history nor to history in abstraction from nature proved satisfactory. As Cooper saw both in the case of the American Revolution and in the whites' conquest of the lands of the Indians, accepting the legitimacy of what happened in the past merely because it did happen is—in effect—endorsing the doctrine that might makes right. To decide what should be preserved and what should be regretted and reformed, it is necessary to appeal to a transhistorical and natural standard. But simply to appeal to nature is to suggest that human beings cannot learn from their experience. Such an appeal thus destroys all grounds for hope of real improvement. Moreover, it leads people to forget the reasons that human beings left the state of nature in order to join civil society. If nature were simply good, and all conventions essentially empty—if not evil, as Hemingway concluded—then there would be no reason to hope for anything better.

By bringing nature and history together, Faulkner not merely united the major elements of this distinctive American tradition. He could also claim to have solved a fundamental problem in the philosophical origins or foundations of the American regime.

Like Cooper, Faulkner observed his compatriots' tendency to lose sight of the need to protect liberty and secure justice, in their frantic search for material prosperity. And further like Cooper, he responded by explicitly reasserting the responsibility of the writer to teach. Like Hawthorne, Faulkner insisted that human beings can learn from their history. Like Melville, however, he showed that each individual will take a different view of that history and that this difference in perspective is a source of division and alienation—as well as of color and beauty. To live is to change. On the basis of this insight, Hemingway concluded that there is no natural basis for any form of enduring social or political union and that human life is essentially solitary. In responding to Hemingway, Faulkner stressed the historical continuity in the consciousness of both individual and nation. Like Bergson, he showed that human perception is not composed of discrete moments or sensations. People understand their present experience in terms of the past, which they are nevertheless simultaneously and constantly reinterpreting in light of current events. This is a dynamic process in which individuals, nations, and the human race as a whole are free not merely to define but repeatedly to redefine themselves.

By applying a Bergsonian understanding of nature as "creative evolution" and of humanity as distinguished by a historical consciousness to emphatically American materials, Faulkner showed that the historicism characteristic of nineteenth- and twentieth-century European philosophy does not necessarily undermine American political principles.[6] On the contrary, such a historical understanding may strengthen them.

By using the arguments of a French thinker to reinterpret American political principles in a more moral and philosophically adequate fashion, Faulkner again followed the example first set by Cooper. And his work thus brought both the fundamentally philosophic character and the political function of classic American literature back to the fore.

Cooper had reinterpreted American political principles in a Rousseauian direction without ever naming the French philosopher in his novels. But in applying such a Rousseauian understanding to American circumstances, Cooper modified the practical meaning and implications of the French philosopher's arguments in important ways, as well. His Rousseauian reinterpretation of American political principles raised certain questions about both the foundation and meaning of those principles—questions that were pursued even further by later authors. Working within the tradition that Cooper originated, authors like Hawthorne and Melville anticipated some of the major insights of later European thinkers like Nietzsche and Freud. Unlike Nietzsche, however, these American novelists tried to use their insights to found liberal democracy on a new and better understanding of human nature.

The distinctively American literary tradition that Cooper initiated thus represents a series of reinterpretations of the meaning not only of American political principles, but also of the philosophic criticisms made of those principles. It is therefore both critical and creative. Although the repeated depiction of their protagonists' withdrawal from civil society to live in the state of nature clearly constitutes a criticism of contemporary American life, these novels do not merely reflect the artists' alienation from middle-class American society—as commentators like Marius Bewley have argued.[7] Nor, because the heroes usually return in the end, do these works constitute sophisticated rationalizations for the American political experiment—as critics like Sacvan Bercovitch have more recently contended.[8] Each successive depiction of human life in the state of nature represents an investigation of the purported basis of the American political creed and a reassessment of the practical meaning of the philosophic claims on which the United States was founded.[9]

Following Cooper's example again, later American novelists did not usually specify the names or arguments of the philosophers that they were using or addressing. As we have seen, they tended rather to incorporate such arguments into the organizing structure or plots of their works. The fact that they did not explicitly present philosophic arguments, as such, in their dialogues or narrative (in the manner of European novelists like James Joyce and Marcel Proust) does not mean that these American novelists did not know the works of the philosophers or that they addressed such issues only unconsciously.[10] Although all the novelists under study here were self-educated, they were widely read. Cooper's expulsion from Yale did not prevent him from studying the works of European political philosophers like Burlamaqui and Montesquieu, to whom he casually referred in his editorials. The list of Hawthorne's borrowings from the Athenaeum library in Salem, Massachusetts, shows that he, too, was an avid reader of the likes of Mandeville and Machiavelli. Melville indicated the results of some of his reading from his friend Duyckinck's library in his allusions to Plato and Spinoza in *Moby Dick*. If Twain did not know about Hobbes's description of the state of nature from reading *The Leviathan,* he certainly knew something about the main outlines of the argument from reading Lecky. Hemingway's reading included *Thus Spoke Zarathustra,* and Faulkner stated his debt to Henri Bergson on several occasions.

These novelists' failure to address the philosophers by name indicates more about the characters of their audience and about their intended effect than about their own knowledge. Visiting the United States at the time that Cooper was writing, Alexis de Tocqueville observed that Americans generally were both an extremely rationalistic and an aphilosophical people. They acted according to the principles of Descartes without even knowing his name.[11] Aware of their readers' antipathy to arguments by authority, our novelists appealed rather to the readers' own experience by enlisting their sympathies through empathetic identification with the protagonists of the stories. The novelists did not wish to convince their readers of the truth or error of any particular philosopher's arguments, in any case. They wished rather to affect—however indirectly—their readers' fundamental understanding of their own and their nation's life.

Historical influence is difficult (if not impossible) to prove, but there is some evidence that this literary tradition has had a broad—somewhat diffuse—popular effect.[12] In *The Closing of the American Mind,*[13] Allan Bloom observed that American political principles—as usually articulated and understood—represent an amalgam of Locke and Rousseau. Although the Lockean influence has been extensively documented and debated, no one has identified a specific source for the Rousseauian elements. Paul Spurlin has shown that Rousseau was widely read in America, both before and after the Revolution.[14] The excesses of the French sequel in 1789 made it impolitic for early American sympathizers like Jefferson to refer explicitly or positively to that revolution and its philosopher. A generation later when Cooper offered a Rousseauian reinterpretation of the principles of the Declaration in his tales of the Leatherstocking, he did not specify his French source by name. Encapsulated in the image of the simple woodsman who withdraws from civil society to live in the state of nature, Rousseau's ideas nevertheless persisted in American fiction—to be interpreted and reinterpreted by later authors and readers. Because these authors disagreed with one other about the political implications of such a fictional depiction of life in the state of nature, the collective impact of their work on popular American attitudes or mores has necessarily been diffuse. Nevertheless, it has been perceptible.

Taken as a whole, these fictional depictions of a man's withdrawal from civil society to live in the state of nature have served to reiterate the major elements of the social contract theory underlying the U.S. Constitution, in the face of European philosophical criticism. The novels have not taken the truth of the "self-evident" propositions of the Declaration for granted, however. On the contrary, by leading their readers to raise questions about the adequacy of the philosophic foundations of the American regime, these novelists have reminded us of the need repeatedly to reconsider the status of the "truths" themselves as well as their practical meaning in ever-changing historical circumstances. They thus invite us to join with them in the ongoing enterprise of political philosophy.

Notes

1. Martin Heidegger, "The Origin of the Work of Art," "What Are Poets For?" and "Poetically Man Dwells," in *Poetry, Language, Thought* (New York: Harper, 1975). As Richard Rorty has observed even more pointedly: "By the early twentieth century the scientists had become as remote from most intellectuals as had the theologians. Poets and novelists had taken the place of both preachers and philosophers as the moral teachers of the youth." *Philosophy as the Mirror of Nature* (Princeton, N.J.: Princeton University Press, 1979), p. 5.

2. Like Rousseau in *The Leviathan* (Indianapolis: Bobbs-Merrill, 1958), Hobbes argued that there were no standards of good and evil in the state of nature itself. Human beings could not be guilty of breaking a law—and so be "evil"—until a law was instituted.

3. See, for example, Harry Levin, *The Power of Blackness: Hawthorne, Poe, Melville* (New York: Knopf, 1958).

4. See Aristotle, *Poetics* (Cambridge, Mass.: Harvard University Press, 1926), passage 1451b.

5. For Twain as for Nietzsche, history consisted essentially in the eternal return of the same. Twain referred explicitly to Nietzsche in an observation included in his posthumous papers, to the effect that every human being has within him or her the potential to be like every other. See Bernard De Voto, ed., *Mark Twain in Eruption* (New York: Harper and Brothers, 1940).

6. Examples of the ways in which Continental thought threatened to undermine American political theory are plentiful. As Edwin Corwin has argued, the legal realists used European historical criticism of social contract theory to show that there was no such thing as a higher or natural law. Woodrow Wilson drew from his studies of Hegel and other German idealists to argue that the separation of powers was outdated and that the United States ought to institute a more scientific system of administration instead. Drawing

from the same German process school of thought, John Dewey tried to substitute a progressive understanding of education and democracy for the more individualistic, rationalistic, and hence legalistic American social contract tradition. And following Arthur Bentley, American social scientists adopted the arguments of the—again—predominantly German logical positivists to declare that all so-called principles were merely expressions of subjective emotional preferences, with no cognitive or factual foundation. Allan Bloom has made much of this "German connection" in *The Closing of the American Mind* (New York: Simon and Schuster, 1987), pp. 141–56; but he does not seem to have noticed the American literary response.

7. See, for example, Marius Bewley, *The Eccentric Design* (New York: Columbia University Press, 1957).

8. See, for example, Sacvan Bercovitch, *The American Jeremiad* (Madison: University of Wisconsin Press, 1978).

9. As Hans Georg Gadamer has argued, every re-presentation of the same story to a new audience living under different historical circumstances necessarily changes its meaning—and gives it new life. *Truth and Method* (New York: Seabury, 1975), pp. 142–50.

10. See Lionel Trilling, "The Meaning of a Literary Idea," in *The Liberal Imagination* (New York: Viking, 1950), pp. 282–93.

11. Alexis de Tocqueville, *Democracy in America* (Garden City, N.Y.: Doubleday, 1964), vol. 2, pt. 1, chs. 1–2.

12. Both Henry Nash Smith, *The Virgin Land* (Cambridge, Mass.: Harvard University Press, 1950), and Richard Slotkin, *Regeneration through Violence* (Middletown, Conn.: Wesleyan University Press, 1978), have traced its effect on and through popular literature.

13. Allan Bloom, *The Closing of the American Mind* (New York: Simon and Schuster, 1987).

14. See Paul Spurlin, *Rousseau in America* (University: University of Alabama Press, 1969).

Bibliography

Abele, Rudolph von. *The Death of the Artist: A Study of Hawthorne's Disintegration.* The Hague: Martinus Nijhoff, 1955.

Adler, Joyce. *War in Melville's Imagination.* New York: New York University Press, 1981.

Anderson, Douglas. "Cooper's Improbable Pictures in *The Pioneers,*" *Studies in American Fiction* 14 (Spring 1986):35.

Arendt, Hannah. *Totalitarianism.* New York: Harcourt, Brace, and World, 1951.

Aristotle. *Poetics.* Cambridge, Mass.: Harvard University Press, 1926.

———. *Politics,* trans. Carnes Lord. Chicago: University of Chicago Press, 1984.

Arvin, Newton. *Herman Melville.* Westport, Conn.: Greenwood, 1972.

Axelrod, Allen M. "The Order of the Leatherstocking Tales," *American Literature* 54 (May 1982): 189–211.

Baker, Carlos. *Ernest Hemingway: A Life Story.* New York: Scribner's, 1969.

Baker, Sheridan. *Ernest Hemingway: An Introduction and Interpretation.* New York: Rinehart, 1976.

Banta, Martha. "Escape and Entry in *Huckleberry Finn,*" *Modern Fiction Studies* 14 (Spring 1968): 70–80.

Barthes, Roland. *Mythologies,* trans. Annette Lavers. New York: Hill and Wang, 1972.

Baym, Nina. "*The Blithedale Romance:* A Radical Reading," *Journal of English and German Philology* 67 (October 1968).

———. "Head, Heart, and Unpardonable Sin," *New England Quarterly* 40 (March 1967): 31–47.

———. "Melodramas of Beset Manhood," *American Quarterly* 33 (Summer 1981): 123–39.

———"Passion and Authority in *The Scarlet Letter,*" *New England Quarterly* 43 (1970): 209–30.

———. *The Shape of Hawthorne's Career.* Ithaca, N.Y.: Cornell University Press, 1976.

Beard, James, ed. *The Letters and Journals of James Fenimore Cooper.* Cambridge, Mass.: Harvard University Press, 1960–68.

251

Beaver, Harold. "Herman Melville: Prophetic Mariner," in Richard Gray, ed., *American Literature: New Readings*. Totowa, N.J.: Barnes and Noble, 1983.

Beck, Warren. *Faulkner*. Madison: University of Wisconsin Press, 1976.

Becker, Carl. *The Declaration of Independence*. New York: Knopf, 1942.

Beecher, Jonathan, and Bienveau, Richard, eds. *The Utopian Vision of Charles Fourier*. Boston: Beacon, 1971.

Bell, Michael Davitt. *The Development of the American Romance*. Chicago: University of Chicago, 1980.

Benardette, Seth. "Sophocles' *Oedipus Tyrannus*," in Thomas Woodard, ed., *Sophocles*. Englewood Cliffs, N.J.: Prentice-Hall, 1966.

Bercovitch, Sacvan. *The American Jeremiad*. Madison: University of Wisconsin Press, 1978.

———. *The Puritan Origins of the American Self*. New Haven, Conn.: Yale University Press, 1975.

Bergson, Henri. *Creative Evolution*, trans. Arthur Mitchell. New York: Random House, 1944.

———. *Time and Free Will*, trans. F. L. Pogson. New York: Harper, 1980.

———. *The Two Sources of Morality and Religion*, trans. R. Ashley Audra. Garden City, N.Y.: Doubleday, 1935.

Berstein, John. *Pacifism and Rebellion in the Writings of Herman Melville*. The Hague: Mouton, 1964.

Bewley, Marius. *The Eccentric Design: Form in the Classic American Novel*. New York: Columbia University Press, 1957.

Blair, Walter. *Mark Twain and Huck Finn*. Berkeley: University of California Press, 1960.

Blitz, Mark. *Heidegger's "Being and Time" and the Possibility of Political Philosophy*. Ithaca, N.Y.: Cornell University Press, 1982.

Bloom, Allan. *The Closing of the American Mind*. New York: Simon and Schuster, 1987.

Blotner, Joseph. *Faulkner: A Biography*. New York: Random House, 1974.

Bohrer, Randall. "Cannibalism and Cosmology in *Moby Dick*," *Studies in Romanticism* 22 (Spring 1983): 65–92.

Boyd, J. P., et al., eds. *The Papers of Thomas Jefferson*. Princeton, N.J.: Princeton University Press, 1969.

Bradford, M. E. *Generations of the Faithful Heart*. La Salle, Ill.: Sherwood, 1983.

Brodhead, Richard H. *Hawthorne, Melville, and the Novel*. Chicago: University of Chicago Press, 1973.

Browne, Ray B. "*Billy Budd:* Gospel of Democracy," *Nineteenth Century Fiction* 17 (March 1963): 321–38.

———. *Melville's Drive to Humanism.* Lafayette, Ind.: Purdue University Studies, 1971.

Burdick, E. Miller. "The World as Specter: Hawthorne's Historical Art," *PMLA* 101 (March 1986): 218–32.

Burke, Edmund. *Reflections on the Revolution in France.* Indianapolis: Hackett, 1987.

Burleigh, Harry T. *Negro Spirituals.* New York: American Museum Science, 1922.

Carrington, George C. *The Dramatic Unity of Huckleberry Finn.* Columbus: University of Ohio Press, 1976.

Carter, Everett. "The Modernist Ordeal of Huckleberry Finn," *Studies in American Fiction* 13 (Autumn 1985): 169–72.

Chase, Richard. *Melville.* Englewood Cliffs, N.J.: Prentice-Hall, 1962.

Clark, Robert. *History and Myth in American Fiction, 1823–52.* New York: St. Martin's Press, 1984.

Clemens, Samuel (Mark Twain). *Adventures of Huckleberry Finn.* Berkeley: University of California Press, 1985.

———. *Autobiography,* ed. Charles Nieder. New York: Harper and Row, 1975.

———. *The Adventures of Tom Sawyer.* Berkeley: University of California Press, 1979.

———. *A Connecticut Yankee in King Arthur's Court.* Berkeley: University of California Press, 1982.

———. *Life on the Mississippi,* in *The Writings of Mark Twain,* Vol. 9. New York: Harper and Brothers, 1889.

———. "Literary Offenses of Fenimore Cooper," *North American Review* 161 (July 1895): 1–12.

———. *The Mysterious Stranger.* Berkeley: University of California Press, 1970.

———. *The Prince and the Pauper,* in *The Writings of Mark Twain,* Vol. 15. New York: Harper and Brothers, 1889.

———. *Pudd'nhead Wilson,* in *The Writings of Mark Twain,* Vol. 14. New York: Harper and Brothers, 1889.

———. *What Is Man?* New York: Harper and Row, 1917.

Coleman, Frank. *Hobbes and America: Exploring the Constitutional Foundations.* Toronto, Canada: University of Toronto Press, 1977.

Conder, John. *Naturalism in American Fiction*. Lexington: University of Kentucky Press, 1984.

Cooper, James Fenimore. *The American Democrat,* ed. George Dekker. Baltimore: Penguin, 1969.

———. *The Deerslayer*. Albany: State University Press of New York, 1987.

———. *Gleanings in Europe: Switzerland*. Albany: State University Press of New York, 1980.

———. *The Last of the Mohicans*. Albany: State University Press of New York, 1983.

———. *A Letter to His Countrymen*. New York: John Wiley, 1834.

———. *Letters and Journals*. Cambridge, Mass.: Harvard University Press, 1960.

———. *The Pathfinder*. Albany: State University Press of New York, 1981.

———. *The Pioneers*. Albany: State University Press of New York, 1980.

———. *The Prairie*. Albany: State University Press of New York, 1985.

———. *The Wept of Wish-ton-Wish*. St. Clair Shores, Mich.: Scholarly Press, 1970.

Cooper, Stephen. *The Politics of Ernest Hemingway*. Ann Arbor: University of Michigan Research Press, 1987.

Cox, James M. *Mark Twain: The Fate of Humor*. Princeton, N.J.: Princeton University Press, 1966.

Crews, Frederick C. "Criticism without Constraint," *Commentary* 73 (January 1982): 65–71.

———. *The Sins of the Fathers*. New York: Oxford University Press, 1966.

Daubner, Kenneth. "The American Culture as Genre," *Criticism* 21 (Spring 1980): 104–6.

Davie, Donald. *The Heyday of Sir Walter Scott*. New York: Barnes and Noble, 1961.

Davis, Sarah I. "The Bank and the Old Pyncheon Family," *Studies in the Novel* 16 (Summer 1984): 150–66.

Dekker, George. *James Fenimore Cooper, The Novelist*. London: Routledge and Kegan Paul, 1967.

Derrida, Jacques. *Speech and Phenomena*. Evanston, Ill.: Northwestern University Press, 1974.

———. *Spurs: Nietzsche Styles,* trans. Barbara Harlow. Chicago: University of Chicago Press, 1978.

Descartes, René. *Discourse on Method,* trans. Laurence J. LaFleur. Indianapolis: Bobbs-Merrill, 1950.

De Voto, Bernard, ed. *Mark Twain in Eruption.* New York: Harper and Brothers, 1940.

Diamond, Martin. *The Democratic Republic.* Chicago: Rand McNally, 1966.

Douglass, Paul. *Bergson, Eliot, and American Literature.* Lexington: University of Kentucky, 1986.

Dryden, Edgar. *Melville's Thematics of Form.* Baltimore: Johns Hopkins University Press, 1968.

Erwin, Robert. "The First of the Mohicans," *Antioch Review* 44 (Spring 1986): 149–60

Fant, Joseph L., and Ashley, Robert, eds. *Faulkner at West Point.* New York: Random House, 1964.

Farias, Victor. *Heidegger et le Nazism.* Paris: Editions Verdier, 1988.

Faulkner, William. *Faulkner at Nagano.* Tokyo: Kenkyusha Press, 1957.

———. *Go Down, Moses.* New York: Random House, 1942.

———. *Intruder in the Dust.* New York: Random House, 1948.

———. *The Sound and the Fury.* New York: Random House, 1956.

———. *The Portable Faulkner.* New York: Viking Press, 1946.

Fenton, Charles. *The Apprenticeship of Ernest Hemingway.* New York: Farrar, Straus, 1954.

Fesselring, Marion L. *Hawthorne's Readings.* Folcroft, Pa.: Folcroft Library, 1975.

Fetterly, Judith. "Disenchantment: Tom Sawyer in Huckleberry Finn," *PMLA* 87 (January 1972): 69–74.

Fiedler, Leslie. *An End to Innocence.* Boston: Beacon, 1955.

———. *Love and Death in the American Novel.* New York: Dell, 1969.

Fisher, Philip. *Hard Facts: Setting and Form in the American Novel.* New York: Oxford University Press, 1985.

Flora, Joseph M. *Hemingway's Nick Adams.* Baton Rouge: Louisiana State University Press, 1982.

Fogle, Richard Harter. "*Billy Budd*— Acceptance or Irony," *Tulane Studies in English* 8 (1958): 107–13.

Foucault, Michel. *Discipline and Punish: Birth of the Prison,* trans. A. Sheridan. London: Allen Lane, 1977.

———. *Power/Knowledge,* ed. and trans. Colin George. New York: Pantheon, 1980.

Franklin, Wayne. *The New World of James Fenimore Cooper.* Chicago: University of Chicago Press, 1982.

Freud, Sigmund. *Civilization and Its Discontents,* trans. Joan Riviere. London: Hogarth Press, 1946.

Gadamer, Hans Georg. *Truth and Method.* New York: Seabury, 1975.

Gillespie, Michael. *Hegel, Heidegger, and the Ground of History.* Chicago University of Chicago Press, 1984.

Ginsberg, Robert, ed. *A Casebook on the Declaration of Independence.* New York: Thomas Y. Crowell, 1967.

Goldwin, Robert A. "Locke," in Leo Strauss and Joseph Cropsey, eds., *The History of Political Philosophy.* Chicago: Rand McNally, 1962.

Green, Martin. *Re-apprisals: Some Commonsense Readings in American Literature.* New York: W. W. Norton, 1965.

Grunes, Dennis. "Preinterpretation and *Billy Budd,"* *Essays in Literature* 13 (Spring 1986): 106–13.

Gwynn, Frederick L., and Blotner, Joseph L., eds. *Faulkner at the University.* Charlottesville: University of Virginia Press, 1959.

Hagemann, E. R. " 'Only let the story end as soon as possible': Time and History in Ernest Hemingway's *In Our Time,"* *Modern Fiction Studies* 26 (Summer 1980): 255–61.

Hall, Lawrence. *Hawthorne: Critic of Society.* New Haven, Conn.: Yale University Press, 1944.

Hane, Norman R. "Nature's Moralist." Unpublished dissertation, University of Chicago, 1968.

Hamowy, Ronald. "Jefferson and the Scottish Enlightenment," *William and Mary Quarterly,* 3rd series, 37 (1979).

Hartman, Geoffrey H. *Criticism in the Wilderness.* New Haven, Conn.: Yale University Press, 1980.

Hawthorne, Nathaniel. *The Blithedale Romance and Fanshawe.* Columbus: Ohio State University Press, 1964.

———. *Complete Short Stories.* Garden City, N.Y.: Hanover House, 1959.

———. *The House of Seven Gables.* Columbus: Ohio State University Press, 1956.

———. *The Scarlet Letter.* Columbus: Ohio State University Press, 1962.

Hegel, G. W. F. *Phenomenology of Mind.* New York: Harper and Row, 1967.

Heidegger, Martin. *The Basic Problems of Phenomenology,* trans. Albert Hofstadter. Bloomington: Indiana University Press, 1982.

———. *Being and Time,* trans. John Macquarrie and Edward Robinson. New York: Harper and Row, 1962.

———. *Introduction to Metaphysics.* New Haven, Conn.: Yale University Press, 1959.

————. *Nietzsche: Nihilism*. New York: Harper and Row, 1982.

————. "The Origin of the Work of Art," "What Are Poets For?" and "Poetically Man Dwells," in *Poetry, Language, Thought*, trans. Albert Hofstadter. New York: Harper, 1975.

————. *The Question Concerning Technology*, trans. William Lovitt. New York: Harper, 1977.

Hemingway, Ernest. *Across the River and into the Trees*. New York: Charles Scribner's Sons, 1950.

————. *Death in the Afternoon*. New York: Charles Scribner's Sons, 1932.

————. *Farewell to Arms*. New York: Charles Scribner's Sons, 1929.

————. *For Whom the Bell Tolls*. New York: Charles Scribner's Sons, 1940.

————. *Green Hills of Africa*. New York: Charles Scribner's Sons, 1935.

————. *In Our Time*. New York: Charles Scribner's Sons, 1925.

————. *Men without Women*. New York: Charles Scribner's Sons, 1927.

————. *The Moveable Feast*. New York: Charles Scribner's Sons, 1964.

————. *The Nick Adams Stories*, ed. Philip Young. New York: Charles Scribner's Sons, 1972.

————. *The Old Man and the Sea*. New York: Charles Scribner's Sons, 1952.

————. *The Sun Also Rises*. New York: Charles Scribner's Sons, 1926.

————. *Winner Take Nothing*. New York: Charles Scribner's Sons, 1927.

Hirsh, John C. "The Politics of Blithedale," *Studies in Romanticism* 11 (Spring 1972): 138–46.

Hobbes, Thomas. *The Leviathan*. Indianapolis: Bobbs-Merrill, 1958.

Hoffman, Charles G., and Hoffmann, A. C. " 'The Truest Sentence': Words as Equivalents of Time and Place in *In Our Time*," in Donald R. Noble, ed., *Hemingway: A Reevaluation*. Troy, N.Y.: Whitston Publishing, 1983.

Hoffman, Daniel G. *Form and Fable in American Fiction*. New York: Oxford University Press, 1961.

House, Kay Seymour. *Cooper's Americans*. Columbus: Ohio State University Press, 1966.

Howe, Irving *Politics and the Novel*. New York: Vintage, 1957.

Hume, David. "Of the Origin of Government," and "Of the Original Contract," in *Moral and Political Philosophy*. New York: Hafner, 1948.

Jaffa, Harry V. "Inventing the Past," *St. John's Review* 33 (1981): 3–19.

————. "Tom Sawyer: Hero of Middle America," *Interpretation* (Spring 1972): 194–255.

Jefferson, Thomas. *Notes on Virginia*. New York: Norton, 1954.

Jehlen, Myra. *Class and Character in Faulkner's South*. New York: Columbia University Press, 1976.

Johnston, Kenneth G. "Hemingway and Cézanne: Doing the Country," *American Literature* 56 (March 1984): 28–34.

Kant, Immanuel. *On History*. Indianapolis: Bobbs-Merrill, 1963.

Kaplan, Harold. *Democratic Humanism and American Literature*. Chicago: University of Chicago Press, 1972.

Kartiganer, Donald M. *The Fragile Thread: The Meaning and Form in Faulkner's Novels*. Amherst: University of Massachusetts Press, 1979.

Kaul, A. N. *The American Vision*. New Haven, Conn.: Yale University Press, 1963.

Kelly, William P. *Plotting America's Past*. Carbondale: Southern Illinois University Press, 1983.

Kesselring, Marion L. *Hawthorne's Reading*. Folcroft, Pa.: Folcroft Library, 1975.

Kirkpatrick, Jeane. *Dictatorships and Double Standards*. New York: Simon and Schuster, 1980.

Kojève, Alexandre. *Introduction à la lecture de Hegel*. Paris: Gallimard, 1947.

Kolodny, Annette. *The Lay of the Land*. Chapel Hill: University of North Carolina Press, 1975.

Kort, Wesley A. "Human Time in Hemingway's Fiction," *Modern Fiction Studies* (1980): 579–96.

Lawrence, D. H. *Studies in Classic American Fiction*. New York: Thomas Seltzer, 1923.

Lefcowitz, A., and Lefcowitz, B. "Some Rents in the Veil: New Light on Priscilla and Zenobia in *The Blithedale Romance*," *Nineteenth Century Fiction* 2 (December 1966): 263–75.

Lettis, Richard, et al. *Huck Finn and His Critics*. New York: Macmillan, 1962.

Levin, Harry. *The Power of Blackness: Hawthorne, Poe, Melville*. New York: Knopf, 1958.

Levy, Leo B. "*The Blithedale Romance:* Hawthorne's Voyage through Chaos," *Studies in Romanticism* 8 (Autumn 1968): 1–15.

Lewis, R. W. B. *The American Adam*. Chicago: University of Chicago Press, 1955.

Lloyd-Smith, Allan Gardner. *Even-Tempered: Writing and Sexuality in Hawthorne's Fiction*. Totowa, N.J.: Barnes and Noble, 1984.

Locke, John. *An Essay Concerning Human Understanding*. London: Dent, 1961.

———. *The Second Treatise of Government*. New York: Liberal Arts, 1952.

Lynn, Kenneth P. "Falsifying Jefferson," *Commentary* (October 1981).

———. "Huck and Jim," *Yale Review* 48 (Spring 1958): 421–31.

———. "Welcome Back from the Raft, Huck Honey!" *American Scholar* 46 (Summer 1977): 338–47.

Lytle,, E. G. Andrew. *The Hero with Private Parts*. Baton Rouge: Louisiana State University Press, 1966.

Mace, George. *Locke, Hobbes, and the Federalist Papers: An Essay on the Genesis of the American Political Heritage*. Carbondale: Southern Illinois University Press, 1979.

McIlwain, Charles Howard. *The American Revolution*. New York: Macmillan, 1923.

Macpherson, C. B. *The Political Theory of Possessive Individualism*. Oxford, England: Oxford University Press, 1972.

McWilliams, Cary. *The Idea of Fraternity in America*. Berkeley: University of California Press, 1973.

McWilliams, John. *Political Justice in a Republic*. Berkeley: University of California Press, 1972.

Madison, James. "On Property," in Marvin Meyers, ed., *The Mind of the Founder*. Indianapolis: Bobbs-Merrill, 1973.

Manierre, William R. "Huck Finn, Empiricist Member of Society," *Modern Fiction Studies* 14 (Spring 1968): 57–66.

Manlove, C. N. "An Organic Hesitancy: Theme and Style in *Billy Budd*," in Faith Pullin, ed., *New Perspectives on Melville*. Kent, Ohio: Kent State University Press, 1978.

Martin, Terence. *Nathaniel Hawthorne*. Boston: Twayne, 1983.

Marx, Karl. *Capital*. London: Everyman, 1967.

———. "The German Ideology," in Robert C. Tucker, ed., *The Marx-Engels Reader,* 2nd ed. New York: W. W. Norton, 1978.

Marx, Leo. *The Machine in the Garden*. New York: Oxford University Press, 1964.

———. "Mr. Eliot, Mr. Trilling, and *Huckleberry Finn,*" *American Scholar* 22, 4 (Autumn 1953).

Matthiessen, F. O. *American Renaissance*. New York: Oxford University Press, 1941.

Maxwell, D. E. S. *American Fiction: The Intellectual Background*. New York: Columbia University Press, 1963.

Melville, Herman. *Billy Budd*. Chicago: University of Chicago Press, 1962.

———. "Hawthorne and his *Mosses,*" *Literary World,* August 17 and 24, 1850.

————. *Moby Dick,* eds. Harrison Hayford and Hershel Parker. New York: Norton, 1967.

Meriweather, James E., and Millgate, Michael, eds. *Lion in the Garden.* Lincoln: University of Nebraska Press, 1963.

Meyers, Jeffrey. "Hemingway's Second War: The Greco-Turkish Conflict, 1920–22," *Modern Fiction Studies* 30 (Spring 1984): 25–36.

Millgate, Michael. *The Achievement of William Faulkner.* New York: Random House, 1963.

Murphy, Kevin. "Illiterate's Progress: The Descent into Literary in *Huckleberry Finn,*" *Texas Studies in Literature and Language* 26 (Winter 1984): 363–87.

Murphy, Richard W. *The World of Cézanne 1839–1900.* New York: Time-Life, 1968.

Nakajima, Kenji. *"Big Two-hearted River" as the Extreme of Hemingway's Nihilism.* Tokyo: Eichosha, 1979.

Nietzsche, Friedrich. *Beyond Good and Evil,* trans. Walter Kaufman. New York: Vintage, 1967.

————. *Genealogy of Morals,* trans. Walter Kaufman. New York: Vintage, 1968.

Noble, David. "Cooper, Leatherstocking, and the Death of the American Adam," *American Quarterly* 16 (1964): 419–31.

Noone, John. *"Billy Budd:* Two Concepts of Nature," *American Literature* 19 (November 1957): 249–62.

O'Connor, William. "Why *Huckleberry Finn* Is Not the Great American Novel," *College English* 18 (October 1955): 6–10.

Okin, Susan. *Women in Western Political Thought.* Princeton, N.J.: Princeton University Press, 1979.

Paine, Thomas. *The Rights of Man and Other Writings.* London: Heron, 1970.

Parrington, Vernon Louis. *Main Currents in American Thought.* New York: Harcourt, Brace, and World, 1927.

Patterson, Mark T. "Democratic Leadership and Narrative Authority in *Moby Dick,*" *Studies in the Novel* 16 (Fall 1984): 288–303.

Peavy, Charles P. *Go Slow Now: Faulkner and the Race Question.* Eugene: University of Oregon Press, 1971.

Peters, Erskine. *William Faulkner: The Yoknapatawpha World and Black Being.* Darby, Pa.: Norwood Editions, 1983.

Pilkington, John. *The Heart of Yoknapatawpha.* Jackson: University of Mississippi Press, 1981.

Plato. *Republic,* trans. Allan Bloom. New York: Basic Books, 1968.

————. *Symposium*. Cambridge, Mass.: Harvard University Press, 1925.

Pocock, J. G. A. *The Machiavellian Moment*. Princeton, N.J.: Princeton University Press, 1975.

————. "The Myth of John Locke and the Obsession with Liberalism," in J. G. A. Pocock and Richard Ashcraft, eds., *John Locke*. Los Angeles: Clark Memorial Library, 1980.

————. *Virtue, Commerce, and History*. Cambridge, England: Cambridge University Press, 1985.

Poeggler, Otto, *Der Denkweg Martin Heideggers*. Pfullingen, FRG: Neske, 1963.

Railton, Stephen. *Fenimore Cooper: A Study of His Life and Imagination*. Princeton, N. J.: Princeton University Press, 1976.

Rawls, John. *A Theory of Justice*. Cambridge, Mass.: Harvard University Press, 1971.

Reynolds, Michael S. *Critical Essays on Ernest Hemingway's "In Our Time."* Boston: G. K. Hall, 1983.

————. *Hemingway's Reading 1910–1940*. Princeton, N.J.: Princeton University Press, 1981.

Ringe, Donald. *James Fenimore Cooper*. New York: Twayne, 1962.

Rogin, Michael. *Subversive Genealogy*. New York: Knopf, 1975.

Rorty, Richard. *Philosophy as the Mirror of Nature*. Princeton, N.J.: Princeton University Press, 1979.

Rousseau, Jean Jacques. *The Confessions,* trans. J. M. Cohen. London: Penguin, 1953.

————. *Emile,* trans. Allan Bloom. New York: Basic Books, 1979.

————. *The First and Second Discourses*. ed. Roger D. Masters. New York: St. Martin's Press, 1964.

————. *On the Origin of Language,* trans. John H. Moran and Alexander Gode. New York: Frederick Ungar Publishing, 1966.

————. *Reveries of a Solitary Walker,* trans. Charles Butterworth. New York: New York University Press, 1979.

————. *On the Social Contract,* trans. Donald A. Cress. Indianapolis: Hackett, 1983.

Samway, Patrick. "*Intruder in the Dust:* A Re-evaluation," in Glenn O. Carey, ed., *Faulkner: The Unappeased Imagination*. Troy, N.Y.: Whitston Publishing, 1980.

Schacht, Paul. "The Lonesomeness of Huckleberry Finn," *American Literature* 53 (May 1981): 189–201.

Schwan, Alexander. *Politische Philosophie in Denken Heideggers*. Cologne, FRG: Westdeutscher Verlag, 1965.

Scorza, Thomas. *In the Days before Steamships*. De Kalb: Northern Illinois Press, 1979.

Scott, Arthur L., ed. *Mark Twain: Selected Criticism*. Dallas: Southern Methodist University Press, 1967.

Sealts, Merton J. *Melville's Reading*. Columbia: University of South Carolina, 1988.

Sedgwick, William Ellery. *Tragedy of Mind*. Cambridge, Mass.: Harvard University Press, 1948.

Seed, David. " 'The Picture of the Whole': *In Our Time*," in A. Robert Lee, ed., *Ernest Hemingway: New Critical Essays*. London: Vision, 1983.

Sherrill, Rowland A. *The Prophetic Melville*. Athens: University of Georgia Press, 1979.

Slotkin, Richard. *The Fatal Environment*. New York: Atheneum, 1985.

————. *Regeneration through Violence*. Middletown, Conn.: Wesleyan University Press, 1978.

Smith, Henry Nash. *The Virgin Land*. Cambridge, Mass.: Harvard University Press, 1950.

Solomon, Eric. "Huck Finn Once More," *College English* 3 (December 1960): 172–77.

Spurlin, Paul M. *Rousseau in America*. University: University of Alabama Press, 1969.

Stephens, Robert O. *Hemingway's Nonfiction*. Chapel Hill: University of North Carolina Press, 1968.

Stern, Milton. *The Fine Hammered Steel of Herman Melville* (Urbana: University of Illinois Press, 1957.

Strauss, Leo. *Natural Right and History*. Chicago: University of Chicago Press, 1953.

Tarcov, Nathan. *Locke's Education for Liberty*. Chicago: University of Chicago Press, 1984.

Tatum, Campbell. "Dismal and Lonesome: A New Look at *Huckleberry Finn*," *Modern Fiction Studies* 14 (Spring 1968): 47–55.

Thomas, Brook. "*The House of Seven Gables:* Reading the Romance of America," *PMLA* 97 (March 1982): 195–211.

Thompson, Laurence. *Melville's Quarrel with God*. Princeton, N.J.: Princeton University Press, 1952.

Thoreau, Henry. *Walden and Civil Disobedience*. New York: W. W. Norton, 1966.

Tick, Stanley. "The Unity of *Go Down, Moses*," reprinted in Linda Welsheimer Wagner, ed., *William Faulkner: Four Decades of Criticism*. Lansing: Michigan State University Press, 1973.

Tocqueville, Alexis de. *Democracy in America,* trans. George Lawrence. Garden City, N.Y.: Doubleday, 1964.

Tompkins, Jane P., ed. *Reader-Response Criticism: From Formalism to Post-Structuralism*. Baltimore: Johns Hopkins University Press, 1981.

Trilling, Lionel. *The Liberal Imagination*. New York: Viking, 1950.

Tully, John. *A Discourse on Property*. Cambridge, England: Cambridge University Press, 1980.

Vickery, Olga. *The Novels of William Faulkner*. Baton Rouge: Louisiana State University Press, 1961.

Waggoner, Hyatt. *Nathaniel Hawthorne: A Critical Study*. Cambridge, Mass.: Harvard University Press, 1963.

Walker, Margaret. "Faulkner and Race," in Evans Harrington and Ann J. Abadie, eds., *The Maker and the Myth*. Jackson: University of Mississippi Press, 1978.

Warren, Austin. "Introduction," to *Nathaniel Hawthorne: Representative Selections*. New York: American Book, 1934.

Warren, Joyce M. *The American Narcissus*. New Brunswick, N.J.: Rutgers University Press, 1984.

Wecter, Dixon. "Mark Twain," in Robert Spiller et al., eds., *Literary History of the United States*. New York: Macmillan, 1948.

White, Morton. *The Philosophy of the American Revolution*. New York: Oxford University Press, 1978.

Williams, Wirt. *The Tragic Art of Ernest Hemingway*. Baton Rouge: Louisiana State University Press, 1981.

Wills, Garry. *Inventing America*. Garden City, N.Y.: Doubleday, 1978.

Wilson, Edmund. *The Shores of Light*. New York: Farrar, Straus, and Young, 1952.

Winters, Yvor. *In Defense of Reason*. Denver: Allan Swallow, 1960.

Witham, Phil. "*Billy Budd:* Testament of Resistance," *Modern Language Quarterly* 20 (June 1959): 115–27.

Wright, Nathalia. *Melville's Use of the Bible*. New Haven, Conn.: Yale University Press, 1957.

Young, Philip. *Hemingway: A Reconsideration*. University Park: Pennsylvania State University Press, 1966.

Zoellner, Robert. *Salt-Sea Mastodon: A Reading of Moby Dick*. Berkeley: University of California Press, 1973.

Zuckert, Catherine. "Law and Nature in *Adventures of Huckleberry Finn*," *Proteus* 1 (Fall 1984): 27–35.

———. "The Political Wisdom of Nathaniel Hawthorne," *Polity* 13 (Winter 1980): 163–83.

Zuckert, Catherine, and Zuckert, Michael. " 'In Its Wake We Followed': The Political Wisdom of Mark Twain," *Interpretation* (Summer 1972): 59–66.

Zuckert, Michael. "Self-Evident Truths in the Declaration of Independence," *Review of Politics* (Fall 1987).

Index

265

ACB0068

5/30/90

PS
374
P6
Z97
1990